READING POPULAR PRINTS 1790–1870

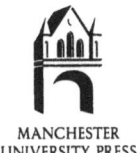

MANCHESTER
UNIVERSITY PRESS

Reading popular prints

1790–1870

SECOND EDITION

B. E. Maidment

Manchester University Press

MANCHESTER AND NEW YORK

distributed exclusively in the USA by Palgrave

First edition published 1996 by Manchester University Press

This edition published 2001 by
Manchester University Press
Oxford Road, Manchester M13 9NR, UK
and Room 400, 175 Fifth Avenue, New York, NY 10010, USA
http://www.manchesteruniversitypress.co.uk

Distributed exclusively in the USA by
Palgrave, 175 Fifth Avenue, New York,
NY 10010, USA

Distributed exclusively in Canada by
UBC Press, University of British Columbia, 2029 West Mall,
Vancouver, BC, Canada V6T 1Z2

British Library Cataloguing-in-Publication Data
A catalogue record for this book is available from the British Library

Library of Congress Cataloging-in-Publication Data applied for

ISBN 0 7190 3371 3 *paperback*

This edition first published 2001

10   09   08   07   06   05   04   03   02   01   10 9 8 7 6 5 4 3 2 1

Typeset by Action Publishing Technology, Gloucester
Printed in Great Britain by
Bookcraft (Bath) Ltd, Midsomer Norton

CONTENTS

LIST OF ILLUSTRATIONS

Additional illustrations in the second edition

the new illustrations appear between pages 173 *and* 175

✑ ACKNOWLEDGEMENTS

Like Keats's Grecian Urn, most books used to be the foster children of silence and slow time. While this book, long in the making, is aptly characterised by slow time, silence is less appropriate. It has been written among the raised voices and hubbub of academic management with a consequently increasing distance from the whispers of teaching and research. In these circumstances, the debts to supporters, enthusiasts, and colleagues who have maintained their belief in my project have become even more important.

My long standing interest in prints was given new focus by being asked to teach part time in the Department of History of Art and Design at Manchester Metropolitan University. The author of this request, Diana Donald, not only gave me the chance to talk with art and design students and engage in dialogue with formal art history, but also taught me an enormous amount about what it means to be a proper scholar of eighteenth-century image making. Meanwhile, my colleagues in the Department of English and History watched with bemused tolerance as I applied much of what they had taught me about how to read texts to a new range of images and representations. Friends and colleagues who were historians, especially Alan Kidd, Ken Roberts, and Terry Wyke, were well aware of my willingness to tackle scholarly challenges for which I was not entirely well prepared, and I owe them much for showing me some of the more creative and interesting ways in which historians think. My English colleagues at Manchester had collectively engaged with cultural studies and its theoretical implications in their teaching and research, and I have learnt much from many of them. My debts to Jeff Wainwright, Margaret Beetham, Trefor Thomas, and Colin Buckley, who had the unenviable responsibility of being my boss, go way beyond scholarly respect into friendship and support at a level of generosity rarely found among the jealousies and petty feuds of academic life. Intellectually, I found working at Manchester, in daily contact with the likes of Alf Louvre, Antony Easthope, Michael Howard, Lawrence Coupe, Elspeth Graham and Jeff Walsh, to say nothing of successive generations of students, a constantly energising, unsettling, and valuable experience. Not so many people will have had the pleasure of working in English, History, and Art History Departments simultaneously. In many ways, it is this triple focus which underpins this book.

The Library, presided over for so long by Professor Ian Rogerson, was both a sanctuary and a primary resource. I found unexpected and, I am sure, undeserved levels of helpfulness, support, and understanding among Ian

Rogerson's staff, without which this book would never have been sustained through its early stages.

In 1990 I moved to Edge Hill College of Higher Education in Ormskirk where I now hold a senior management post. Putting aside the issue of whether any true scholar could even think of being an educational manager, especially in these fraught times, the College has none the less allowed me to pursue my research and writing interests. I have not found that increasing distance from the day-to-day activity of teaching, however much it may have diminished me in other ways, has affected my interest in or enthusiasm for research. Within the inevitable limits imposed by its nature and function, Edge Hill has supported my work, especially in its latter stages. Mark Flinn and John Simons, among senior colleagues, have been ingenious as well as understanding in providing me with a modicum of 'slow time' in which to complete this book. Ruth Jenkinson, the Head of Library Services, and Andrew Sackville have been endlessly encouraging in both practical and personal ways. Rod Pye has helped me prepare the illustrations with a characteristic mixture of skill and good humour. Pauline Martland not only taught me word processing but also gave up time and energy to help me present my manuscript in a proper form. Pam Snellgrove has efficiently managed travel and other support from the School of Humanities and Arts. John Townsend, Head of Management Information Systems, and his staff magically provided me with much needed help at a crucial moment. Within the Programmes Unit, Sue Orrell and Jane Hilton have given me help with the preparation of the manuscript, and my long serving and long suffering colleagues, Frances Scattergood and Mandy Holland, have taken the stresses and strains of my occasional absences and far more frequent absent-mindednesses with good grace and generosity.

Like all scholars, I owe many debts to Libraries and other repositories who have not even known that they have helped me. I have, as a usually anonymous and insignificant visitor, used many libraries and collections, among them the Ashmolean Museum, Lancaster University, University of Central Lancashire, Manchester Central Reference Library and a host of local libraries in the north-west. I have never been treated with anything less than courtesy, and I owe much to the expertise of staff in many of these institutions. Booksellers and print dealers have similarly taken their response to requests way beyond the commercial, as well as providing me with a great deal of pleasure along the way. John Worthy of the Rochdale Book Company, Laurie Hardman of Broadhurst's in Southport, Alan and Joan Tucker in Stroud, the Halewood family in Preston, and George Kelsall in Littleborough are long standing allies. Others, less well known to me personally, have made major contributions to this book – The Print Room in Bloomsbury, for example, found me several 'educated dustmen' prints through a combination of a good card index and a long and effective memory. They must have wondered why I wanted them. To all unacknowledged 50p bins, silverfish specials, dusty print shops, antique fairs, and other sources of old and recent images, I here give collective thanks.

I give even more unreserved thanks to Maxine Melling, who has redeemed me, and this project, into good sense, proportion, and happiness.

Another version of chapter 4., called 'Domestic ideology and its industrial enemies' has appeared in C. Parker (ed.), *Gender Roles and Sexuality in Victorian Literature* (Scolar Press 1995), 25–56.

ॐ PREFACE

Like all such projects, this book has arisen from a number of motives and preoccupations. Partly, it is the product of curiosity, and increasingly compelling interest in explaining prints and images which had hung on my walls or sat in my bookshelves for many years without explication. In finding out about these images, I discovered how complex and interesting the social activity of producing popular prints and illustrations was and is. Equally, I discovered that the act of reading images is no less complicated. So one source of this book is a kind of wondering curiosity, a naïve pleasure in finding out, which is related to, but not quite the same thing as, academic investigation. The complexity which I find in the apparently simple and unselfconscious pictures studied in this book is not solely one constructed by the 'play' of contemporary theoretical debates (the 'dialogism' or 'heteroglossia' of competing genres, discourses, and ideologies found in all texts which seek to construct social meanings). It is also a product of the vast weight of empirical evidence, manifested in the insistent presence of huge quantities of popular imagery to be found at every level of society from the end of the eighteenth century up to the advent of photography as a widespread means of illustration. While it seemed foolhardy even to imagine mapping the main contour lines for a history of popular printmaking in this period, it did seem possible right from the start to think in terms of detailed and extended readings of popular prints. Such readings form the central activity of what follows.

It is important to insist that the prints selected for discussion are not intended to be representative of either the history of printmaking or of the central preoccupations of the societies which produced them, although the persistence and frequent recurrence of some of the images may well imply a widespread contemporary cultural or political importance. The prints have been selected from the huge range available to even the casual seeker because they acknowledge, indeed are structured out of, tensions between various representational codes, and suggest the variety and complexity of the visual and narrative traditions which intersect in them. One charge which might be made against the selection procedure used here is that it has been dominated by a search for complexity, but in fact one argument of the book is that such complexity can be found, unbidden, in even the crudest, simplest, and least self-conscious wood engraved vignette. The narrative, representational, and emblematic discourses which inform cheap, mass produced engravings and woodcuts are too easily hidden by their apparent simplicity of form.

While to some extent they share a common subject matter – that of the depiction of working or 'ordinary' people at both work and at leisure – the prints studied here have been chosen largely because they permit and encourage a series of questions about the act of interpretation. Such self-consciousness is not meant to intimidate interpretation nor indeed to restrain the pleasures of looking at prints but rather to bring to popular prints some of the seriousness and purpose of academic methods of study. This seriousness and purpose presupposes the value and complexity of the material to be studied.

How, then, might an interested student, equipped with some knowledge of social history and art history, and open to some of the difficulties surrounding representation and interpretation opened up by contemporary theoretical debates, set about an explanation of these particular images? I answer this question through the example of a series of exemplary, but I hope not excluding or dogmatic, readings. In chapters 2 to 5 of the book I show how I set off in pursuit of information and then of a theoretical position from which to offer a reading of a group of images which sought to represent the same subject. Thus the organising principle of each chapter is the reading and interpreting process, but underlying that principle is the often quite extensive empirical research required to unearth the range of prints discussed. Further below this empirical research lies another set of assumptions about the inhibiting nature of 'canons' of 'great' or 'complex' texts which should be foregrounded as the most sophisticated and rewarding ways of investigating the past. Accordingly this book is a polemical one, which makes a large number of theoretical and methodological assumptions, but which also engages with the social history of printmaking and its various genres. All these potentially conflicting interests are tackled together, chapter by chapter, in pursuit of the dangerous pleasures of detailed explication, pleasures undaunted by, but I hope fully aware of, the post-modern resistance to single or final explanations.

The following detailed accounts of individual prints or groups of prints are not meant to be definitive, especially because they depend on describing simultaneously the interrelations between the differing codes of the literary, the visual, and the political. The explicatory material assembled round each print in order to explain its possible meanings is meant to suggest how a student or interested spectator might develop his or her understanding further through a disciplined pursuit of analogies, traditions, and similarities. While open to the possiblities of multiple interpretation, these readings are not meant to put forward the associative free play of iconographical allusion, resemblance, or esoteric comparison as a useful method. Too often modern theoretical adulation of the 'open' text or image as a construct of the reader's sensibility is merely self-regarding connoisseurship under another name, yet the need for wide ranging attention to narrative pattern, recurring formal devices, and visual analogies is a pressing one. It would be, for example, impossible to make much sense of the accounts of artisans returning to their family homes after work discussed in chapter 4, without recognising that the theme has been widely represented in painting from the sixteenth century on. Yet the pursuit of precise visual antecedents may not ultimately be anything more than antiquarianism. Therefore, the emphasis in this book is firmly on visual representation as a process which does involve the production of social meanings, and hence raise issues about class and power. Equally, though, I wish to regard explanation as a process, too, and this book is merely a stage in that process. The next stage is in the hands of the reader.

The abbreviation BMC is used throughout to refer to F.C. Stephens and M.D. George, *Catalogue of Political and Personal Satires Preserved in the Department of Prints and Drawings in the British Museum* (London, British Museum 1870–1954).

✎ PREFACE TO THE SECOND EDITION

This book was primarily written to interest, inform, and perhaps enthuse those readers, students, and scholars whose main academic interests do not include graphic images, but who may well encounter or seek out prints in pursuit of their own kinds of historical explanations. Grateful as I am to those several reviewers who chose to regard this book as a scholarly monograph or as an imperfect history of popular prints, my primary aim was to suggest to *students* some of the rewards which might be gained from 'reading popular prints'. I have been gratified by those readers who have written to me, especially as their backgrounds have ranged from economic history through art history and cultural studies to English. With these diverse kinds of people in mind I am especially pleased that this book has proved popular enough to justify re-publication in a cheaper format.

In the five years since the book came out there have been a number of major publications in the field. Some of these have been ground-clearing and, indeed, ground-breaking surveys like Timothy Clayton's *The English Print 1688–1802* (Yale University Press 1997) and Diana Donald's *The Age of Caricature – Satirical Prints in the Age of George III* (Yale University Press 1996). Others have included heavily revised reprints of essential reference books such as Ian McKenzie's *British Prints* (Woodbridge Antique Collectors' Club 1998) and Simon Houfe's *Dictionary of Nineteenth Century Book Illustrators* (Woodbridge Antique Collectors' Club 1996), although, despite many new illustrations, the latter has been stripped of much of its invaluable Introduction and now stresses illustration at the expense of caricature. Peter Lord's *Words with Pictures – Welsh Images and Images of Wales 1640–1860* (Llandysul Gwasg Gomer 1995) discussed a wealth of images little known outside Wales. Several other significant publications derived from and accompanied exhibitions. Sheila O'Connell's *The Popular Print in England* (British Museum Press 1999) was the most wide-ranging of these, but equally significant has been the specialist attention given to individual, often little known, artists and engravers. David Alexander's *Richard Newton and Caricature in the 1790s* (Manchester University Press 1998) underpinned an exhibition at the Whitworth Art Gallery, Manchester, an exhibition which also became the occasion for a two-day conference on eighteenth century prints. Equally welcome was an exhibition at the Strang Print Room at University College, London of the work of C.J. Grant which gave rise to an excellent catalogue edited by Richard Pound. Other more theoretically orientated approaches to the interpretation of popular imagery have included Peter

Sinnema's *Dynamics of the Printed Page* (Aldershot Ashgate 1998) which offers detailed analysis of the textual organisation and significance of *The Illustrated London News*.

With all this new work, there was an obvious temptation to substantially re-write this book, but this edition reprints the original text in the belief that the reader will bring his or her own range of images to the discussion, and that further detailed discussion of my chosen images was unnecessary. Nonetheless, I have encountered many images which might have found a place in my original discussions if I had known them – my ignorance of them is, I hope, clear evidence of the richness of the field – and four of the most interesting are now reproduced between pages 173 and 175 of this edition.

Two of these images offer further graphic formulations of the narrative of the 'returning workman' which forms the subject of chapter 4. Both images are taken from the large format, cheap weekly temperance magazine *The British Workman*, one from 1866 and one from 1867. The magazine, which was aimed at an artisan readership, published some of the largest and most ambitious mass circulation wood engravings ever seen in Victorian Britain. The other two images, which offer additional, extremely sophisticated, formulations of the suicide images discussed in chapter 5, are drawn from two mid-Victorian periodicals which were largely read by middle-class readers. The first, by Matt Morgan, accompanies an outraged article concerned with the criminalisation and uncomprehending denunciation of female suicides to be found in the satirical magazine *The Tomahawk* in 1868. The second illustrates a sensationalist verse narrative 'Found Drowned' in *Tinsley's Magazine* in the same year. The poem challenges the drowned woman's seducer to face up to his complicity in her death.

These additional images are offered not just to emphasise how many powerful, complex and sophisticated images are to be found in Victorian periodicals but also to encourage the reader to make use of what is still a vastly underused scholarly resource – the huge mass of popular graphic images through which Regency and Victorian society formulated its ideas and its anxieties.

Brian Maidment
University of Salford

CHAPTER 1

Prints as history
AND THE HISTORY OF PRINTS

Studying prints

A self-conscious study of prints poses the student a range of immediate problems. Prints might be discussed as an aesthetic or art-historical category, but they are every bit as complex and interesting as a branch of social history. Read as an aesthetic category, prints have tradition-ally been regarded as 'lesser' forms and genres, incapable of representing either deep feeling or abstract concepts, let alone aesthetic complexity, with any hope of success. Why have artists as brilliant as Rowlandson or George Cruikshank been marginalised by art history because they worked as engravers, etchers, and illustrators? Given this uncertainty over the aesthetic status of prints, art history has been only partially able to construct proper models for the inter-pretation of prints which acknowledge their particular technical and social history, their distinctive iconographical, emblematic, and repre-sentational traditions, and their aesthetic potential. There are still grounds for arguing that art history has never understood, and has certainly under-valued, the print as a source of pleasure and interest.

If we ascribe prints to social history, then the interpretative issues are no less complex. Historians have only slowly learnt from art history the concepts and terminology which allow them to acknowledge the complex formal and iconographical mediations through which prints represent historical events. Prints must be allowed a historical status beyond the illustrative or the evidential. A further necessary challenge to the historian concerns the widespread belief in the primacy of the written and the authority of the verbal as forms of historical evidence. As this book suggests, the relationship between the verbal and the visual, always a close and dynamic one, becomes even more complex as a result of the early nineteenth-century development of the mass circulation wood engraving.

The student faces further issues to do with the way in which contemporary historiography structures the past. Picture editors and television researchers can only use what they can find, thus raising all sorts of problems about the typicality and representativeness of the visual record. Re-constructing readerships and audiences is equally demanding. How can we differentiate between images meant to amuse, to divert, to persuade, or to inform? Only, perhaps, by looking beyond overt statements of prevalent attitudes to a more subtle and ambiguous rhetoric of gesture, posture, emblem, and allusion. Even if it is possible to identify the 'purpose' and 'audience' of any particular image, it is still difficult to guarantee that the intended audience would have understood the graphic codes used even in simple prints. The temptation is to believe that even relatively unsophisticated late eighteenth and early nineteenth-century audiences, poorly versed in the complexities and figures of written discourse, were none the less better able to interpret icon, emblem, and visual pun. Thus it might be possible to see visual and graphic culture between 1790 and 1870 as a more potent means than the printed word of democratising social understanding. Yet such a hypothesis requires a detailed understanding of the motives and intentions of printmakers and distributors to be substantiated, and evidence of this kind is not easy to find.

This book is written on the understanding that these issues are live ones, but probably incapable of resolution, even when the period studied extends only from 1790 to 1870. The introductory chapter which follows shapes the questions baldly posed above into some kind of scholarly order, so that the main contours of debate become visible and the main protagonists and their writing can be identified. The Bibliography is organised as an annotated study guide which is intended to reinforce this chapter's account of the nature and scope of the key interpretative issues which confront anyone interested in 'reading' prints. This opening chapter is followed by four detailed readings of groups of prints made and distributed between the French Revolution and the advent of photography as a major mode for the reproduction of images, brought together by a common concern to describe and interpret a particular historical event or social narrative. These four chapters are meant to exemplify how one interested student has sought to mediate between a range of competing interpretations.

The status of prints

Prints in general have never enjoyed a high status in the gallery, the auction room, or the Art History course. Despite the aspirations of some printmakers, notably in eighteenth-century attempts to reproduce the formal and tonal complexity of oil painting[1] or in contemporary art market attempts to establish prints as original and significant productions by major artists,[2] prints have remained as 'lesser' art works. Their authenticity as 'art' has invariably been undermined by the element of mechanical reproduction involved in their making.[3] The 'craft' mediations which define printmaking processes would appear unambiguously to disrupt any direct relationship between artist and artefact, between genius and canvas. Prints, by their nature as multiple reproductions of images, attack the notion of artistic uniqueness by insisting on publicising the technical process through which idea becomes image. At the bottom of prints, especially eighteenth and nineteenth-century prints, you find a cluster of names – artist, engraver, publisher, sometimes more – so that the creative credit has to be shared out.[4] The idea of art as the unmediated expression of the artist's inner life and compulsions is thus destroyed by prints, which acknowledge both a complex of makers and an implied commercial exchange with an audience in their actual forms. Prints have to be made – they do not happen spontaneously as the fall-out of genius. They are made to be sold.

Although the ambition to reproduce paintings may initially have been an attempt to democratise art and make high art traditions available to a mass audience, it also required printmakers to develop and use increasingly sophisticated methods to reproduce the complex colours and tones of oil painting or watercolour. The period studied by this book covers eighty years in which many such developments took place, most obviously in the exploitation of wood engraving techniques and the development of lithography and other modes of colour printing. While prints from this period may show immense tonal complexity (see illustration 3) and deploy colour printing techniques in startlingly effective ways, the great strength of printmaking in the first half of the nineteenth century lies in a general acceptance that line rather than tone or colour is the medium through which printmaking, given the reprographic methods available, worked most effectively.

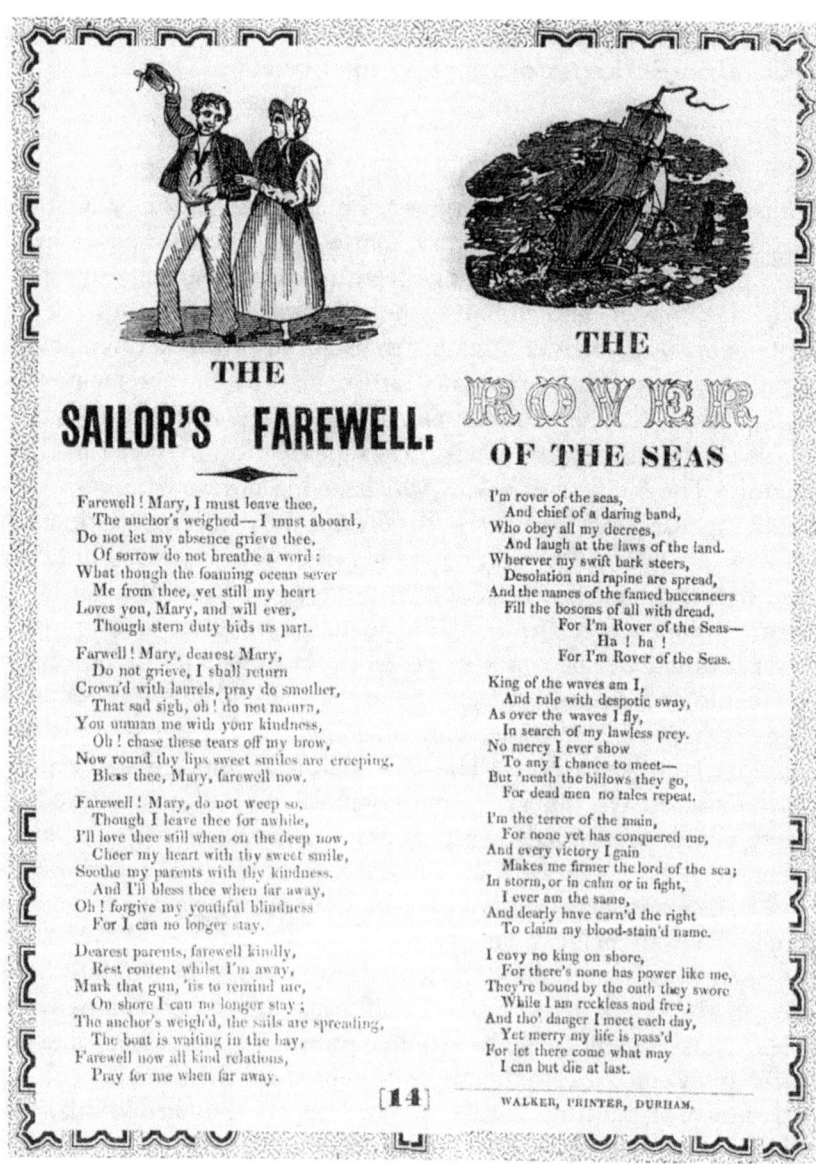

1 Woodcut illustration to a ballad sheet printed and issued by Walker of Durham. A typical anonymous broadside song-sheet, one of the classic commodity texts of the nineteenth century. The text was set together with the wood engraved illustrations and the 'display' typographic ornamentation.

Of course, these remarks assume that prints and printmakers might have had artistic aspirations in the first place. Yet when, as I have done, the definition of a print is extended to include illustration, then even the most casual survey suggests that most prints have little interest in becoming 'art' as opposed to illustration, decoration, or explanation. The vast majority of prints produced in this period derived from immediate, and often ephemeral, social purposes. Their function was one of social utility, of serving a perceived social need. Late eighteenth and early nineteenth-century prints are, then, explanatory, expository (illustration 6), satirical (illustration 4), topical (illustration 7), or topographical (illustration 3). They embody the values and beliefs of their makers and their viewers, and belong, in a key sense more to social history than to the history of art. But to make an absolute distinction between the self-consciously artistic and the necessarily social robs prints of their own social and aesthetic history as self-conscious and distinctive representational genres and modes. Prints do not describe or delineate the social in an unmediated and simple way. The history of prints is also the history of a complex dialogue between social history and the history, conventions, and representational capacity of the various genres and forms of printmaking.

So this is not a book which shows much respect for the artistic reputation of the artists and engravers it studies. Graphic works by 'great' artists like Blake, Rowlandson (illustration 11), and Doré (illustrations 29 and 31) do form part of the discussion, and well known and historically important printmakers like George Cruikshank (illustration 4), Robert Seymour (illustrations 16–18), and William Heath provide many of the images described in my text, but well known artists like these are vastly outnumbered by lesser known names, especially by that divertingly various and productive printmaker 'anon'. This is not to deny that the popular images discussed in this book intersect in important ways with traditions of high art representation – in chapter 4, for example, the graphic images of workmen returning home from labour drawn from tracts, book illustration, and periodicals, crucially evoke the long tradition of oil paintings of cottage doors, and bring not just Constable and Morland, but also Burns and Goldsmith into the equation. Similarly, in chapter 2, crude broadside engraved images of the fire at the Albion Mill require comparison with those made by Girtin and Turner as complex watercolours and oils. It is hoped and intended that the reader of this book will bring his or her knowledge of the wider art historical tradition to bear on the relatively humble and unselfconscious images which form the main focus of attention here. The extent to which popular images *depend* on

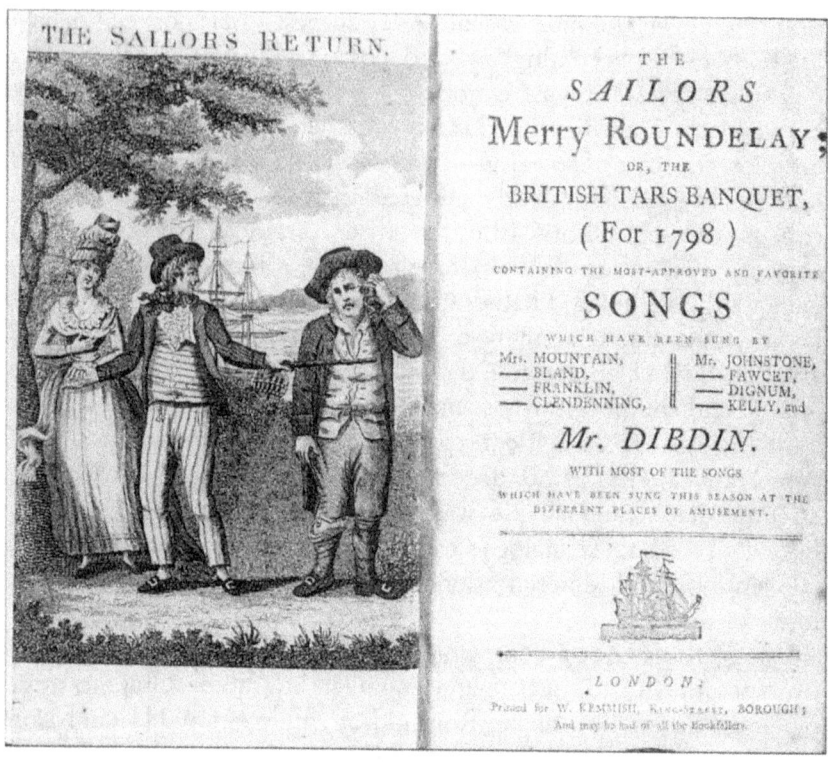

2 This late eighteenth-century songbook title page spread to *The Sailor's Merry Roundelay* (1798) retains a copper engraving to give an air of respectability to a vernacular text. While a small wood engraved vignette has been introduced into the title page itself, the frontispiece has been separately printed off a single plate.

an awareness, however unacknowledged, of high art traditions is one that can only be hinted at in many of these discussions.

Evaluations of the artistic success and the aesthetic qualities of the images studied here are relevant here only in so far as they define the particular discourses and audiences in which the prints are mobilised. Of the prints discussed in detail, it is obvious that some offer more sophisticated and aesthetically successful images than others. But the argument of my book depends on the acknowledgement of a variety of representational possibilities, a repertoire of potential interpretations, being available to image makers as a resource for the depiction of any particular event or subject, some of which will be artistically sophisticated, but many of which will be crude, populist, and simplified in both their graphic formulations and their social analyses. Any relationship between aesthetic success and the effective

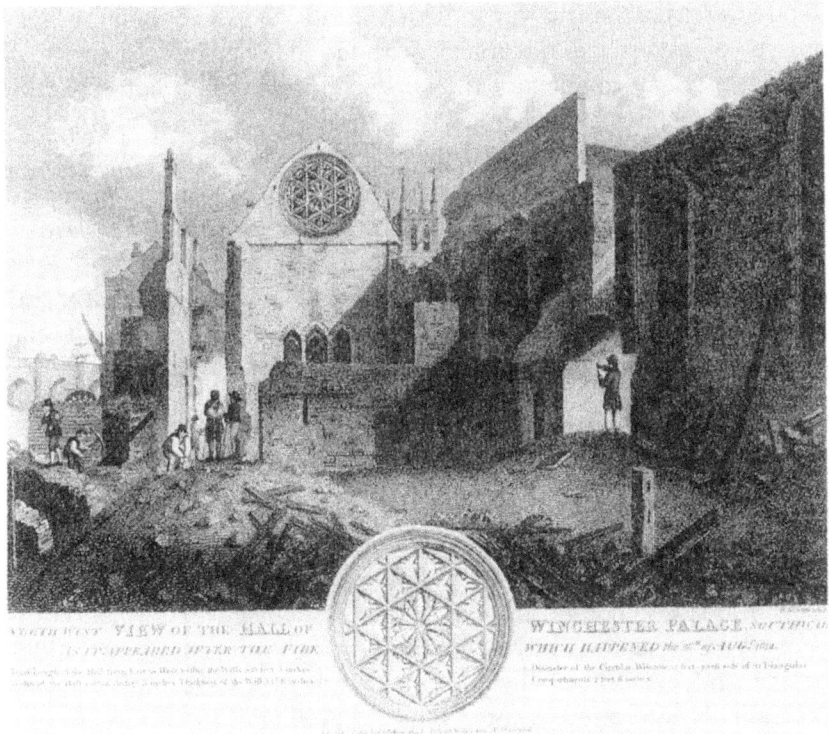

3 A tonally sophisticated copper engraving by B. Howlett depicting the aftermath of a London fire in 1814 (see chapter 2). The addition of a small vignette to complement the main image is worthy of note.

production of social meanings remains, as far as I am concerned, unproven. Indeed, it is plausible to argue that 'simple' images which derive from crudely held graphic conventions and social stereotypes offer the student a better understanding of widely held cultural assumptions and values than those offered by the ironies, subtleties, and contradictions of, say, Rowlandson or Gillray.

The interpretative model used here thus foregrounds the vernacular and the commonplace, and is interested in competing representational possibilities rather than unified and successful outcomes. This model of 'competing possibilities' shapes the chapters which follow, building each round differing graphic accounts of similar social events or phenomena. It also deliberately privileges the 'historical' against the 'aesthetic' not because there isn't a case to be made for the aesthetic quality of prints, but rather because it seems crucial to me to offer a critique of the way in which prints have been used for illus-trative purposes by historians without due reference to their representational complexity. I believe, quite simply, that it is the weight of social history held within these prints which gives them their power to interest and engage the contemporary student. However, this kind of history cannot be explained solely by reference to other sources, especially the printed word. The codes, conventions, and representational traditions of the printed image are themselves as representative of ideology as anything they seek to depict. By this token, a crudely drawn woodcut may be as freighted with social complexity as a self-consciously elegant design by Rowlandson.

Prints as history

Are prints a reliable source of historical evidence for the historian? What are the dangers of historians constructing an interpretation of historical events from written and oral sources, and then looking for illustrations which confirm or amplify this argument? How can prints be more subtly and successfully used in ways beyond the merely illus-trative and evidential? Over recent years historians have become increasingly interested in these kinds of problems. In two interesting review articles which discuss one of the major recent publishing ventures in the field of reprinting graphic images,[5] the historian Roy Porter raises a series of substantial issues for the historian who wishes to engage seriously with prints as a form of historical evidence. These are issues which are important not just for historians, but for all students of popular imagery.

The first issue Porter raises is the relationship between the 'visual' and the 'written' as forms of cultural history. Porter argues that, inevitably, historians privilege written and verbal evidence as the mainstay of historical interpretation, thus relegating visual material to an illustrative or confirmatory role. This model is confirmed by a vast array of illustrated popular history texts, often extremely well researched and with sophisticated texts by eminent scholars, where the illustrations while seeming to be decorative in function actually begin to construct a historical model of 'the Georgian Age' or 'Victorian London' or whatever.[6] However careful and scholarly these books might be, the danger is that their visual construction of the past will depend more on the pragmatic availability of images for reproduc-tion and their decorative qualities than on any deep and careful evaluation of their power to 'represent' or 'reveal' that part of the past which the book seeks to describe. The past becomes merely what the picture editor can find and afford.

This kind of a model in which the verbal is crassly extended and confirmed by the visual of course ignores the crucial interdependence of text and image which is central to the nature of most print genres.[7] This interdependence is not only an issue of historiographical significance, but also one which is of immediate pragmatic and theoretical importance in trying to read off the meaning of prints. In some kinds of single plate prints, especially copper engravings, etchings, and lithographs, the large visual image is annotated only with written information about artists, engraver, publisher, and date and place of publication. In other genres, notably caricature, the verbal invades the graphic to construct the overall image. The crowded captions, speech balloons, labelling, and emblematic written commentary of a Gillray or Rowlandson caricature provide one obvious example of this process, as do the kinds of emblematic title pages, crowded with both verbal and visual elements, studied in chapter 4. Here the 'visual' construction of the page is as much dependent on typography and layout as on the illustration. Word and picture are bound together in a single image. The steel engraved vignette, dropped into the text, most famously exemplified by Turner's illustrations for Rogers's *Italy* (1830) and *Poems* (1834) offer another formulation of the text/image complex.[8] More complicated still are the illustrations for the Victorian novel, where the status of the illustration, most famously formulated in Dickens's and Thackeray's serial issues (illustration 8), varies enormously from purely decorative capitals through illustrative vignettes to a sequence of powerful single page images which seem almost to construct a 'counter' or 'meta' narrative to the main text.[9] One central theme of this book will be the increasing ease with which in the early Victorian period illustration and text could be combined on a single page due to both the technical development of illustrative processes and a growing sense of the need to reinforce word with image in a barely, or newly, or just literate culture. This issue will be pursued in a later section of this chapter.

Porter's main argument about the interrelation of word and image is a different one, however:

> On deeper reflection, it proves no accident that it has been literary historians – whose primary schooling lies in verbal hermeneutics – who have opened our eyes to the lexicons of the pictorial. For despite our clichéd stereotypes, word and picture were never antitheses or alternatives, still less rivals. It was never words for the literate and

pictures for the unlettered. There is little evidence within English culture from the seventeenth century on of the production of visual images independent of writing, targeted at those who could not read. What was normal, at all levels from the patrician to the plebeian, was the marriage of word and image. That 'mutuality' may be tacit ... But very commonly the interleaving of the verbal and visual is quite explicit, as with illustrated chapbooks, broadsheet ballads, illustrated novels and biblical texts, trade advertisements, catchpenny prints or funeral monuments.

In other words, the production of visual images in post-Gutenberg society was principally not aimed at sub-literate starers, but at those who already formed the readership for anything from bills to books. To see pictures as a sort of baby-food mode of communication, pap for those whose minds could not digest real words, would be to misread the function of the visual image in emergent commercial culture.[10]

As Porter notes here, along with much else of interest, it has been literary historians, used to notions of verbal codes and the complex ways in which language 'represents' or 'constructs' perception, who have begun to read graphic images not just as failed paintings or unmediated forms of historical evidence, but as complex acts of representation which both draw on and reveal the cultural and ideological assumptions of their makers and their audiences. If historians have been, as Porter suggests, slow to acknowledge the complexity of graphic images as a source, there has been increasing recent acknowledgement of the problems of representation together with, to take another of Porter's points, growing awareness that prints are not aimed at a less literate or sophisticated audience than written discourses. He summarises the issues concerning representation in the following terms:

Now, clearly, no historian will naively believe that political prints give us an uncontaminated, unideological, objective 'snapshot' from which we can 'read off' the past. Visual material is no less value-laden than verbal, and the historian must be perennially on guard for the ideology behind the image ...

The hopes of quarrying prints to archaeologise the material culure of the past – what were coffee-houses and brothels, mobs or hustings actually like? – raises terrifying issues, ones which historians have by and large shirked. It is helpful to state that what such materials primarily offer us is not a window on 'reality', but a record of the shorthand artistic conventions deployed by the engraver and taken 'as read' by his viewers ... Do the gestures, body language, clothes and accoutrements of the patricians and plebeians depicted in the prints reflect the actual theatre of Georgian life? Or do they only tell us about the stock symbols deployed to facilitate identification? It is hard to tell ... [11]

Porter's argument about the ways in which prints always 'represent' or mediate historical detail through aesthetic and gestural convention is given even more impulsion if the subjects of study prove to be aesthetically more ambitious and self-conscious than political caricature. Doré's widely recognisable and complex wood engraved illustrations to Blanchard Jerrold's *London: A Pilgrimage* (1872) provide a good example of images which have come to be given almost iconic status as a documentary record of the Gothic horrors of Victorian London. Yet, as Alan Woods showed as long ago as 1978, 'Doré at times displayed not merely a disregard for, but an actual hostility to detail, preferring what he wanted to be there to what was there ... His whole method of working, indeed, was incompatible with accuracy of detail ...'.[12] Woods goes on to show the relationship between the 'real' and the 'fabulous' in Doré, and how Doré's apparently naturalistic images are filtered through a range of artistic conventions like the picturesque and the grotesque. The same tensions between apparent social realism and the artistic conventions of the fantastic appear in Doré's illustrations to Hood's poems which are discussed in chapter 5.

These brief citations from historians suggest the central critical issues here. The first is that prints, however documentary their mode or literal their intentions, can never be entirely naturalistic descriptions of the past. The second is that prints, to use Porter's phrases, use 'shorthand artistic conventions' which are 'taken as read' by the intended viewers. Clearly we, as students of prints, have to decode these conventions and common interpretative assumptions. Thirdly, prints, as much as any other medium of communication, are essentially ideological formations which, whether consciously or unconsciously, are shaped by the cultural values and social aspirations of both make and audience. Fourthly, historians have become increasingly aware of these kinds of interpretative problems over the last fifteen years. Porter's essay in *Past and Present*, quoted above, was written as a response to a major publishing project aimed at reproducing and annotating in a scholarly way the vast resources of political and social caricature held in the British Museum. As Porter points out, this project could only be worthwhile if the editors of each volume understood the dangers as well as the opportunities of using prints as a form of historical evidence. It is worth showing how this shift of historical focus away from the subject being represented to the processes of representation themselves has changed the way in which history has engaged with the past. The recent bi-centenary of the French Revolution provides an exemplary study.

Partly because the revolutionaries themselves had understood so well the importance of emblems, symbols, and visual codes, to say nothing of language, as forms of political and social argument and action, the visual remains of the Revolutionary period are staggeringly rich. Given additionally the depth of the emotional and philosophical engagement of European artists and writers in Revolutionary events, it is not surprising that a number of ambitious visual histories and exhibitions were undertaken during the bi-centenary period. Studies like Aileen Ribeiro's book on dress codes in the Revolution,[13] which draws extensively on contemporary paintings, engravings, and fashion plates, or Christopher Hibbert's social history *The Days of the French Revolution*,[14] which had been first published in 1980, but was re-issued with an abridged text by Penguin in 1989 with the addition of a wide array of graphic sources, showed the popular potential of the visual resources available in the field. Emmet Kennedy's *A Cultural History of the French Revolution*[15] showed a similar impulse to combine an ambitiously popularising text with a wide array of contemporary prints, drawings, and other visual evidence. It would not be fair to say that the illustrations in all three of these texts are largely decorative in function or that they are 'merely' illustrative of features of the Revolutionary period described in the text. Ribeiro, at least, is largely dependent on visual sources to be able to make an historical argument at all. None the less, I think it is legitimate to say that none of these studies is much concerned with the 'problems' of visual sources. They are used as an agreeable prompt to the reader to attend to a narrative drawn almost exclusively from written sources.

A number of other bi-centenary projects and publications did, however, seek to foreground the visual as a major site for academic study. Such activity included David Bindman's amazing exhibition and catalogue, *The Shadow of the Guillotine – Britain and the French Revolution*,[16] the exhibition of 'French Caricature and the French Revolution 1789-1799' held in California and supported by a lengthy catalogue edited by James Cuno,[17] and Darnton and Roche's *Revolution in Print – The Press in France 1775–1800*,[18] which developed an exhibition catalogue into a more extended scholarly investigation of the subject than is usually the case. The tone for all three of these extraordinarily rich exhibitions is set by Bindman's Preface to *The Shadow of the Guillotine*. Bindman takes a general

anxiety about the historical usefulness of satirical prints as his starting place:

> The starting place for the idea of this exhibition was a review by Roy
> Porter ... in which he complained that satirical prints had been too
> often used 'as visual documentation for a political narrative, rather
> like a Georgian version of the Bayeux Tapestry', and that we must
> 'analyse these prints not just as "evidence" but as "art", with its own
> conventions for expressing moral messages'. It is easy to imagine a
> French Revolution exhibition along the lines deplored by Porter, with
> the major events represented by prints and paintings, regardless of
> their conventions of representation and the attitudes of their produc-
> ers. Another possibility, in which the works in the exhibition are
> chosen for their artistic quality rather than their historical interest
> seems equally unsatisfactory. The aim of the present exhibition has
> been to avoid both extremes ... [which] has led to an emphasis on the
> variety of visual material ... Such a range of objects, often highly
> partisan in their intentions, inevitably raises the question of the
> persuasive power of images, not only in their own time but also in
> ours.[19]

Bindman's insistence on 'the persuasive powers' of prints bring us back
towards ideology. As one reviewer of *The Shadow of the Guillotine* exhibition noted, 'its true subject is the history of distortion, the process by
which an extremely complex series of events, and the vast political
issues which they raised, were boiled down by the forces of propaganda
to a series of stereotypes'.[20] In tackling the 'history of distortion',
Bindman, Cuno, and Darnton and Roche all stress the ways in which
an understanding of modes of production, audience, and representational codes are a necessary means of seeking to align the history of
graphic images with the history of ideology.

So from the historian come a number of key ideas and conceptual frameworks which are necessary to the 'reading' of popular prints.
These include the concepts of ideology, representation, stereotype,
and propaganda. Further key ideas include the notion of prints as a
form of social persuasion, the consciousness of the intersections
between visual and verbal, graphic and written, and the nature and
status of visual evidence as a historical record. Although all the subsequent chapters draw on this repertoire of issues and concerns, chapter
3, which describes the cultural aspirations of manual labourers in a
newly class-conscious society, is the most direct discussion of the relationship between ideology and printmaking, and the chapter which

owes most to historical models of power and control within early industrial society. Equally, though, as Porter has so perceptively noted, it has been literary historians who have described 'the lexicon of the pictorial', and shown how verbal and visual codes can equally be deconstructed by the alert student. 'The idea that profundity can be verbalised but not visualised is surely a typical fallacy of the word-bound academic for whom the Word is God, and who can be as patronising to pictorial as to "preliterate" cultures'.[21] With all these warnings and cautions in mind, we should indeed patronise popular prints if we thought of them either as crassly evidential or as too simple to explain the complex ideologies within the social groups which created them. In other words, there is no such thing as a simple image.

The histories of prints

This book, as already stated, is not a history of printmaking or print-makers between 1790 and 1870. While it may be possible to piece that history together from the different kinds of studies listed in the Bibliography, the resultant narrative would still be a tentative and inadequate one.[22] There are many potential histories of prints, and probably the best that can be done in a brief introduction like this is to sketch those possibilities, and stress the wealth of further sources contained within the Bibliography.

At one obvious level, the history of prints must include some account of the major technical and economic developments of graphic media within a particular historical period. This technical history will also need to consider the relative autonomy within and between the various genres of printmaking. The chapters which follow stress the development of wood engraving rather than the development of, say, steel engraving or any persistent Victorian traditions of caricature. They also suggest a move away from prints as single images to the notion of prints as illustration. Even tendencies as large and easily evidenced as these might be disputed – many key technical changes did not result in any immediate popularity or widespread dissemination of images made by a particular reprographic method.

But some obvious features of the period between 1790 and 1870 can be fairly confidently described. The most important of these is the introduction, and eventual dominance of, end-block wood engraving as a mode of illustration.[23] More detailed discussions of the major Victorian applications of and assumptions about wood engraving are contained in chapter 5, where it is argued that the dominance of wood engraving in Victorian image making is comparable to the use of the photograph in contemporary society. Crucially, though, the wood engraving must be understood both as a naturalistic representational medium through which Victorians sought to describe and delineate their increasingly complex and technological world (illustration 5) *and* as a shorthand non-naturalistic visual code built out of long traditions of popular illustration in broadsides (illustration 1), reprinted fiction, pamphlets, and tracts. Wood engraving vastly extended the possibility of integrating text and image into the same printed page, using cheap and technically simple methods. In contrast to the most commonly used methods of printmaking in the eighteenth century – etching, copper engraving, steel engraving, mezzotint, and aquatint – which required any circumambient text to be delicately engraved on to the plate, wood engraving allowed a typeset page to be integrated with a wood engraved image and printed in a single process. In our own age of sophisticated photo-reprographic methods, where layers of typeset images and texts can be overlaid or superimposed at will, it is hard to recover the force and centrality of the wood engraving revolution in mass image making. This revolution was not just brought about by the vastly enhanced durability of wood engraved blocks over metal engraved plates, which allowed long print runs to be taken from a single block, nor by the new cheapness and speed with which vast numbers of copies of an image might be produced. The most profound revolution brought about by the massive use of wood engraved illustration was the way in which wood engraving presupposed an intense relationship between an image and a written text. Many wood engraved images (given that the size of blocks available was limited by the dimensions of the available tree trunk) could not fill a printed page. Even where several small blocks were locked together to form a single larger image, wood engraving was largely used to illustrate a text rather than to provide a single autonomous image. So Victorian wood engraved images assume a literate, indeed a reading, public.

A further implication of these massive developments in the capacity, speed, and cheapness of image making was the emergence in London of a series of trades and trade organisations built round wood engraving. A number of studies have traced the dependence of the London engraving trades on the tutelage and sponsorship of Thomas Bewick, the great pioneer of commercial wood engraving both as practitioner and entrepreneur.[24] Many of Bewick's pupils moved into the jobbing markets developing in London, and formed the pool of labour and skill necessary to launch the emblematic new illustrated ventures of the 1830s and 1840s like *The Penny Magazine* and *The Illustrated London News*. The network of engravers, entrepreneurs, speculators, and editors which underpinned the mass literature of the early Victorian period can be glimpsed by a detailed reading of Engen's *Dictionary of Victorian Wood Engravers*,[25] but the full chain of overlapping interests is hard to disentangle.[26] The interdependence of the emergence of mass circulation popular literature and the rise of the commercial wood engraving is thus one of the key historical narratives which underpins this book.

As well as the wood engraving, the period between 1790 and 1870 sees the invention and dissemination of lithography as a reprographic medium.[27] The crayon-like effects and pastel colours available through lithography particularly suited single plate caricature – one of the central images studied in chapter 3 is an 'early' use of lithography to maintain a decaying tradition of single plate caricature. Much more widely exploited in France than in Britain for satirical purposes by artists like Gavarni and Daumier, lithography none the less added an important element to the repertoire of available printmaking methods, if only because the unique textures and colours of the lithograph self-consciously announced the way in which the image was constructed. As well as the artist-made lithograph, the commercially produced chromolithograph, one of the first methods to take coloured illustration on past hand colouring for a mass audience, was widespread by the mid-Victorian period. Indeed, the chromolithograph might be described as the characteristic popular image making medium in America in this period.[28] The vignette has already been described as an important new genre. By the end of the period described by this book, photo-reprographic methods were becoming widely available.[29] Apart from generic technical developments, there are other obvious material factors bearing on the development of the print and illustration trades, which might include the price of paper or the nature of regulation and censorship within topical journalism. Additionally, the role of new professionals like the art editor, a new phenomenon in the early Victorian period, would require careful consideration.

Even from this grotesquely simplified summary, the difficulties of providing a brief history of printmaking techniques which is based upon technical change are obvious. While it is possible to chart genre-by-genre development, a wide range of reprographic media are available at any one time, and their relative significance can only be understood by introducing a socio-historical element to the discussion.

You only need to try to look for headline historical summaries to see the limitations of a technical history of prints. Should the period discussed by this book be called 'between the decline of the single plate engraved or etched print and the advent of photography'? Or is it rather 'the rise of the wood engraving'? Or 'the advent of lithography'? Or 'the death of caricature'? Or 'illustration not prints'?

The most usual way in which the socio-historical is fitted into this discussion is through the invention of an *emblematic* history of the printed image, in which major changes are described through highly visible 'representative' or 'characteristic' moments of change or break-through. The period discussed in this book is particularly rich in these emblematic moments. You could focus, for instance, on the work of the Religious Tract Society in the last decade of the eighteenth century, where a propagandising middle class seized on the mass production techniques, popular forms, and effective pyramid distribution methods of cheap street literature and subverted them to its own purposes. Acute understanding of the effectiveness of volunteer distribution networks was matched by a recognition of the value of wood engraved vignettes as both an effective sales device and as an emblematic mode of communicating values.[30] Or you could look at the Hone/Cruikshank pamphlets which celebrated the Queen Caroline controversies in 1819 and 1820 (illustration 4). Here, what masqueraded as children's toy books or popular nursery rhymes turned out to be a brilliantly apt appropriation of popular forms to new and sophisticated political purposes.[31] Then there are the really famous moments – the inaugura-tion of *The Penny Magazine* as a form of cultural propaganda (illustration 6);[32] the foundation of *Punch* which emblematically repre-sents the transmutation of eighteenth-century traditions of political caricature into the more genteel formulations of the cartoon;[33] *The Illustrated London News*, which brought the possibility of *topical* illus-tration into play;[34] *The Pickwick Papers*, a book which transformed some robust traditions of eighteenth-century engraving into illustra-tions fit for a more cautious bourgeois audience;[35] and many more.

A number of successful books on prints work within this tradi-tion of constructing a history of image making through 'breakthrough' moments of change, including the extremely valuable texts by Ivins, Mayor, and Anderson.[36] The chapters which follow, however, deliber-ately refuse to focus on famous 'emblematic' or 'representative' moments in the history of printmaking, preferring instead to work back from unselfconscious and unambitious groups of images towards wider significances. Such a technique allows a less forced and determining model of what is or is not 'representative' to emerge. The ways in which images are 'characteristic' of their time and genre in technique and iconography is something which requires careful consideration. It may be that the least ambitious and least self-conscious images are in fact the most representative. Certainly there is no attempt here to select images for study on grounds of any obvious intrinsic significance in the history of printmaking. None of the images studied in this book are radical in technique or innovatory in any formal sense. Just as they are not selected on the grounds of any perceived aesthetic quality, nor are they chosen to construct any emlematic history of the development of printmaking technique. It is their matter of fact ordinariness, their spontaneous response to an ephemeral social event or commercial opportunity, which makes them attractive as a subject of study. They offer a way into history not by their specialness, but by their ordinariness.

The above statement is, of course, somewhat disingenuous.

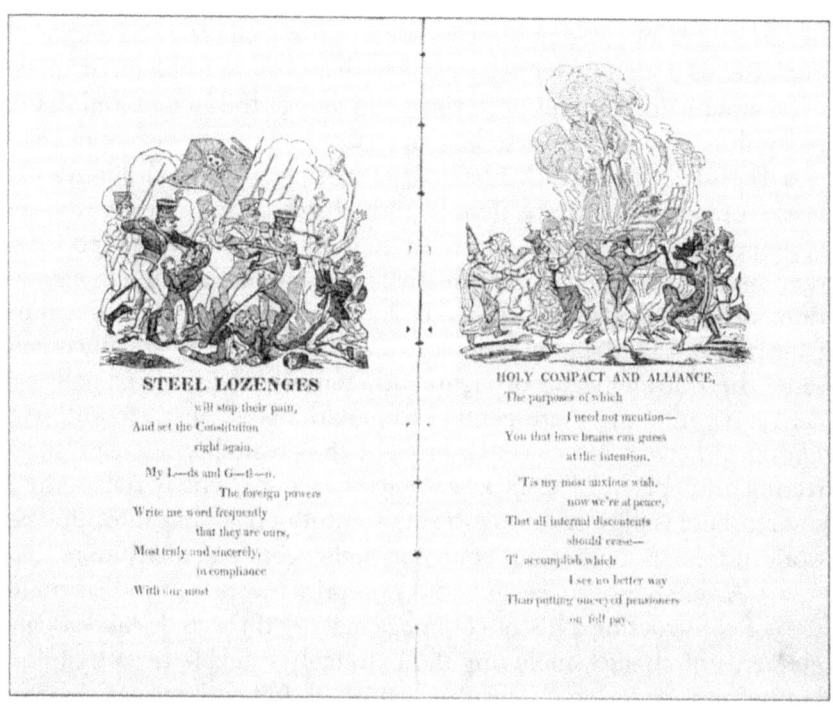

STEEL LOZENGES

HOLY COMPACT AND ALLIANCE,

4 Cruikshank's famous woodcut images for William Hone's political pamphlets dating from 1819 and 1820 provide strong evidence of the power of sophisticated artists to subvert and appropriate simple graphic media into complex meanings.

What I do ask these images to do is to offer us a way into the history of ideology, that is, into the ways in which meanings and values are constructed, negotiated, transferred, and received within a complex industrial society. The model is thus a conjunctural one. These prints exist, I argue, at points of intersection or conjunction between the propagandising aspirations of powerful social groups which can utilise image making to their own purposes and the technical, commercial, and iconographical traditions of printmaking. In seeking to represent the immediate, the topical, and the ephemeral within their own culture, these images instead describe for us the complex and not entirely conscious exchange of cultural values which is characteristic of discourse. Such discourses are dependent on representational codes which we can never decipher with absolute confidence. So much of the exchange between printmaker and audience is taken for granted, so much assumed within the image itself, that we are always tempted to replace these potentially inscrutable assumptions with our own

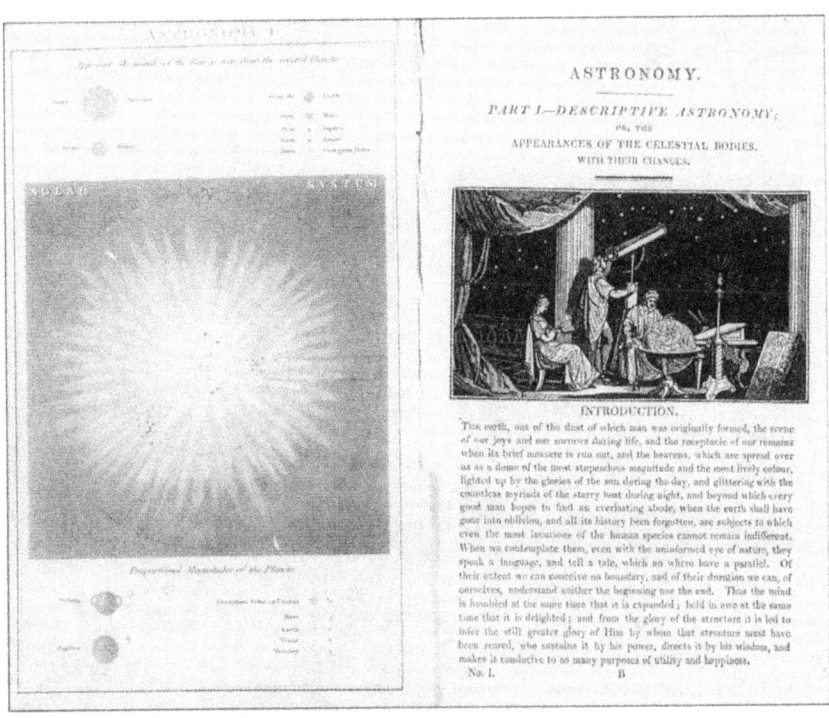

5 An early example of the publications of Charles Knight, one of the great entrepreneurs of 'useful knowledge'. *The Library for the People* combined different reprographic techniques, using both eighteenth-century traditions of copper or steel engraved explanatory diagrams and vernacular wood engraved vignettes more often associated with novels and broadsides.

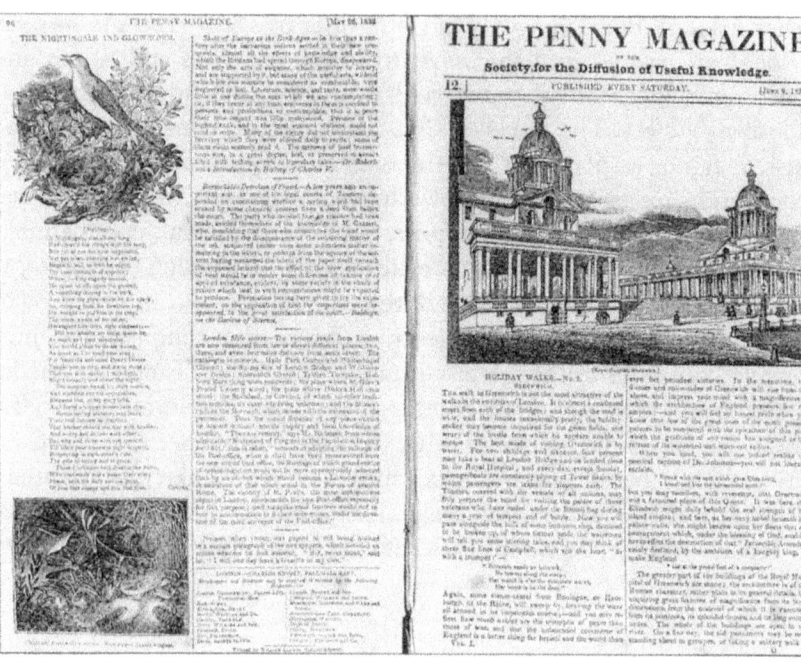

6 Through *The Penny Magazine* Charles Knight established the large wood engraving as the dominant means of depicting and explaining an increasingly complex world to artisan readers.

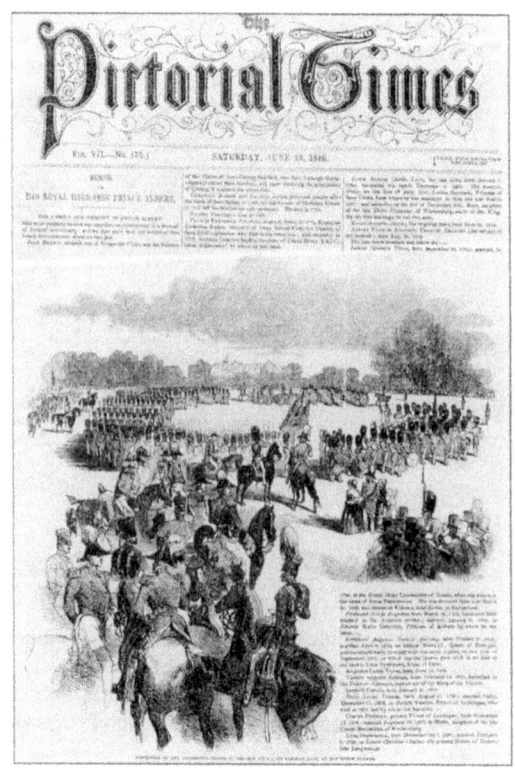

7 By the late 1840s, the success of *The Illustrated London News* had produced a range of topical weeklies illustrated by spectacular large wood engravings. This issue of *The Pictorial Times* from 1846 is characteristic of a number of similar periodicals.

preoccupations and interpretative hubris. The discourses of popular prints inevitably include our own contemporary beliefs about interpretation as well as the historically coded fields of significance in which the prints were constructed and shared. It is worth describing some of the motives which have led recent scholars and students to prints as a field of study before plunging into the dangerous pleasures of interpretation.

The recovery of popular images

In my first teaching post at the University of Leicester during the early years of the 1970s, I was able to glimpse the editing and production of Dyos and Wolff's extraordinary volumes which comprised *The Victorian City*.[37] I remember particularly the excitement generated by the visual sources – the photographs, prints, and paintings which punctuate the text and form the subject of several of the essays. It is only twenty-five years ago that the use of such historical sources seemed revolutionary, a startling exercise in 'history from below', a

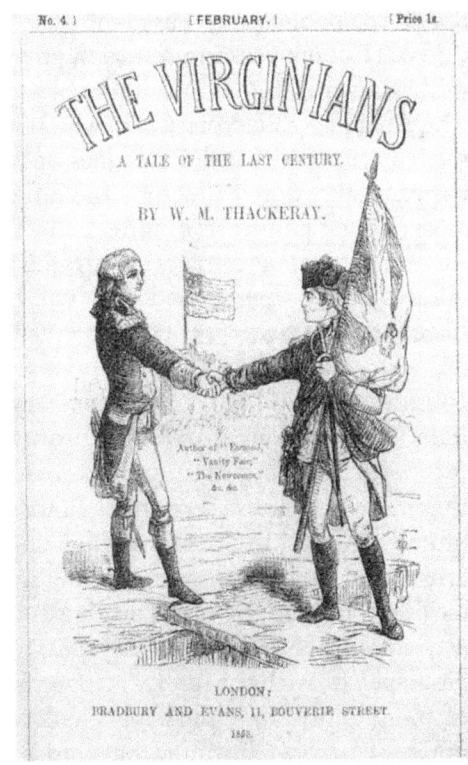

8 The serialised novel depended on a readily identifiable cover for marketing purposes. Thackeray designed his own cover for *The Virginians* (1858), which was printed in a distinctive yellow causing the author to refer to 'his jaundiced parts'.

new way of seeing and constructing the past. The recovery of a staggering array of Victorian popular imagery from unpopularity,
condescension, and neglect has been characteristic of the last thirty
years, although the motives which underlie these acts of recovery are
various. Collectors have played an important part, especially emergent
middle class connoisseurs who have been forced by economic reasons
to look beyond expensive oil paintings or antiques. While there has
always been a strong market in the major wood engravers and illustrators like Millais, Cruikshank, or Doyle, important publications like the
Moxon edition of Tennyson or *Dalziel's Illustrated Goldsmith* still
remain within the reach of moderate means. As collectors have
replaced connoisseurship with expertise, and shifted their interests
from the sophisticated to the vernacular or the mass produced, specialist interest in, say, chromolithographed popular illustration or
children's lesson books has flourished. Great collections of vernacular
material have become well known to specialists and fellow collectors,
either through deposit in a major library (like the Johnson collection
of printed ephemera in the Bodleian Library, Oxford, which formed
the basis for Louis James's *Print and the People*),[38] or through extensive
illustrated publications based on the collections (like the Opie collection of children's literature which provided *The Nursery Companion* as
well as several studies and books of essays).[39] The work of groups like
The Antique Collectors' Club, which has published a range of key listings, dictionaries, and catalogues of mass circulation printed images
basically aimed at collectors, have furthered this kind of interest in
mass popular culture as a 'collectable' field.[40]

　　But a number of other strands of interest need to be kept in
mind. Some of these are educational. Striking images are important to
history school textbooks both to create a pleasurable diversion from a
dry text, and to show the variety of sources a good historian needs to
consider. Within higher education, the post-war rise of Marxist historians, interested in structuring history from 'below', resulted in new
interest in the forgotten and the overlooked, the commonplace and
the taken for granted within Victorian culture. Certain strands of
prurient interest in the half-hidden underworlds of Victorian sexuality,
crime, and prostitution, originating in unhealthy obsessions with the
Gothic formulations of urban destitution, resurfaced in newly scholarly form in Steven Marcus's *The Other Victorians* or in Hudson's
biography of Arthur Munby.[41] Conservative nostalgia for a cosy Britain
of fairground and nursery, chalk downs and Regency terraces
progressed from illustrated Batsford books celebrating the vernacular

past in the 1930s, through *The Saturday Book*, Shell County guides, and the photographic essays of Edwin Smith into the current obsession with gentrified versions of an artisan past. In all these projects, anti-quarianism combines with a conceptual yearning to replenish the present from the past. The central activity on which to build this vision has been the recovery of as much of the past as possible, especially visual evidence of how things were.

This introduction has already shown how suspicious we need to be of the accuracy of any version of the past constructed out of visual images. We run the danger of constructing only our own fantasies and yearnings. But it would be foolishly self-denying to throw away the rich variety and energy of the images from the past assembled, for whatever reasons, over the last forty or fifty years. This book denies self-denial, and, I hope, encourages every student to dive in to the vast sea of eighteenth and nineteenth-century mass produced images which cram libraries and record offices. Do what I did – begin anywhere, with your own walls or bookshelves, and see where you get taken by whatever image you first find. I have been taken to some startling places by the prints pictured here. I hope you will join me there.

Notes

1   There are many discussions of the artistic ambitions of prints to simulate, evoke, or imitate painting. Susan Lambert's *The Image Multiplied: Five Centuries of Printed Reproductions of Paintings and Drawings* (London, Trefoil Publications 1987) is the study most obviously relevant to this book. Her opening chapter on 'The Status of the Reproduction' suggests the complex equivocations contained in the word 'original'. Carol Wax's *The Mezzotint* (London Thames and Hudson 1990) describes the history and development of one of the most ambitious print genres which was used especially for portraits and landscapes. The tonal depth of the mezzotint and the way in which it requires the artist to work from dark to light made it particularly suitable for the rendering of paintings into mass reproducible form. For studies of representative eighteenth-century painter/printmakers who sought to extend their market by exploiting prints both as versions of their painted works and as 'originals' see: D. Alexander 'Kauffmann and the print market in eighteenth-century England' in W. W. Roworth (ed.), *Angelica Kauffmann* (London, Reaktion Books 1992), 141–78 and M. Webster, *Francis Wheatley* (London, Routledge and Kegan Paul 1970), 53–86. Also relevant are the many studies of Hogarth's reluctant recognition that his oil paintings were less commercially and critically acceptable than his prints.

2   Pat Gilmour's *Artists in Print* (London, BBC Publications 1981) describes not only contemporary printmaking techniques but also some of the issues of what constitutes an 'art' print, or an 'original' print. Her book is particularly interesting as it accompanied an ambitious television series aimed at encouraging

the understanding of the qualities of prints as an aesthetic medium. I found the series informative and exciting, and it certainly confirmed and legitimised my own interest in the study of prints.

3   Walter Benjamin's famous essay 'The Work of Art in the Age of Mechanical Reproduction' from *Illuminations* remains a most interesting meditation of the print and the photograph, delineating ideas of 'authenticity' and 'uniqueness' as conceptual starting places for the study of prints. Benjamin shows how mechanical reproduction liberates the art work from ritual into politics, and hence renders irrelevant any discussion of its transcendent or autonomous value. Other useful studies of the ways in which the development of mechanical modes of reproduction in the nineteenth century transformed art images include W.M. Ivins, *Prints and Visual Communication* (Cambridge, Harvard University Press 1953); G. Wakeman, *Victorian Book Illustration – The Technical Revolution* (Newton Abbot, David and Charles 1973); C. Ashwin 'Graphic Imagery 1837–1901: A Victorian Revolution', *Art History*, vol. 1, no. 3, September 1978, 360–70; and Aaron Scharf, *Industrialisation and Culture* (Milton Keynes, Open University Press 1971), section 3. For a more general introduction to the relationship between art and the marketplace see J. Wolff, *The Social Production of Art* (London, Macmillan 1981).

4   Thomas Hearne's topographical and antiquarian engravings provide particularly interesting examples of the ways in which several artists and engravers might collaborate in the production of a single print. In engravings like 'Lanercost Priory' of 1780, for example, the print declares Hearne to be the artist and W. Byre to be the engraver. But the small solitary figure in the print, a tiny but detailed representation of a friend of Hearne's, was engraved by another specialist engraver W. Woollett (see D. Morris, *Thomas Hearne and his Landscape*, London, Reaktion Books 1989). Within the world of professional wood engraving in the 1840s and 1850s it was commonplace for various specialists to work on particular elements within the block.

5   Roy Porter 'Prinney, Boney, Boot' in *The London Review of Books*, 20 March 1986, 19–20: and 'Seeing the Past' in *Past and Present*, February 1988, 186–205. See also, for this part of the chapter, the whole of the 'Prints as social history' section of the Bibliography.

6   I am thinking particularly of J.H. Plumb's *The First Four Georges*, first issued as an unillustrated 'straight' work of scholarly history but later released by Book Club Associates as an extremely successful and good looking text illustrated from a variety of contemporary sources. Asa Briggs's collection of essays by eminent historians like James Joll and F.M.L. Thompson, first published in 1970, was re-issued in a profusely illustrated form as *The Nineteenth Century – The Contradictions of Progress* by Thames and Hudson in 1985. Such remakings of scholarly texts as illustrated books for a more general reader is a staple technique of book clubs.

7   There is one scholarly periodical, *Word and Image*, specifically dedicated to this inter-relationship between the written and the visual. Despite a tendency to aestheticism, it is a periodical which contains many articles of interest to readers of this book.

8   The vignette is luckily a form whose origins in the early nineteenth century have been excellently explored, especially by Jan Piggott, *Turner's Vignettes* (London, Tate Gallery 1993) and by Charles Rosen and Henri Zerner, 'The Romantic Vignette and Thomas Bewick' in *Romanticism and Realism* (London,

Faber and Faber 1984). Both these studies describe the ambitious early use of the vignette as one means of pursuing the Romantic sublime. However, as chapter 4 suggests, a later shift from steel to wood engraving resulted in the widespread use of the vignette form in a vast range of Victorian contexts.

9 See J.R. Harvey, *Victorian Novelists and Their Illustrators* (London, Sidgwick and Jackson 1970). There are several studies of individual novelists and their illustrators – Trollope, Dickens, and Hardy, for instance. A good brief exemplary study of the inter-relationships between text and illustrations is provided by Michael Mason's 'The Way We Look Now: Millais's illustrations to Trollope' in *Art History*, vol. 1, no. 3, September 1978, 309–40.

10 Porter, 'Seeing the Past', 188–9.

11 *Ibid.*, 200–1.

12 Alan Woods, 'Doré's *London*: Art and Evidence' in *Art History*, vol. 1, no. 3, September 1978, 343.

13 Aileen Ribeiro, *Fashion in the French Revolution* (London, Batsford 1988).

14 Christopher Hibbert, *The Days of the French Revolution* (London, Penguin, abridged and illustrated edition 1989).

15 Emmet Kennedy, *A Cultural History of the French Revolution* (New Haven, Yale University Press 1989).

16 David Bindman, *The Shadow of the Guillotine: Britain and the French Revolution* (London, British Museum 1989).

17 James Cuno (ed.), *French Caricature and the French Revolution* (Los Angeles, Grunwald Centre for the Graphic Arts 1988).

18 Robert Darnton and Daniel Roche (eds), *Revolution in Print: The Press in France 1775-1800* (Berkeley, University of California Press 1989).

19 Bindman, *Shadow of the Guillotine*, 9.

20 Andrew Graham-Dixon, 'La Revolution glorieuse' in *The Independent*, 16 May 1989.

21 Roy Porter 'Prinney, Boney, Boot', 19.

22 I have found the Introduction to Houfe's *Dictionary of British Book Illustrators and Caricaturists 1800–1914* (Woodbridge, Antique Collectors' Club, revised edn 1981) the most useful starting place, but further sources are provided by the 'General history of prints' section of the Bibliography.

23 See the sections on illustration and wood engraving in the Bibliography. R.M. Slythe's *The Art of Illustration 1750–1900* (London, The Library Association 1970) and Wakeman's *Victorian Book Illustration* provide much solid information on technical processes and their development.

24 A section of the Bibliography is devoted to Bewick.

25 R.K. Engen, *Dictionary of Victorian Wood Engravers* (Cambridge, Chadwyck-Healey 1985).

26 It is quite instructive to try to draw up charts of the interconnections between early Victorian engravers and their associates and pupils. Bewick's pupil Ebenezer Landells for example can, through various projects and employers, be linked to Edmund Evans, Robert Landells, Birket Foster, H.G. Hine, the Dalziel Brothers, Dickens's *Master Humphrey's Clock*, R.E. Branston, and J.H. Vizetelly. Put simply, Landells knew and worked with almost all the major entrepreneurs and engravers of his period. More work needs to be done on the inter-relationships between the various firms of engravers and entrepreneurs of print culture.

27 M. Twyman, *Lithography 1800–1850* (Oxford, Oxford University Press 1970) is

the standard history of the medium, but see the Lithography section of the Bibliography.

28   See P.C. Marzio, *The Democratic Art – Pictures for a Nineteenth Century America* (London, Scolar Press 1980).

29   For an account of photo-reprographic methods see Wakeman, *Victorian Book Illustration.*

30   See R.D. Altick, *The English Common Reader* (Chicago, University of Chicago Press 1957) for an account of the development of tract literature.

31   See Edgell Rickwood (ed.), *Radical Squibs and Loyal Ripostes* (London, Adams and Dart 1971) and Marcus Wood, *Radical Satire and Print Culture 1790–1822* (Oxford, Clarendon Press 1994).

32   Of the many accounts of the development of *The Penny Magazine* see Altick, *English Common Reader*, C. Fox, *Graphic Journalism in England During the 1830s and 1840s* (New York, Greenwood Press 1988), and P. Anderson, *The Printed Image and the Transformation of Popular Culture* (Oxford, Clarendon Press 1991).

33   M.H. Spielmann, *The History of Punch* (London, Cassell 1895) remains the standard history, although many other commentaries are available.

34   See Fox, *Graphic Journalism* and Anderson, *The Printed Image.*

35   See Harvey, *Victorian Novelists and their Illustrators.*

36   A. H. Mayor, *Prints and People: A Social History of Printed Pictures* (New York, The Metropolitan Museum of Art 1972); W.M. Ivins *Prints and Visual Communication* (Cambridge, Harvard University Press 1953); and Anderson, *The Printed Image.*

37   H.J. Dyos and Michael Wolff (eds), *The Victorian City: Images and Realities* (London, Routledge and Kegan Paul, 2 vols, 1973).

38   Louis James, *Print and the People 1819–1851* (London, Allen Lane 1976).

39   Iona and Peter Opie, *The Nursery Companion* (Oxford, Oxford University Press 1985). See also *The Treasures of Childhood* (London, Pavilion Books 1989) by the same authors.

40   Simon Houfe's *Dictionary*, which appears in so many of the notes in this volume, is a typically valuable product of The Antique Collectors' Club publishing programme.

41   S. Marcus, *The Other Victorians* (London, Weidenfeld and Nicolson 1966); D. Hudson, *Munby: Man of Two Worlds* (London, John Murray 1972).

CHAPTER 2

Conflagration!

THE BURNING OF THE ALBION MILL, SOUTHWARK IN 1791

Prints, paintings, and illustrations

This chapter describes a group of representations of a subject common in both popular visual culture and in ambitious eighteenth and nine-teenth-century painting – a spectacular urban fire, or 'conflagration'. The images discussed are indeed drawn from a startling variety of sources and levels within image making, and the intention of the chapter is to describe the competing meanings offered by these diverse depictions of the same event. But the fire at the Albion Mill was more than a commonplace street event. Correspondingly, the images which seek to describe the event also press beyond the commonplace. Not only was the cause of the fire at the Mill open to question, but the Mill had also established for itself a complex network of emblematic or symbolic meanings, representing to various groups in society such different possibilities as triumphant technological progress, radically changed economic organisation based on mass production, a violent attack on the economic survival of farmers and working people, or a sublime monument to human ingenuity. The Mill was a triumph, an insult, or a tragedy depending on your point of view.

In describing the representations of the fire at the Albion Mill, this chapter, unlike the ones which follow, does undertake to compare 'high art' images with those drawn from the lower reaches of popular culture. The aim of this comparison is not to establish a hierarchy in the aesthetic quality of the images, but rather to establish retrospec-tively a struggle for control over the meaning of the event. This is the only place in this book where direct discussion of watercolours and paintings is a central concern, although an awareness of potentially competing traditions of representation in oil paintings and water-colours is necessary for all discussion of popular prints.

This chapter is also the only one to discuss graphic images made before the widespread introduction of wood engraving and lithography as reprographic methods. In the 1790s, most printmaking, apart from crude woodcuts, essentially comprised single plate images, most usually copper engravings, steel engravings, etchings, aquatints, and mezzot-ints. Images of this kind are generally not dependent on a written text, as any accompanying text has to be engraved free hand into the plate. The varying inter-relationship between image and text is an important issue in this chapter. The watercolours discussed here are entirely without text, as the images themselves are intended to render language redundant through the power of painting to evoke the beyond-language code of the sublime. All the graphic images, however, draw extensively on accompanying written texts. In some cases, the text offers extensive, but separate, elucidation of the image, as in Ackermann's *Repository* or Smiles's *Lives of the Engineers*. Charac-teristically this pattern of image and separate explanatory discussion belongs in the late eighteenth century to ambitious polite discourses like serious magazines, illustrated albums, or books. In other cases, most obviously those drawn from the 'lowest' forms of social discourse like broadsides, the text and image are drawn or brought together within the single page, either by using crude woodcuts which could be reproduced as part of a typeset page or by engraving the commentary actually into the plate, so that it actually forms part of the graphic image.

One feature of this chapter is that all these kinds of images are discussed: paintings which construct a visual language of their own; single plate illustrations to an extended but separate accompanying text; engravings which use written text as part of the actual construc-tion of the visual image; and broadsides which combine a crude woodcut vignette with a printed text. These four methods of organis-ing the relationship between word and image form an interesting paradigm – images which seek to be beyond language; images which seek to illustrate an extended text; images which include words as part of the image; and images which belong with, but are distinct from, a surrounding text.

This book describes the widespread superseding, in mass culture at least, of single plate images by a cultural addiction to an inter-relatedness between image and text. Even before the early nineteenth century, when this change is driven by the widespread introduction of end-block wood engraved methods of producing illustrations which could be incorporated into the typeset page, the relationship between text and image, commentary and illustration is a complex and diverse one. In examining the startlingly diverse images described in this chapter, it is important to understand that it is not just the visual representation which constructs meaning, but the whole organisation of text and image into generic or commodity forms. Of the images discussed here only the watercolours are innocent of text. We clearly need to abandon all idea that prints are self-explanatory, that every picture tells its own story, when faced with the overwhelming evidence that few graphic images come without their accompanying freight of words, words which may seek to explain, locate, date, or divert. One of the pleasures of prints is that they are never far from language. We may properly talk of 'reading' prints, without referring exclusively to iconographical or symbolic codes.

The Albion Mill

The Albion Flour Mill, built in 1783–86 at the south-east or Surrey end of Byrne's lovely Blackfriars Bridge in London, was a famous and profoundly significant building even before it caught fire (or was, as many believed, deliberately burnt down) on 2 March 1791. The iconic status of the building was constructed through a combination of different meanings. Albion Mill was significant as a large-scale corn mill in a central metropolitan site, built to designs by Samuel Wyatt in a Palladian style which 'civilised' its industrial function in the manner of many early factory buildings. But this conventionality was only skin deep. Albion Mill was built to a new specification to house new technology, specifically Boulton and Watt's rotary steam engine, the use of which would revolutionise flour production methods. The needs of this progressive technology made fresh functional demands of the building: accordingly, complex constructional methods were required to accommodate the machinery. The detailed architectural studies of Skempton[1] and Robinson[2] allow the progressive elements in the conception, planning, building, and re-planning of Albion Mill to be easily summarised.

When it was built, the building was unique in two ways. The first was Wyatt's use of an enormous foundation raft to underpin the entire building. Skempton describes this in the following way: 'the weight was distributed as uniformly as possible over the whole area of the ground in order to minimize settlements, and especially to avoid differential settlements ... Moreover, the weight of excavated earth was equal to about one-half of the entire building load, so the net pressure imposed on the ground was greatly reduced. So far as I am aware this foundation raft had no precedent.'[3]

The second unique feature was that of size. No building of this scale had ever used timber framing, infilled with masonry, rather than load bearing masonry walls. Again to cite Skempton's conclusion, 'the timber framing was quite exceptional in its height and the large area of flooring supported without any internal walls.'[4] In addition to these unique features, Albion Mill also embodied a number of transitional elements in that process which moved factory production into its modern phase. The first element was the move towards independent framing as the structural solution to producing large, wall free, load bearing spaces for factory floors. The second, related, element was the implicit awareness of cast iron as a possible material for such framing, an awareness made clear by Wyatt's proposal to rebuild Albion Mill in a 'fire-proof' form after it had been burnt down,[5] with cast iron as the main structural material. The third element was the way in which these features were defined, or made necessary, by the need to accommodate new machinery, specifically the circular motion steam engine patented by James Watt in 1781,[6] and developed in partnership by Wyatt's friends Watt and Boulton. Albion Mill was the first time that steam power had been applied to the large-scale production of corn, and thus came to represent, in the popular consciousness at least, a classic case of machinery destroying the need for a larger labour force.

Against these popular views, Albion Mill could be, and was, read as a heroic symbol of the Industrial Revolution, combining the engineering skills of Watt and Boulton with the planning abilities of Wyatt and Rennie, and exemplifying the new technology, new modes of factory organisation of production, and the new financial structures and investment patterns of the modern capitalist era. Certainly, the building was represented in this way in the most famous graphic portrayal of the Mill, an engraving from the *New London Magazine* (see the List of images at the end of the chapter). This engraving had a much wider public impact through its use as an illustration for a book which did much to define the Industrial Revolution as a heroic technological narrative, Samuel Smiles's *Lives of the Engineers*[7] (illustration 9).

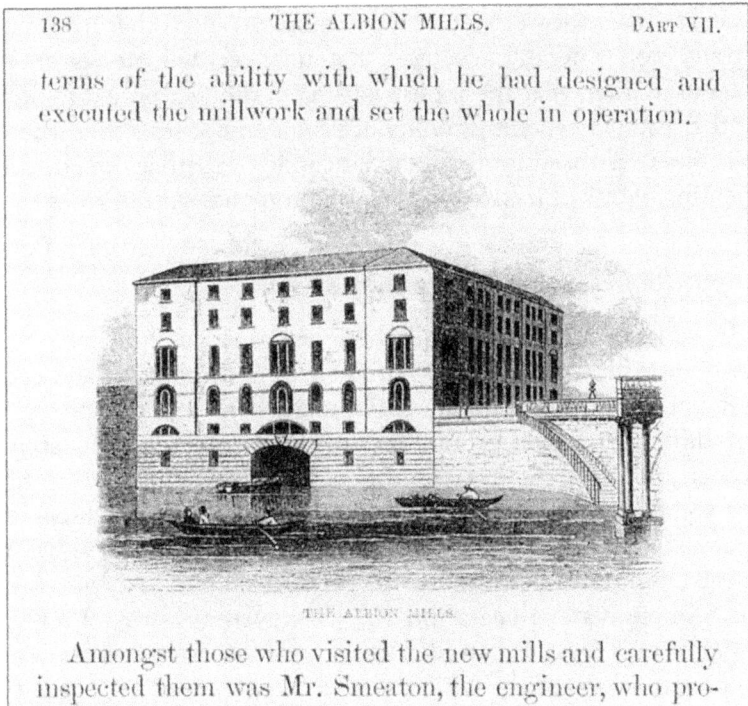

138   THE ALBION MILLS.   PART VII.

terms of the ability with which he had designed and
executed the millwork and set the whole in operation.

THE ALBION MILLS.

Amongst those who visited the new mills and carefully
inspected them was Mr. Smeaton, the engineer, who pro-
nounced them to be the most complete, in their arrange-
ment and execution, which had yet been erected in
any country; and though naturally an undemonstrative

9 Anonymous wood engraved vignette. 'The Albion Mill', an illustration to
Samuel Smiles's *Lives of the Engineers*, (1862) after a copper engraving first
published in *The New London Magazine* in July 1790.

But against Smiles's bid for a heroic industrial meaning for
Albion Mill, many of the prints I wish to study here offer a different
possibility – that the Mill served as a focus for popular anxiety over the
effects that new industrial developments would have not just on the
labour market but also on the price of popular commodities. As an
application of industrial modes of production to corn-milling, Albion
Mill entered popular consciousness through a crucial, and totemic
commodity – the loaf of bread. Modern historians may assert that
contemporary popular opinion was wrong in believing that new technology was responsible for rises in bread prices during this period, but
the discourses of popular politics largely depend on the symbolic
constructions of meanings, and the graphic representations of Albion
Mill offer an explicit site where the meaning and social significance of
the Mill were contested. As we shall see, the popular prints of the time

accepted, or at least exploited, a number of beliefs that historians now would not generally accept – that new technologies destroyed the labour market, that the industrialising of production led to price rises rather than cheapening commodities,[8] and, not least, that the Albion Mill was destroyed by disaffected incendiaries rather than by the over-heating of one of its two working Boulton and Watt engines.[9]

Representational possibilities

Given its significance in all these areas, it was inevitable that the Albion Mill as structure, as spectacle, and as political and economic symbol, would form the subject of many contemporary prints, framed in differing discourses for differing audiences, in the attempt to construct or reinforce one of the many potential meanings offered by so complex a building. The central image I wish to discuss here is Samuel Collings's copper engraving dated 1 April 1791 which was issued both as a folding plate in a periodical (*The Attic Miscellany*) and as a single plate (illustration 10). However, as a way of reading this engraving, I wish to consider in some detail a range of contemporary representations of the Mill and the competing graphic traditions in which they express themselves.

The combined resources of Skempton, who has drawn heavily on the Boulton/Watt correspondence in the Guildhall Library, the British Museum *Catalogue of Political and Personal Satires*, and the watercolours and drawings by James Moore and his protégé Thomas Girtin in the Ashmolean Museum, Oxford, the British Museum, and Newport Art Gallery, provide an interesting and complex set of repre-sentations of the Albion Mill. These images are numbered in the accompanying image list, and will henceforward be referred to by using their numbers on this list in square brackets. Although no claims for comprehensiveness can be made, the fifteen images used in this chapter fall within a widely diverse range of generic categories. (See the List of images cited at the end of the chapter. Images discussed but not illustrated are referred to by a number in square brackets.) The first genre is that of a documentary topographical and architectural repre-sentation, which is both informative and celebratory in purpose [1, 2 and 12]. The second comprises prints of the fire which drew on both picturesque and sensational popular traditions in order to present the burning of the Mill as an urban spectacle [3 and 9]. The third genre is the result of extending the picturesque elements of the scene into more ambitiously 'sublime' images of the burnt out shell of the Mill,

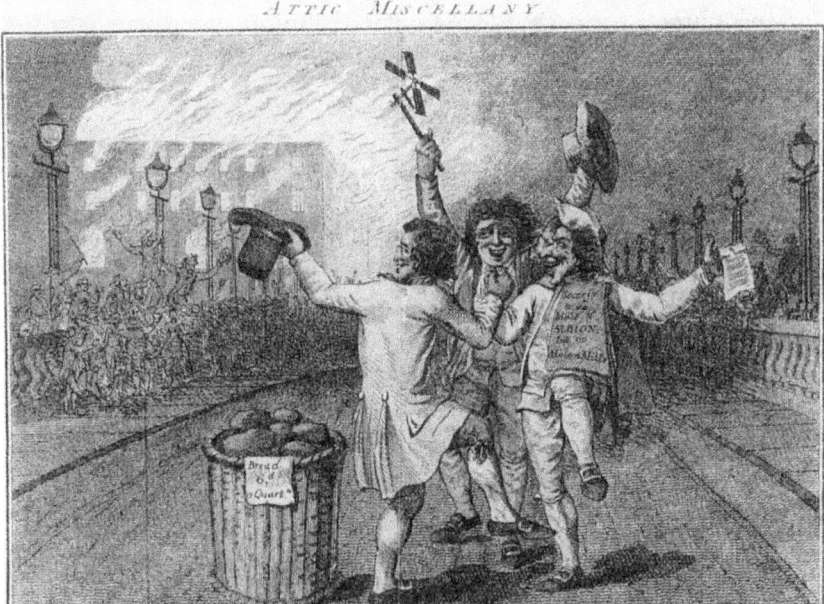

10 S. Collings engraved by Barlow, Etching. 'Conflagration! or the Merry Mealmongers' in *The Attic Miscellany*, 1 April 1791.

thus constructing an allegorical account of human frailty [8, 10, 11, 13 and 14]. The fourth is made up of engravings mainly in the caricature tradition which sought to situate the burning of the Mill within contemporary discourses about popular protest mainly through juxta-position of representations of common people against the burning Mill [4, 5, 6 and 7]. These four representational modes are not, of course, entirely distinct or exclusive, but their use does raise crucial questions about how far generic expectations and traditions do construct, or even constrain, what might be said within that mode. A further issue raised by this categorisation is the extent to which images made by a particular technique can be associated with a corresponding list of particular meanings. How far, in short, does the medium delimit, rather than permit, the resultant image? In this particular list, the picturesque list is suggested by lithographs and aquatints, the sublime through watercolours and pen and wash, the topographical through line engraving, and the satirical through often crude line engraving or through woodcuts. It is tempting to regard this evident association between chosen genre and subsequent technique as a paradigm for printmaking more generally, but this is a connection which needs careful appraisal.

The heroic

The aim of *The New London Magazine* engraving [1], as already suggested, was to offer both an informative and celebratory view of Albion Mill. The place of publication, an illustrated metropolitan journal, stresses the discourse of this print as urbane, polite and tradi-tional. The tradition invoked here is that of classical and neo-classical architectural draughtsmanship, that tradition by which the rational geometric planning of Palladio, Vitruvius, and their followers was transformed to the library folios of eighteenth-century people of taste. The engraving deliberately stresses, as a virtue, the tension between a functional industrial building (made explicit by the laden lighter entering the tunnel-vaulted loading bay) and the facade as expressing the balance, symmetry, and the poise of an elegant town house. In Girtin's watercolour [12], where the Mill building is part of a panorama looking out of the surrounding townscape, away from the river, the functional elements are completely suppressed so that the building expresses only its geometrical precision and urbanity. Interestingly, the Mill was eventually rebuilt, after the fire, on its street front at least, as housing for the gentry.[10] Hence, the industrial and functional novelty of the building is represented in [1], as the artist intended, through an appeal to civilised progress, an inevitable, polite transition from rural windmills to an urban large-scale productivity which shaped itself rationally into neo-classical facades which did not disrupt the texture of urban life. Edgar Jones argues that this alliance between early indus-trial architecture and neo-classical codes of civility and progress was a relatively unusual one in the pre-1800 phase of factory building:

> 'Initially entrepreneurs employed builders or millwrights, rather than architects to design their new plant. Using local materials and tending to follow vernacular tradition, they introduced Palladian features ... when these could be afforded or might perform a useful role. It was only in the case of a particular site (close to the City of London) or elevated role (the Royal Arsenal) that industrial buildings received special attention.... In a period when entrepreneurs and mill design-ers were largely preoccupied by structural questions and organising a building's practical operation, it was scarcely surprising that architec-ture occupied a low priority.'[11]

Given this tendency towards severe functionalism, Wyatt's presenta-
tion of his huge Albion Mill as a symmetrical neo-classical
composition, with a rusticated basement, recessed central bays, and
sophisticated string coursing, can be read in a number of ways. Partly,
as Jones suggests, it may have been a response to a particularly prominent and sensitive site already dominated by a fine neo-classical
bridge. Partly, Wyatt may have wished to conceal the revolutionary
implications of the machinery housed in his factory by using the
rhetoric or architectural gentility. Most probably, though, the building
was meant to reflect the conventional but powerful claims of classical
analogy by representing the confident civility, imperialism, and
economic power of the Greek and Roman world in architectural
terms.[12] This analogy was, of course, a commonplace within the
genteel discourses of late eighteenth-century polite culture, and it was
one still available to Samuel Smiles over fifty years later when he
translated this grand image into a small wood engraved print for his
mid-Victorian readership (illustration 9). The medium may have been
changed into a more familiar vernacular one but the heroicising
purpose of the image – industry as part of rational, civil, social progress
– remained the same. Unfortunately for Smiles, as for Wyatt, the ideological codes of neo-classical assertion were being challenged by a
whole variety of interpretative possibilities, which had been brought
into sharp focus by the spectacular fire of 1 March 1791.[13]

Spectacle

One graphic response to the fire was to exploit its picturesque implications, a tendency which can be easily identified in Edy's lithograph [3]
and in Pugin and Rowlandson's aquatint (illustration 11), which was
published long after the fire in 1808. These two images seem to me the
least interesting of those discussed in this chapter because they rob the
scene of its social content and instead concentrate on a traditional
sense of visual pleasure in urban spectacle. However, the print by
Pugin and Rowlandson, drawn from Ackermann's *Repository*, needs to
be situated within the subtle delineating function of the *Repository*,
which builds a vision of a zoned and distinctly class divided metropolis
rather than the indiscriminate street culture which is so often represented in eighteenth-century prints. The divisive river separates out
the powerfully symbolic mass of St Paul's from the crowded industrial
street scene in Southwark. Even allowing for this muted ideological
perception, however, the main interest in these two prints is the

tension between a vernacular mode of subject (street spectacles were a staple subject for broadside woodcuts) and the polite techniques and presumably sophisticated audience for lithography and aquatint. This discrepancy between mode and method is not, however, explored with any great energy in these two prints. Their main relevance for this essay is as a reminder that there was a representational possibility that the fire at Albion Mill could be delineated as a non-political event. Just how difficult it was to sustain such an ideologically bland representation of the burning mill can be judged by turning to the ostensibly similar, but in fact very different, watercolours and drawings by Moore and Girtin.

The sublime

Moore was a gentleman amateur artist of some talent. He is better remembered as Girtin's friend and sponsor than as an artist in his own right. His three pencil, pen and wash drawings in the Ashmolean Museum [13], [14], and [15], sketched immediately after the fire, and contained in an album of rather trim and dry drawings of churches and

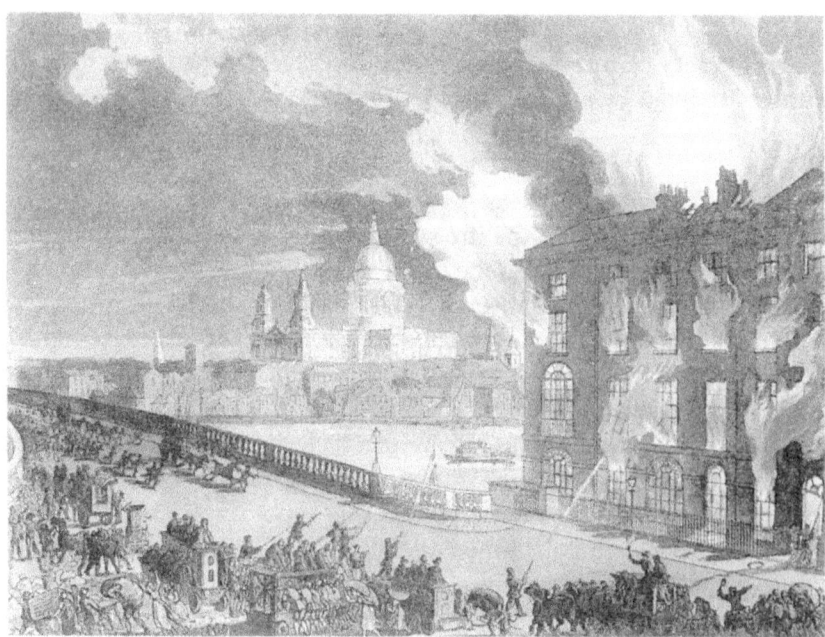

11 Pugin and Rowlandson aquatint, engraved by J. Bluck. First published in Ackermann's *Repository of Arts*, 1 September 1808, and then in *The Microcosm of London*, 1808–10.

other buildings, move interestingly beyond the picturesque formulations of Edy and Rowlandson.

Moore's drawings employ symbolic, allusive representational traditions in which the jagged ruins, heaped masonry, and fractured geometry of gear wheel, millstone, gantry and hoist aspire towards a sublime exposition of the vanities of human progress. This sudden weightiness is a startling event not just in the Ashmolean album, but in Moore's work generally, which comprised stolid topographical draughtsmanship within much less vivid modes. Moore's drawings of the Albion Mill press towards an almost Piranesi like abstraction and symbolism – Albion Mill as a grand ruin is explicitly rendered through its precarious tiered arches as a Roman aqueduct or, more obliquely as a battleground between the geometrical *braggadocio* of functional industrial architecture and the uncontrollable natural forces of fire and gravity. These drawings are conservative, but extremely vivid, eighteenth-century exercises in the rhetoric of hubris, in which the Albion Mill is presented as a gigantic *memento mori*, rendered vigorously by Moore's awed appreciation of the grandeur of scale on which this particular conflict between industrial society and nature has taken

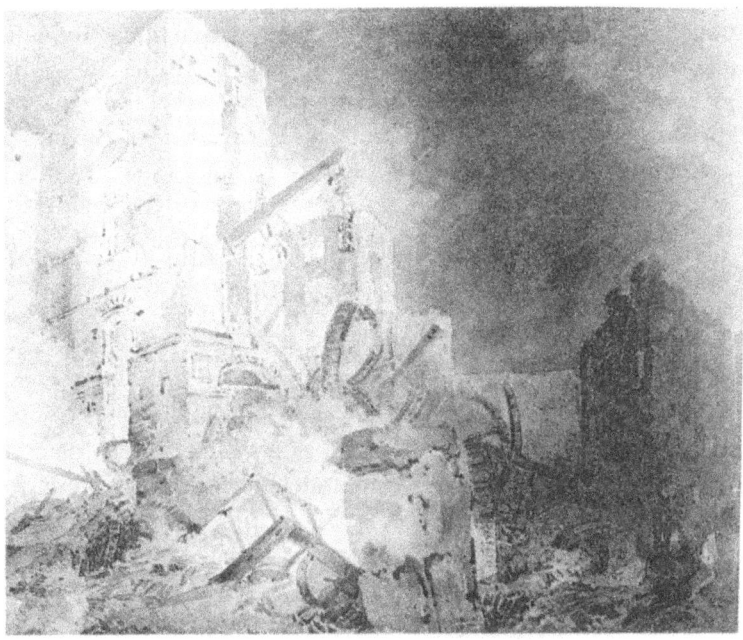

12 Watercolour by Thomas Girtin. 'Albion Mills after the Fire', 1791–92.

place. Interestingly, Girtin's Newport watercolour (illustration 12) is a rendering of Moore's least dramatic, most documentary image.

If at one level the fire at Albion Mill could be perceived as a dramatic, even picturesque, urban spectacle, at another level it could be rendered in a tradition of the sublime – a reverent meditation on the relationship between human endeavour, at its most civil and urbane, and the chastening powers of Nature. It is, of course, to both these traditions (urban spectacle and sublime revelation of natural power) that Constable and Turner allude in their interestingly comparable paintings of the burning of the Houses of Parliament in 1834.[14] Behind Constable and Turner lies the sublime tradition of rendering fire as newly visible energy through its metaphorical association with industrial process – a tradition readily apparent in the work of de Loutherbourg, Wright of Derby, and John Martin.[15] The ambitious splendours of the Albion Mill are easily rendered through this sublime moralism, a tradition in which human presence is registered through humankind's most prodigious endeavours (the factory or the blast furnace) only to be dwarfed by natural powers. Wright's famous painting of Cromford's Belper factory almost buried by surrounding trees and hills characterises a representational mode which sought to place industrial process at a level above that of individual human consequence.[16] Hence Moore and Girtin describe the Albion Mill as an unpeopled ruin, coded into symbolic messages about human smallness. The reinstatement of human scale, and of the political context of the scene, into the representation of the fire comes most forcibly in the caricatures which provide a diverse account of the feelings, actions and attitudes of the urban crowds which are so obviously absent from Moore's drawings.

Caricature

The caricature versions of the fire at Albion Mill [4, 5, 6 and 7] are unanimous in regarding the event as a dramatisation of conflicting social interests, but disparate in their expression of opinion and in their artistic method. Indeed, the varying degrees of sophistication from Collings's complex etching, down through simple line engraving to re-used woodcut is a reminder of how loose a term 'popular prints' may be, especially as two of these satirical prints depend on highly developed written texts, and the other two are festooned with captions and other verbal messages as an aid to interpretation.

'The Albion Mill on Fire' [4], the first of the dated prints to be published (on 10 March 1791, not much more than a week after the fire) is a topical broadside. The text is predominantly narrative, and the woodcut is a depiction of a conventional street scene, lacking any true topographical specificity. The Mill's architectural sophistication is reduced to crude symmetry and the streetscape in the background is rendered in schematic shorthand. The fire engines, much ridiculed in the late eighteenth century both for their tardy arrival and for their ineffectuality, are shown in all their clumsiness with a sly visual joke at the right hand fireman's expense as he is shown apparently pissing on the fire. The image is vivid and dramatic, with a fine pall of dark smoke, but ultimately only forms a crudely simplified and conventional street drama, apart, that is, from the presence of the two impish devils, one fiddling on the balustrade while Albion burns, the other helping on the fire by means of a pair of bellows. The presence of the devils makes political readings of the print available. Are the devils meant to represent the malicious spirit of 'the people' who, even if they have not caused the fire, none the less regard it with pleasure as an instrument of divine retribution against presumptuous and corrupting new technology? But, even allowing this possibility, the print is only marginally political, and not at all radical. That 'very few did sorrow show' is reported as a visible fact rather than as social commentary. The possibility of arson, which was widely suspected at this time, is not even mentioned or implied. The popular belief that the Mill had caused a rise in bread prices, discussed in stanza six, is presented as unconfirmed popular opinion rather than as supported argument. Even the conventional valedictory couplet is cautious:

> That the poor with plenty may abound
> Tho' the Albion Mills burnt to the ground.

'Tho' rather than 'because' – the unwillingness of text and image to interpret and judge is clearly demonstrated here.

In summary 'The Albion Mill on Fire' [4] is a collation of conventional motifs and tropes, essentially topical and narrative in organisation. The political and economic implications of the event are acknowledged through cautiously introduced and unsupported popular opinions but are never organised into anything approaching a sustained, coherent point of view. Popular pleasure at the fire is noted, but not debated. This print, then, is a basic commodity text, with text and image highly interdependent, which allows the widest possible range of viewers or readers to respond to the drama and excitement of the fire without having their particular interpretation of the event subjected to scrutiny or challenge. Here we see a commodity text suppressing social meaning in order to fulfil the tastes of the largest possible audience. This suppression of interpretation is quite unlike the print published by Fores, 'A Bonfire for the Poor' [5], where the aim is neither decorative nor sensational but overtly ideological.

'A Bonfire for the Poor' is an extremely crude line engraving packed with verbal interpretative information. It offers, surprisingly, quite an accurate (if poorly drawn) architectural summary of the Mill, and reduces the fire, so visually prominent in [3], [9], and [4], to some wisps of smoke and peripheral flame billowing from the side and basement of the building. The emphasis here is neither on the building itself, nor on the street spectacle, but on the social and political meaning of the events described, which are represented in vigorous populist terms. The devils here are openly identified with the sketchily indicated crowds on the stairs and on the bridge to the right of the print, with the mass of people inciting the devil in his attempts to encourage the flames with his bellows. The devil, however, remains diabolically manipulative of his sudden popularity – 'what they save in Bread they spend in Gin', he remarks, properly alert to the many available routes to damnation. But this cynical moment apart, the print vindicates, indeed asserts, popular delight in the destruction of the Mill. The left hand barge in the foreground carries four of the Mill's proprietors or managers, in a state of dejected agitation and all too eager to disclaim responsibility. As one oarsman remarks to another, 'They look D...d sulky about it'. More oblique, but even more damning, are the moored barges laden with, on the left 'Pot80 Flower' and, on the right, imported 'Indian Wheat'. The implication is a double one: that the owners of Albion Mill adulterated their flour, and secondly that they used imported wheat when home grown supplies were available. Thus, as the sub-title has it, was 'the shame of Albion exposed'.

This crude, almost illiterate, print clearly pre-supposed a disaffected popular audience, and seems to have operated in a discourse below that of a polite caricature. The publisher of this print, Fores, issued more sophisticated topographical and sporting prints later in his career,[17] but little evidence of cultural ambition appears here, any more than it does in 'The Bakers Glory' [7], a slip-sheet broadside which married a polemical doggerel text to an earlier woodcut.[18] George suggests that the woodcut might be seventeenth century in origin, in which case it must have supplied the image for many disparate texts.[19] The verse tells of millers, bakers, and the ordinary populace flocking to the scene of the fire and rehearsing a series of grievances: the Mill increased the price of flour through monopolising the market, it made country millers redundant, it adulterated the flour it produced, and stockpiled much needed supplies of corn in order to manipulate the market. The text offers these popular views without any attempt at fairness, and, despite a faintly apologetic conclusion:

> I hope these lines that I have penn'd
> None will affront ...

is in fact unabashed in its polemic intentions:

> The case is plain for to be seen
> The price of bread so dear to see
> Let's hope it will much cheaper be.

So both this broadside and [5] suggest the existence of outspoken representations of the Albion Mill fire as a providential triumph for popular justice. The case against the Mill is rehearsed with both coarse humour and with direct accusation, presumably for an audience of tradespeople, artisans, and labourers. Collings's sophisticated representation of 'Conflagration' (illustration 10) can only be properly read against these popular interpretations of the event. Typically for this period it is in caricature and popular prints that social meanings are most vigorously contested. Prints like these are particularly important given Dorothy George's comment that at this time 'the problems of poverty are barely touched on'.[20]

Samuel Collings and the Albion Mill

As is often the case with caricaturists of the late eighteenth century, it is extremely hard to define an appropriate social locale or ideological consistency (or even precise biographical facts) for Samuel Collings.[21] He was clearly deeply engaged in London literary and artistic life in the ten years before his death in 1791, working for *The Wit's Magazine*, *The Carlton House Magazine*, and, especially *The Attic Miscellany*, which was edited for at least some of its life by the prominent self-taught radical dramatist and novelist Thomas Holcroft. Little attention has been paid to the particular qualities of Collings's work except in so far as he collaborated with more famous artists: with Blake, who engraved a series of elaborate social satires drawn by Collings and published by Harrison in *The Wit's Magazine* in 1784;[22] with Morland, for whom Collings wrote verses and suggested subjects in the late 1780s;[23] and, most famously, with Rowlandson, who collaborated with Collings on the series of twenty extremely funny plates for *The Picturesque Beauties of Boswell*, published by E. Jackson in 1786.[24] It is hard to pull together the separate threads of Collings's work. His collaborations with Blake and Holcroft suggest that he had access to late eighteenth-century radical artisan culture, and Dorment argues that even the apparent conservatism of Morland's prints and Collings's verses for 'Fruits of Early Industry' might be read as an ironic attack on middle class values.[25] Against this view of Collings as a plausibly radical figure, many of his small Attic Miscellany personal satires were blatantly anti-radical, notably a vigorous attack on Joseph Priestley.[26] 'Conflagration' too is most obviously read as a conservative image.

Only tentative conclusions are possible. Collings seems to have been a professional hack writer and artist, willing to subordinate personal conviction to commercial commission, and making his living as an editor and contributor to periodicals, especially those with a theatrical interest.[27] He drew for a wide variety of engravers as the occasion arose, and was ambitious and accomplished enough to exhibit work at the Royal Academy.[28] If Henry Angelo's account of him is to be believed, he was a gregarious and amiable metropolitan figure:

> Collins [sic], well known in the region of Covent Garden and sometime editor of the *Public Ledger*, was a lively satirist, both with his pencil and his pen ... a great tavern goer, and known to all the dons of the green-room, kept late hours. His fate was lamented, he being found dead on the steps of an hotel. Collins was known to be no economist: great, then, was the surprise of his convives on discovering that he, scribbler and caricaturist, should die with sixty pounds in his purse which was found in his pocket.[29]

The rakish cosmopolitan evoked here may seem to me to belong both stylistically and morally more to a declining Hogarthian line of urban representation than to the increasingly savage, politicised, personal caricature tradition of Gillray and his followers. Dorment points to the Hogarthian resonances of the Morland prints,[30] and Collings drew one pair of prints, 'The Disinherited Heir', very much in the tradition of Hogarthian moral narratives.[31] Collings's preferred subjects, too, centred on lively scenes crowded with people in the Hogarthian manner. In the amused geniality of his densely urban and tonally complex prints, Collings stands in obvious contrast to the vivid line and grotesque exaggeration of many of his contemporaries. He belongs to a more genteel discourse which is as close to, say,

Wheatley's sentimental 'Cries of London' or to idealising mezzotints after Hamilton and Morland as to the scratching caricatures of Gillray or Newton. Yet if the world of his drawings seems urbane and genteel, his contacts with radical figures like Blake and Holcroft cannot be ignored. In short, the social and ideological basis of Collings's work remains ambiguous and difficult to define either through contextual information or through a study of his prints.

In style, Collings shows something of the warm gregariousness already noted. His figures are seldom exaggerated into total grotesques, and the energy and vigour of his scenes never becomes manic or unhealthy. His larger compositions are complex for caricatures, and are entirely dependent on visual modes of representation except for added verses or captions. Collings seems never to have incorporated verbal elements into his actual drawings. Despite Essick's charge of clumsiness,[32] his drawings show a high degree of finish, aspiring to the fullness and incidental variety of ambitious line engraving. Usually, as in the Albion Mill print, a frieze of fully realised characters is set against a sketchier, greyer, less differentiated backdrop. Many of these effects are gained by vigorous cross hatching. Of especial interest here is Collings's particular visual language for representing the common people who appear so frequently in his prints. Collings makes little use of the racial and bestial elements central to Gillray's work – thick lips, ridged receding foreheads, receding chins, all adding up to a simian effect. Collings shows plebeian origins through wild, longish hair, huge elongated chins and deformed noses, with heads generally too big for their bodies. Obvious sources for these idioms are hard to locate – perhaps Hogarth's illustrations to Butler's *Hudibras* form as close a source as can be found.

But at least as important as Hogarth as a source for Collings's style is the theatre and the various traditions of theatrical illustration, exemplified in the late eighteenth century by such publication as Bell's *Shakespeare* of 1774–78 which was illustrated by copper engravings taken from actual performances. Collings's interest in the theatre is evident in a number of ways: from his acquaintance with Holcroft, one of the best known popular dramatists of the day; from his connection with magazines designed to institute theatrical reviewing as a central component in each issue;[33] from Angelo's remark, already cited, that Collings was 'known to all the dons of the green-room'; from his series of studies of theatrical gesture and expression in *The Attic Miscellany*;[34] and from a print which responded to the dramatic events of the French Revolution by satirising theatrical melodramas which misrepresented the actual historical events.[35] The closed, box-like settings of many of Collings's prints resemble proscenium arch stage sets, while the exaggerated gestures of the caricatures are striking in their closeness to contemporary engravings of acting styles.

One further possible influence on Collings's drawing style may be conjectured. Holcroft, among his many and varied accomplishments, had in 1789 translated Lavater's key book on physiognomy,[36] a book which offered a formal account of the relationship between moral character, appearance, and facial expression. The existence of such a relationship was presumed, if not theorised, by many printmakers and caricaturists from Hogarth on. While Collings does not develop in his graphic work any of Lavater's ideas in a way that Gillray does, his access to debates about the representation of character through physical appearance should certainly be borne in mind in attempting to decode his engravings.

All these contextual issues raised by Collings's work – the political ambiguity of his caricatures, his refusal to adopt the extreme vocabulary of contemporary political and personal caricature, the evident zest and bonhomie of both his life and work – seem to me to add up to a warning not to bring to 'Conflagration' any firm preconceptions about its, or indeed *The Attic Miscellany*'s, likely perspective on the events delineated. The discourse of Collings's drawings seem to me, in contrast to Essick's dismissive equation of it with trashy, opportunistic, vernacular printmaking, essentially polite and genteel, bringing the resources of theatrical prints, popular physiognomy, and Hogarthian moralism to bear on subjects drawn and engraved with more care and sophistication than most popular prints. One only has to glance at 'A Bonfire for the Poor' [5] to see what a really crude popular print looks like. In confronting the polite with the vernacular, Collings is only furthering the cultural negotiations which had provided the energy which underpins, for example, Gay's *Beggars Opera*, Burns's 'Cotter's Saturday Night', Tim Bobbin's *Human Passions Delineated*, John Kay's Edinburgh portraits and, at a more sublime level, Blake's own lyrics.[37] But if the level of Collings's discourse is relatively easily available to scrutiny, his political and ideological position is far harder to assess. It is to these difficulties of interpreting 'Conflagration' that we must now turn.

The first thing to say about Collings's print is that it is the only image of the Albion Mill assembled here to centre on the people involved rather than on the street spectacle provided by the burning Mill or its ruins. Collings's etching focuses on three rural figures, probably millers, the 'Merry Mealmongers' of the sub-title, who are dancing an unrestrained rustic measure presumably to celebrate the destruction of the much hated Mill. One man carries his hat, another a child's toy windmill which is deliberately silhouetted against the flames given off by its urban, industrial equivalent. The third man has a slip ballad sheet over his shoulder proclaiming, with considerable ambiguity, 'Success to the Mills of Albion, but no Albion Mills', and a 'new song' sheet in his hand. By the dancing men is a bin of newly cheap bread priced at 6d for a quartern loaf. On the bridge's balustrade a rapturous crowd delight in the sight of the fire. The caption concludes with the comment 'a new dance as it was performed with Universal applause at the Theatre, Blackfriars, March 2nd 1791'.

The most coherent way of reading these elements is to regard the print as an attack on the crude and unthinking popular reaction to the destruction of the Mill. A group of ignorant rustics, Luddites almost, are naively delighted at the destruction of a symbol of new and progressive technology which, as they wrongly believe, is responsible for both the loss of traditional jobs and the high price of food. The crudeness of this response is thus satirically conveyed through the violent and unthinking intemperance of the popular reaction, the clod-hopping, grinning clumsiness of the dance, the reactionary jingo-ism of the ballad sheet, and the ironic description of the 'Universal applause' of popular reaction to the catastrophe. Such a reading of the print as a denunciation of popular reaction is, however, crucially dependent on two elements – the satirical delineation of the three central characters and the implicit political and historical resonances of the image.

Certainly, the three central characters are derided, with their rustic clumsiness only emphasised by the awkward setting of the left-hand head on its owner's shoulders, and the grotesquely extended nose and chin of the left-hand dancer, although it may be that the dancers are wearing carnival masks to hide their identity. All three have the flowing wild locks of hair characteristic of Collings's plebeian charac-ters, yet their bodies are sturdy and well proportioned, if coarsely dressed. If Collings's print is an attack on unthinking excess, it is a surprisingly restrained one. But the key element here, it seems to me, is Collings's recall of other images of burning buildings and rejoicing crowds. In particular, given his known connections with major late eighteenth-century printmakers, Collings may well have known Boydell's famous print of 1790, engraved by J. Heath from a now lost oil painting by Francis Wheatley of the 1780 Gordon Riots.[38] This print clearly overtly celebrates the heroic deeds of the Volunteers in quelling disorder, and the fire and the crowds are carefully balanced against a neatly ranked, uniformed yeomanry in order to offer a narra-tive of anarchy overcome by order. Despite Collings's apparent lack of interest in drawing political subjects, he did respond to the events of the French Revolution and drew a satirical account of a radical, Joseph Priestley, whose house had been set alight by an intemperate mob.[39] As the recent French Revolution bi-centenary exhibitions have clearly demonstrated, it would not have been difficult for Collings to have seen many, mostly celebratory, prints of the storming of the Bastille made up of graphic motifs comparable to ones used in his Albion Mill print.[40] These analogies should not be taken too far, but the possibili-ties are clear enough to permit a coherent reading of 'Conflagration' as a satire on the misplaced violence of popular reaction to the burning of the Mill. Important here, too is the implicit guilt Collings creates by juxtaposing the discontented populace so firmly against the flames. At this particular moment, a few weeks after the fire, many people still believed the fire to be the work of malcontent incendiaries, and Collings certainly retains this possibility in his print. 'Conflagration' then might read as a genteel satire, published in a polite metropolitan journal, denouncing the reactionary and unthinking violence of an ignorant populace, who are seen not so much as mongers of meal as mongers of anarchy.

But I think several elements in 'Conflagration' serve to contra-dict, or at least to complicate, its apparent conservatism. The first of these is Collings's willingness to reject the obvious picturesque and sublime representational traditions available to him in favour of an explicitly social and political idiom. In his version of the fire, crowd and spectacle, onlookers and event, are seen to have a predominantly economic relationship. Their juxtaposition is not primarily an act of aesthetic judgement, nor even a crudely polemic contrast, but rather one which acknowledges economic grievance and social discontent even as it seeks to contain them. The pure energy of the figures, too, complicates the print, especially as they are so consciously linked to the pleasures of popular carnival through the depiction of broadsides[41] and the allusion to the streets of Blackfriars as a 'theatre'. Even the child's toy windmill, redolent of holidays and fairs, points ambiguously both to its wielder's childishness and to his capacity for simple plea-sure. Typically for Collings, the print celebrates the pleasures of urban street culture even as it derides them as metaphors of childish, igno-rant, anarchic political and economic perceptions. Ridiculous as these

clumsy figures are intended to be, they none the less bring a vital presence to the scene, and Collings seems to have had difficulty in
deciding whether their delight is properly child-like and innocent or
else dangerously irrational, even seditious.

Conclusion

Interpretation of course, depends heavily on the preconceptions of
the spectator. Yet as I hope I have shown, these preconceptions are
not necessarily easy to define. Lacking a clearly evolved tradition for
representing common people, Collings avoids the racial and bestial
physiognomy developed by Gillray which is still being used in the
single plate caricatures of the 1820s and 1830s described in chapter
3, using instead his own less exaggerated form of grotesquery. But any
derision for popular opinion and radical politics is to some extent
offset against his Hogarthian pleasure in street scenes, in theatrical
gesture, and in the ambiguous delights of urban life. Equally, Collings
rejects a series of representational traditions available to him in
depicting London fires – picturesque aquatints, sublime watercolours
or oil paintings, polemically crude line or wood engravings.
Acknowledging that genre and generic expectations can overdeter-
mine what can be said, Collings pursues his own idiom, drawing on
both vernacular and polite elements to offer his own interpretation
of a complexly symbolic event. Yet he himself is inevitably
constrained by the genteel discourse of *The Attic Miscellany* and its
presumed readership. It is clear that the dangers of reading simple
historical meanings into prints like these are acute. While it may be
true, in general terms, that the caricatures of the fire at Albion Mill
do suggest, as Dorothy George claims, 'the attitude ... of the poorer
classes',[42] it is also evident that caricatures were only one of a number
of graphic discourses in which the meaning of the event was negotiated with the public. Even within that caricature discourse, as
'Conflagration' shows, political, social, and generic meanings remain
disconcertingly unstable.

List of images cited

[1] 'The Albion Mill, Blackfriars Bridge'
     Anonymous engraving; engraved by Eastgate.
     The New London Magazine vi (July 1790), 329.

[2] 'The Albion Mill' (illustration **9**)

Anonymous wood engraved vignette drawn after [1], in Samuel Smiles, *Lives of the Engineers* (London, John Murray 1862), vol. 2, 138.

[3] 'A View of the Albion Mills on Fire'
Coloured aquatint. Drawn and engraved by J. Edy.
Cited by Skempton, 'Samuel Wyatt and the Albion Mill', 40.

[4] 'The Albion Mill on Fire'
Anonymous engraving. Published by C. Sheppard, 10 March 1791.
BMC, VI, No. 8020.

[5] 'A Bonfire for the Poor, or the Shame of Albion Exposed'
Anonymous coloured engraving. Published by S.W. Fores, 1 April 1791.
BMC, VI, No. 8021.

[6] 'Conflagration! or the Merry Mealmongers' (illustration **10**)
Etching. Drawn by S. Collings, etched by Barlow.
The Attic Miscellany (London, Bentley & Co.), 1 April 1791.

[7] 'The Bakers Glory, or, The Conflagration'
Anonymous woodcut with broadside text.
BMC, VI, No. 8023.

[8] 'View of the Ruins of the Albion Mill'
Watercolour. Signed SW. 1803.
Guildhall Library. Cited by Skempton, 'Samuel Wyatt and the Albion Mill', 40.

[9] 'Fire in London' (illustration **11**)
Aquatint. Drawn and engraved by Pugin and Rowlandson.
Aquatint by J. Bluck.
Published by Ackermann's *Repository of Arts*, 1 September 1808,
as part of *The Microcosm of London* (2 vols).

[10] 'Albion Mills after the Fire' (illustration **12**)
Watercolour by Thomas Girtin. 1791–92?
Newport Museum and Art Gallery.

[11] 'Albion Mills after the Fire'
Watercolour by Thomas Girtin. 1791–92?
Lost, but cited by T. Girtin and D. Loshack, *The Art of Thomas Girtin* (London, A. & C. Black 1954), 14.

[12] 'Albion Mills'
Watercolour by Thomas Girtin. 1797–98?
British Museum. See Leslie Parris, *Landscape in Britain c.1750–1850* (London, Tate Gallery 1973), 83.

[13] 'Albion Mills'
Pen and wash by James Moore. 27 February 1791.
Ashmolean Museum, Oxford.
D. Blayney Brown, *Catalogue of the Collection of Drawings in the Ashmolean Museum* 1982), 1395.

[14] 'Albion Mills Southwark, immediately after the fire'
Pen and wash by James Moore. 1791?
Ashmolean Museum, Oxford.
Blayney Brown, *Catalogue*, 1396.

[15] 'Albion Mills'
Pen and wash by James Moore 1791?
Ashmolean Museum, Oxford.
Blayney Brown, *Catalogue*, 1397.

Notes

1 A.W. Skempton, 'Samuel Wyatt and the Albion Mill' in *Architectural History*, vol. 14, 1971, 53–73. Skempton lists many of the plans and constructional drawings in the Guildhall Library.

2 J.M. Robinson, *The Wyatts: An Architectural Dynasty* (Oxford 1979), 44–8.

3 Skempton, 'Samuel Wyatt and the Albion Mill', 55.

4 *Ibid.*, 55.

5 *Ibid.*, 47–8.

6 Robinson, *The Wyatts*, 45. See also H.W. Dickinson and R. Jenkins, *James Watt and the Steam Engine* (1927), 164–8.

7 Samuel Smiles, *Lives of the Engineers* (London, John Murray, 2 vols., 1862), II, 134–42. The whole section of Smiles's book on Rennie is relevant to this chapter.

8 See the commentary by M.D. George in *BMC*, VI, Introduction and Nos 8020–8023.

9 Robinson, *The Wyatts*, 47.

10 *Ibid.*, 49.

11 Edgar Jones, *Industrial Architecture in Britain 1750–1939* (London, Batsford 1985), 46.

12 *Ibid.*, 22–3. This section of his book is called 'The hierarchy of decorum and Palladianism'.

13 Robinson says (p. 46) of the Albion Mill fire, apparently without irony, that it was 'the most picturesque of the period'.

14 An extremely detailed description of Turner's oils and watercolours of the scene can be found in R. Dorment, *British Painting in the Philadelphia Museum of Art* (Philadelphia, Museum of Art 1986), 396–405. Dorment concentrates his discussion on the Philadelphia oil listed by M. Butlin and E. Joll, *The Paintings of J.M.W. Turner* (New Haven and London, Yale University Press, revised edn., 2 vols, 1984) at number 359. See also no. 364. Dorment shows many of the sketches and also two contemporary engravings of the scene. A crude Catnach engraving of the fire can be found in T. Gretton, *Murders and Moralities – English Catchpenny Prints 1800–1860* (London, British Museum 1980), 62–3. See also K. Solender, *Dreadful Fire! – Burning of the Houses of Parliament* (Cleveland, Museum of Art 1984) and *1666 and Other London Fires* (London, Guildhall Art Gallery 1966).

    The bridge/fire/crowd combination in Turner's Philadelphia oil is described by Dorment as both a theatrical and an accurate representation of the scene. Both the Philadelphia and the Cleveland oils combine the artist's interests in sublime manifestations of natural forces with his analytical account of fire reflected in water. Both pictures also show a less sophisticated obsession with street spectacle.

    More precisely relevant to this chapter, both in mode and in date, is Turner's watercolour 'The Pantheon, the Morning after the Fire' now in the Tate Gallery and dated 1792. The picture was shown at the Royal Academy in that year. As a representation of a neo-classical building devastated by fire, Turner's watercolour shares obvious thematic concerns with Girtin and Moore, but is very different in its considerable interest in the crowd of bystanders, both genteel and vulgar, gathered to witness the scene. Here again, Turner's interest in crowds and street spectacle brings this picture as close to vernacular prints as ambitious watercolours or oils on sublime themes. None the less, Turner did additionally draw the ruined interior of the Pantheon (which, interestingly enough, had been designed by James Wyatt) in an unpeopled, allegorical mode very similar to that used by Girtin and Moore in their drawings, drawings which Turner may well have known. The contrast between the two Turner accounts of the Pantheon is interestingly made in Solender, *Dreadful Fire!*, 12–13. Both are reproduced on p. 12. The continuity between the images used in this chapter and Turner's later sophisticated re-workings of these early representations is one well worth further exploration.

A further interesting comparison here is with George Jones's watercolour 'Fire on the Thames' of *c*. 1808. Jones was a close friend of Turner's, and eventually acted as one of his executors. 'Fire on the Thames' has interesting structural similarities to [5], although the manner is, of course, in the sublime tradition of Turner, Moore, and Girtin. See Christopher White, *English Landscape 1630–1850* (New Haven, Yale Centre for British Art 1977), 107 and plate CLVI.

15   Of particular interest here are Wright's several pictures of artisan cottages on fire. See B. Nicolson *Joseph Wright of Derby: Painter of Light* (London, 2 vols, 1968), I, 269–70 and J. Egerton, *Wright of Derby* (London, Tate Gallery 1990), 182. Wright here seems to be playing with the elevating potential of the sublime manner. Even the most humble picturesque scene may be transformed by the violent manifestations of natural power into visionary and powerful moments worthy of large-scale paintings. Discussions of the representation of industrial scenes can be found in F. Klingender *Art and the Industrial Revolution* (London, 1947, revised by A. Elton 1968) and in the catalogue of the 1968 *Art and the Industrial Revolution* exhibition at Manchester City Art Gallery. Klingender in particular was concerned to show how new industrial forms and landscapes re-surfaced obliquely in ambitious mythological and heroicising paintings.

16   See the *Art and the Industrial Revolution* catalogue, 34.

17   Fores was a famously opportunistic and vigorous print seller, quick to exploit any new fads in popular taste. Later in his career he became prominent as a publisher of coaching prints. See Nicholas Bentley, *The Victorian Scene* (London, 1968), 236–7. Collings did, however, draw for Fores on occasions.

18   The text of this broadside is reprinted, along with the Pugin/Rowlandson aquatint and *The Gentleman's Magazine* description of the Mill, in Roy Palmer's *A Ballad History of England* (London, Batsford 1979), 72–3. Palmer compares the Albion Mill fire to another in a weaving factory in Knott Mill, Manchester, in 1790. Although, as Palmer notes, the Manchester fire was recorded in verse, I have been unable to trace any pictorial accounts of it.

19   BMC, VI, p. 871.

20   BMC, VI, xxix.

21   Collings fails to appear in most of the standard dictionaries of printmakers and caricaturists. The brief entry in William Feaver's *Masters of Caricature* (London, Weidenfeld and Nicolson 1981) says merely that Collings 'is considered among

the minor caricaturists' (p. 52). Even the date of his death is not clear. The *DNB* entry gives 1790? which cannot be right given that he engraved 'Conflagration' in March 1791, which is the year of his death given by Feaver.

22 See R.N. Essick, *William Blake, Printmaker* (Princeton, Princeton University Press 1980), 47–8 and plate 25. Essick is extremely dismissive of Blake's 'purposely crude and heavy style of etching' in these prints which he attributes to Blake's growing commercial awareness of the marketplace. Essick, despite his contempt for this work as 'rough', acknowledges that Collings and Blake were using 'Hogarthian motifs' and that the prints show Blake's (though apparently not Collings's) 'feeling for life in the London streets and sympathy with the tastes of common men'. M.D. George in *Hogarth to Cruikshank – Social Change in Graphic Satire* (London 1967), 72–3, reproduces and discusses the Collings/Blake 'May Day' print, suggesting its importance to any reading of Blake's *Songs of Innocence*.

23 Dorment, *British Printing in the Philadelphia Museum of Art*, 231–3.

24 Feaver, *Masters of Caricature*, 52.

25 Dorment, *British Painting in the Philadelphia Museum of Art*, 233.

26 *Attic Miscellany*, 1 July 1791. 'Doctor Phlogiston' is number 4 in a series of 'Political Portraiture'. The print is signed 'Annabel Scratch', a witty allusion to Hannibale Caracci, regarded as the first recognisable caricaturist. Both George and Feaver believe that Collings drew the many prints which bear the 'Annabel Scratch' signature, and both stylistic and circumstantial evidence confirm this attribution.

27 Henry Angelo, *Reminiscences* (1830) 1904 edn, 1, 333, suggests that Collings was 'sometime editor of *The Public Ledger*'. This is presumably the periodical described by Walter Graham which ran from September 1771 to 10 June 1772. The paper contained a 'Theatrical review' department which Graham notices both for its comprehensive coverage of theatrical events and for setting a precedent for a newspaper, rather than a periodical, covering the theatre (W. Graham, *English Literary Periodicals*, 1930, reprinted edn New York, Octagon Books 1966, 347).

28 Feaver, *Masters of Caricature*, 52.

29 Angelo, *Reminiscences*, I, 333.

30 Dorment, *British Painting in the Philadelphia Museum of Art*, 232–3.

31 BMC, VI, Nos 7814 and 7815.

32 Essick, *William Blake, Printmaker*, 48.

33 See Graham, *English Literary Periodicals*, chap. XII, *passim*.

34 See, for example, the petulant, snuff-wielding fop of 'Damme' (*Attic Miscellany*, 1 May 1791) or the absurd mixture of obsequiousness and expectation shown in 'How to Look Amorously' (*Attic Miscellany*, 1 July 1790).

35 See D. Bindman, *The Shadow of the Guillotine* (London, British Museum 1989), 90. Collings is cited as 'Collins'.

36 Lavater's most famous treatise, *Essay on Physiognomy for the Promotion of the Knowledge and the Love of Mankind*, was published in London in 1789. For a discussion of the influence of Lavater's ideas, and especially of his development of codes for describing character through physiognomy, see Judith Wechsler, *A Human Comedy: Physiognomy and Caricature in 19th Century Paris* (London, Thames and Hudson 1982), especially 22–6.

37 For some account of the relationship between Burns's work and popular illustration see chapter 4. D. Donald and B.E. Maidment's edition of Tim Bobbin's

Human Passions Delineated (Oxford, Hanborough Press 1990) contains an account of the cultural ambiguities of Collier's work. For John Kay see H. and M. Evans's *John Kay of Edinburgh* (London, Paul Harris, 2nd edn 1980). The popular sources of Blake's lyrics are discussed by Heather Glen in *Vision and Disenchantment* (Cambridge, Cambridge University Press 1983).

38   Bindman, *Shadow of the Guillotine*, 82.
39   Bindman, *Shadow of the Guillotine*, 90 and *Attic Miscellany*, 1 July 1791. Bindman (113) suggests that another print with satirical references to Paine is by Collings, but the date (1796) makes this impossible.
40   Bindman, *Shadow of the Guillotine*, 86, for example.
41   The broadside epigram 'Success to the Mills of Albion but no Albion Mills' has a Blakean ring to it, evoking a visionary and mythical past in which the nation of England might be defined in a number of quite different ways. Debates instigated in the 1780s and 1790s by the 'philosophical radicals' and taken over by the Chartists over what constituted 'true' patriotism are also relevant here. Collings is obviously alert to the symbolic possibilities of the name 'Albion'. The Mill's builders, including Wyatt, must have been similarly conscious of the wide ranging allusions created by calling their building 'Albion Mill'.
42   BMC, VI, xxix.

Educated dustmen:

DIRT AND DISRUPTION IN THE PURSUIT OF KNOWLEDGE IN REGENCY AND EARLY VICTORIAN BRITAIN

Printmaking traditions between 1820 and 1840

This chapter concerns the making and interpretation of both comic stereotypes and of cultural clichés. The stereotype to be considered is that of the uneducated manual labourer attempting to engage in self-improving reading, thereby bringing on himself the contempt, mockery, or grudging admiration of the educated classes. I have centred this discussion on the precise image of the 'educated dustman', largely because this stereotype appears to have an identifiable origin in popular culture in the 1820s and 1830s and can subsequently be traced through various modes of transmission. The clichés derive from an attempt within the discourses of middle class culture to formulate complex intellectual, cultural, and political developments within the labouring classes into comprehensible formulations: 'the march of intellect', 'the pursuit of knowledge' (sometimes 'under difficulties'), and, later, 'self-help'. These acts of formulation a were central part of the attempt within a newly coherent and ideologically self-conscious, propagandising middle class to understand, analyse, and ultimately direct the emergence of working class culture. The 'march of intellect' and the 'pursuit of knowledge' were understood by middle class cultural theorists as acts of both cultural and political assertion.

It is within the context of these ideological battles of the 1820s, 1830s and 1840s that the images studied in this chapter need to be situated. As I suggest, the available images of 'educated dustmen' show a surprising variety of responses within middle class image making.

Educated dustmen might be represented as eighteenth-century comic proletarian grotesques, as politically motivated challengers of the status quo, or as legitimate, even heroic, warriors in the battle for social progress. If the most obvious graphic formulations were derived from tolerant, good-humoured goodwill, both a more violently denunciatory and a more openly celebratory possibility were available to the writers and artists of the period. To my mind, the overall effect of these images when read alongside each other is one of fracture. To me, they suggest the variety, uncertainty, and contradictoriness of middle class ideology of the 1830s and 1840s in responding to the cultural and political challenges posed by the emergence of literate, self-educated working people who might begin to speak and write on their own behalf. It is necessary to say something of the nature and extent of the dialogues established in the period between 1820 and 1840 in order to discuss important issues of cultural politics before moving on to look at those graphic images which specifically engage with those dialogues.

At one level, this chapter is an exposition of prints as a form of social history. The most detailed accounts of images of educated dustmen are provided by Dorothy George's *From Hogarth to Cruikshank – Social Change in Graphic Satire*[1] and Celina Fox's *Graphic Journalism in England During the 1830s and 1840s*[2] in which, as the titles suggest, historical realities (attitudes, events, and changes) are read off from prints. In other words, the content of prints is read off as an unproblematic depiction of what happened or of what people thought and believed. I hope the opening paragraph of this chapter has sophisticated this model to some extent by pointing to conflicts and uncertainties within the images constructed by prints and by the insistence that prints construct their social meanings more through negotiation with their audience than through any more overt form of power. But another entire set of interpretative possibilities need to be brought into play here alongside, or more properly intersecting with, the complex dialogue between social reality and the representation of that reality. This possibility concerns the printmaking tradition itself, and major changes which are clearly taking place at the same time as the social events described by these prints. These changes are worth listing in a crude form. Firstly, in this period the single plate caricature (usually a line engraving or an etching), with its explanatory captions, multifarious emblematic detail, and often complex or esoteric contemporary allusions, is in decline. Even where it continues, there is a major change in the representational medium, with the etching or engraving giving way to the lithograph, and, in ambitious and expensive book-making, the copper engraved or etched illustration giving way to the steel engraving.[3] Secondly, the woodcut and the wood engraving, which had been long associated with popular and vernacular media (or with forms like the tract in which less literate social groups were being addressed or propagandised from above) began to move towards the cultural mainstream.[4] There were technical reasons for this shift as well as major developments in literacy and the nature of the potential audience. For whatever reason, the 1830s see the wood engraving appearing in many sophisticated places and being used to establish a number of important discourses which were aimed at cutting across differences of class and levels of literacy. The wood engraving, to take obvious examples, is central to mass 'useful knowledge' journalism,[5] to metropolitan satirical magazines like *Figaro in London* and *Punch*,[6] and, increasingly, to the novel in some of the many serialised forms which were emerging into prominence in the 1830s.[7] Thirdly, single plate engraving does survive, but largely through being accommodated to the serialised novel where the relationship between printed text and illustration is subject to considerable experimentation and development, especially in the 1830s. In particular, the available choice between steel engraving, etching, or wood engraving as alternative means of illustrating fiction suggests a tension between populist and bourgeois ambitions. Even within these forms, there are important variations – the vignette dropped into the text offers a considerably different form from the separate page plate bound in at the appropriate textual moment.[8]

These crudely stated possibilities – the slackening of the caricature tradition, the rise of the woodcut into mass or even genteel culture as an expository or emblematic as well as a diversionary medium, and the continuation of a single plate engraving tradition in a new association with the bourgeois novel – suggest a period of volatility and confusion within popular image making in the second, third, and fourth decades of the nineteenth century. These uncertainties are as much about the functions and audience for various modes of reproducing images as about the social issues which formed the subject of printmaking. This particular chapter looks at images produced not just across the spectrum of social opinion but also belonging to a variety of different media. Just as in the discussion of the representations of the fire at the Albion Mill differing interpretations of the event could be cautiously linked to different printmaking media, so, in this chapter, it is crucial to retain a sense of the ways in which the ostensible political and social content of these prints intersects (or possibly collides) with their chosen method of making and reproduction. The central figure in this chapter, Robert Seymour, was a figure who in one respect represents the protean energy of the unaffiliated late eighteenth-century jobbing caricaturist who would draw and engrave caricatures with evidently contradictory, and equally acerbic, social or political views. But Seymour, despite the evident variety of his work and the interesting ability to work in both etched and wood engraved media, also represents the newly emergent subordination of the engraver to the author, or, more strongly put, of image to text, which characterised the mainstream of Victorian engraving. The pressures brought to bear on Seymour by Dickens's *Pickwick Papers*, where the young but extremely confident author overrode the aspirations and reputation of his relatively eminent engraver in order to produce a publication built on words rather than images, were not just emblematic of a considerable change in the marketplace, but may well have contributed to Seymour's anxieties and his eventual suicide.[9]

A recognition of the verbalness of Victorian culture, which includes a considerable dependence on narration as a form of social explanation, is something which underlies all the discussions in this book. Almost all the images discussed in later chapters show images alongside or, more usually, situated within texts. Often, especially in the vignette form characteristic of much wood engraved illustration, the boundary between text, page, and image is not an entirely clear one.[10] This major shift from a belief in the sufficiency of the graphic image to one where image is defined by text is one which must be kept in mind in reading the images in this chapter. Often allusions to novels, plays, or other verbal inter-texts will offer more by way of explanation than social or historical information. This chapter concentrates on images drawn from a period between 1826 and 1841 when the volatility of graphic modes was at its most obvious. Instead of using Dorothy George's model of analysis and explication, where a direct correlation is sought between verifiable social events and their representation in contemporary prints, it may be more productive to look at the intersection between represented event and mode of representation, especially when those modes of representation are themselves undergoing profound change. The issue is well summarised by Norman Bryson:

> Representation of work and leisure cannot be examined solely against the background of data describing the structural changes of work, leisure, and their interrelation with the domestic economy, but must

be seen also against the second background, of representation as an evolving structure modifying according to laws operative within its own provenance. The problem is one of understanding the articula-tion of a technical process against the history of social formation, of charting one material evolution in the sphere of practice against its reflection and refraction in a further domain of practice.[11]

The 'laws operative' with the 'provenance' of printmaking in the third and fourth decades of the nineteenth century are complex ones, a complexity immediately exemplified by the variety of graphic media which appear in the following discussion.

This chapter considers both a lithograph and a line engraving which appear at the tail end of a single plate caricature tradition which had used line engraving and etching as its dominant media; comic etchings which had been originally drawn as single plates, but which were re-used in conjunction with a later literary text and re-packaged as a work of pseudo-narrative; and a woodcut associated with a popular songbook, which was itself dependent on the mass marketing of plays, play-texts, and surrounding merchandise. All these very different prints focus on a single subject, that of the social implications of the emergent figure of the educated (or, more accurately, the self-educat-ing) dustman. Clearly, in these complex circumstances, it is difficult to align readings of these prints as a form of social history with a reading of them which acknowledges them as exemplifying radical change in the history of representation itself. As Bryson concludes: 'how the problem is resolved will depend crucially, therefore, on how we under-stand the terms "reflection" and "refraction" in connection with the sign.'[12] If a simple model of reflection (the prints as a reflection of social realities) will not serve, then we need to pursue the complex refractions between content and form, between social commentary and self-reflective awareness of the history of their own formal consti-tution, which together structure the meaning of these prints.

The cultural politics of the 'march of intellect'

The two most helpful introductions to the prints about the 'March of Intellect' and the advancement of popular knowledge in the 1830s and 1840s are those by Dorothy George[13] and Celina Fox.[14] George, in a chapter devoted to the widest possible range of formulations of graphic versions of the 'March of Intellect', situates images of educated dustmen within the general context of scientific, technological, and educational changes which were taking place, and subject to ironic analysis, in the Regency and early Victorian period. These prints describe the potentially heroic idea of 'progress' being subverted by a characteristically ironic awareness of the actual absurdities, distortions and grotesqueries which accompanied social advances. Most of the images cited by George remain within a relatively genteel caricature discourse, in which the views of a sophisticated metropolitan audience are represented back to itself via the refracting (as well as reflecting) mirrors of graphic satirical convention. Fox's project is a different one. Her aim is to show the ways in which graphic images became democratised not through any wish or ability within the labouring and artisan classes to appropriate the meanings, codes, or powers of printmaking, but rather through the recognition within the middle and governing classes of the potential power of popular imagery as a way of representing, negotiating, or enforcing their preferred value systems. Organisations like the Religious Tract Society had long been aware of the need to annex the power of popular illustration as part of their social and devotional project. But the 1830s and 1840s saw the sudden and dramatic emergence of illustrated educational, expository, and 'improving' journalism into the mainstream of cultural negotiation, an emergence famously and emblematically announced by, in their own different ways, *The Penny Magazine*, *The Saturday Magazine*, *Punch*, and *The Illustrated London News*.[15] Yet, at a simple level, it is hard to see how the apparently realistic, ostentatiously explanatory and educational wood engraved or woodcut images used in periodicals like *The Penny Magazine* might be read as essentially political in their meaning. What is needed here is some sense of the ways in which popular imagery might negotiate or formulate opinion between differing social groups. To make these formulations, however crudely, it is necessary to define some of the major ways in which early Victorian disputes over cultural power might be theorised.

A simple Marxist model would argue that cultural power is impelled by economic power.[16] The control of economic power through ownership of the modes of production allows the dominant economic groups and interests to impose their cultural will through the forces of social coercion, which include the Church, the army, and the judiciary as well as the legislature. Using such a model, culture becomes part of the social 'superstructure' separate from, but entirely determined by, the economic base of the society. This kind of analytical model has, in the wake of Marxist theorists like Gramsci, been significantly disputed and modified. Many recent Marxist theorists have argued that culture, far from being detached from the central socially determining forces of economics, is a site where a profoundly significant struggle for social meanings, and hence social power, is enacted. Culture is the site where ideology is produced, and ideology (those value systems by which a class or group within society seeks to replicate and extend its own power) need not necessarily be constrained by entirely economic determinants. In short it may be possible to construct power not only through economic dominance but also through the 'discourses' of social control offered by culture.

If this culturalist reading of the sources of power in society is correct, then it may well be that classes or groups retain power not solely, or perhaps not even predominantly, through their control of the forces of social coercion, but rather through their power to disseminate their ideology through culture. Such a dissemination involves a crucial notion of 'consent', with value systems being not so much imposed as negotiated. Differing social groups with apparently diverse economic interests may well seek to find and express areas of shared belief. This process bears the technical name of 'hegemony'. Most readings of this idea of ideological and social consent would see it as a subtle, but none the less profoundly powerful, form of social control. While a powerful social group apparently seeks to share its own values with a less privileged one, and thus enable the less powerful group to hold some sort of equality in the culture of the dominant group, in fact the dominant group seeks only to extend its own interests by 'incorporating' or assimilating the less powerful group into its own processes and purposes.

In the 1830s and 1840s in particular, it is possible to identify a moment of very obvious hegemonic struggle in which an aggressively propagandising middle class, in its attempts to turn new-found economic and cultural influence into Parliamentary, legislative, and municipal power, sought an alliance with emergent groups from within the labouring and industrial classes (usually identified as 'artisans' or, in more recent historiography, 'the labour aristocracy'). The middle classes presented this alliance as a mutually beneficial one, in which the artisans, through education, career advancement, thrift, and self-management, would support the middle class drive towards social dominance and be rewarded by increased access to middle class culture. Cultural rewards, of course, are not the same thing as financial and political ones, yet the attractiveness of the alliance to both sides is obvious enough, given the stress on cultural, educational, ethical, and moral values which shaped the middle class dialogue with artisans. As we have seen, this dialogue formulates itself into many kinds of cultural artefacts – magazines like *The Family Economist* (which is the main subject of the next chapter), tracts, self-improving literature, exemplary biographies, and, by no means least, woodcut and wood engraved illustrations, which provide the focus of the next two chapters.

Crudely simple as this set of historical models might be, it does suggest the likely potency of the figure of the educated dustman at this historical moment in the 1820s and 1830s. Here is a figure from the lowest stratum of the urban proletariat, who thus potentially represents all the disruptive, indeed revolutionary, potential of the alienated urban poor, comically reversed into an emblem of the new potentialities of social mobility gained through cultural rather than political, advancement. It is just this equivocation between the 'political' and the 'cultural' which is of central concern within middle class ideology during the 1830s. Needing the support of potentially disruptive artisans as political allies in their quest for legislative and social power, the middle classes had to find some form of cultural (but crucially not political) inducement to persuade artisans to join their cause through a shared ideology. The looming figure of the dirty, physically vigorous, rough, uncultured dustman had to be accommodated within middle class ideology. Given that the prints studied in this chapter belong largely to the polite discourses of middle class debate rather than to the propagandising negotiations between classes which inform the images studied in the next chapter, it may be helpful to summarise the possible ways in which the (largely invented) figure of the 'literary dustman' might be read within available middle class ideologies.

The educated dustman as a stereotype

One set of potential readings is to do with threat, where the physical presence of a burly, oddly dressed, smelly, uncivilised dustman is elided easily into the political threat of the 'great unwashed', the alienated and volatile urban dispossessed, through the use of specifically political codes of representation to construct the image. Such politically coded prints would be circulated to act as a warning to the middle classes of the destabilising potential of the increasingly ambitious and educated labouring man within an industrial society. In images like these, fear of social disorder overwhelms any more hegemonic strategies. 'The Rival Mag's' (illustration 13) in my view falls into this category. Other prints, less obvious and brutal in their attack on the dustman figure, might use scorn, derision, or disdain as their dominant mode, turning

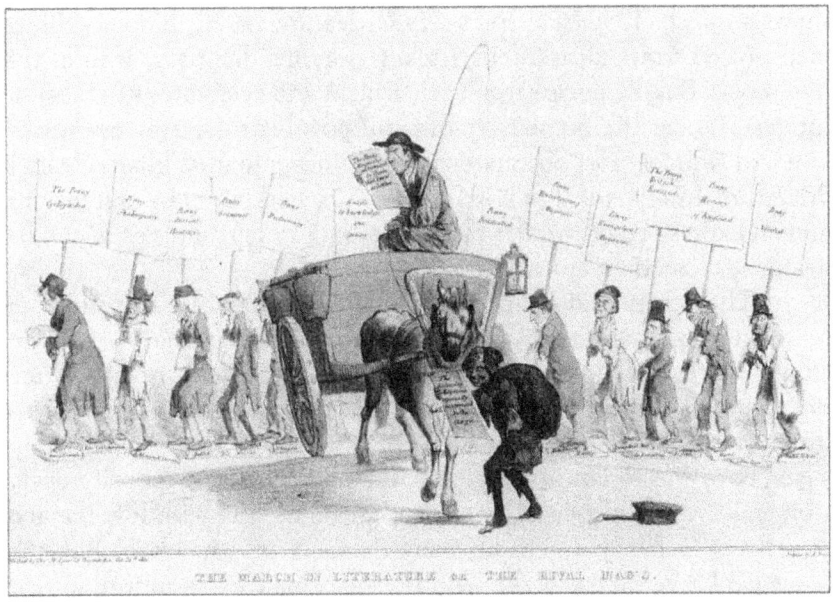

13 Anonymous coloured lithograph. 'The March of Literature or, the Rival Mag's' (Thomas McClean), 25 October 1832.

the cultural ambitions of working men into pretentious and ludicrous assaults on the status quo, and hence dismissing the cultural advancement of the working classes as little more than presumption. Such modes of belittlement depended on shared assumptions between artist and audience over the actual extent of the threat to social stability posed by the education of the poor.

Against these confrontational or oppositional images of the educated dustman more accommodating images were possible, in which the cultural challenge of the ambitious proletarian was dispersed into a genial recognition of comic reversal. In all the prints which situate the educated dustman as an essentially comic figure, the precise tonal configuration of the image is important. There are necessary distinctions to be made between satire, sarcasm, irony, invective, comic disdain, and wry recognition.

Another way of figuring the educated dustman is as a celebratory symbol of what Dorothy George describes as 'the rationalist view of progress'.[17] Several of the illustrations she prints in *From Hogarth to Cruikshank* concerned with 'The March of Intellect' satirise the fantastic inventiveness of the age.[18] Sometimes this satire is fiercely critical of the consequences of mechanical inventiveness. An 1829 caricature by 'Sharpshooter', for example, called 'The Scavenger's Lamentation'[19] shows a massively heroic street cleaner leaning on his broom while a mechanised street cleaning cart takes away his dignity as well as his livelihood. But of course satire both attacks and celebrates its object of interest. Under the humour, it was still possible to convey a sense of awe and wonder. The dustman eating a pineapple in William Heath's 'March of Intellect' [7] is both a satire on working class pretensions and an expression of wonder that something so rare and scarce can be available to such an ordinary person.

The prints studied in this chapter inevitably use this range of representational and tonal possibilities. In particular, they depend on tropes of reversal – symptoms of sophisticated or genteel culture discovered unexpectedly in the lives of the poor and vulgar. This discovery is essentially a humorous one. As George puts it, 'The jest in such prints was to connect the remarkable movements for self-education and the emergence of a new working class elite with low-life and poverty, which, by tradition, were subjects of comedy.'[20] But the comedy of reversal easily slipped into the comedy of irruption, so that proletarian claims on genteel culture could be read as politically threatening rather than as comic reflections of a topsy-turvy world. Indeed, under all these prints lies the continuing problem of how violent change is interpreted – do you contain a world turned upside down within an essentially comic world view, or do you celebrate change as an opportunity for energising turmoil, or do you fear change as a manifestation of social disorder and potential anarchy? When street musicians perform (or attempt to perform) Rossini, bricklayers read massive tomes from the St Giles's Reading Society [11], and dustmen take piano lessons from their fathers [7 and 10], or sponsor ballet lessons for their children [14], how is it possible to construct an orderly view of culture at all?

'The March of Literature, or The Rival Mag's' (1832) and the attack on mass popular education

'The March of Literature, or The Rival Mag's' (illustration 13) [1] is unsigned and the print is given no attribution by Dorothy George. An immediate reaction would be to ascribe it to John Doyle, a prolific producer of thinly satirical lithographs mainly during the reign of William IV.[21] Doyle was well known by his signature 'HB', a version of his monogram by which he sought, ineffectually, to conceal his true identity. Doyle is not well regarded by scholars of the English carica-ture tradition,[22] and his work is usually seen as signalling a transition from vigorous Regency invective to genteel and pompous early Victorian modes of humour. This loss of vigour is also to be remarked technically – the bite of the copper engraved or etched line giving way to the less well defined, dispersed, crayon-like effects of lithography. Equally, the compacted and energetic compositions of Gillray and Rowlandson in Doyle's prints are dispersed into awkward and stiff figure groupings. All these comments might well apply to 'The Rival Mag's' which, I want to argue, should be read as a conservative and retrogressive allusion to a fading caricature tradition rather than any herald of new Victorian graphic traditions.

There are, however, a number of reasons for being cautious about the attribution of 'The Rival Mag's' to Doyle, despite the appropriate publisher (Thomas McClean) and a plausible date (25 October 1832). Nearly all of Doyle's plates were in fact signed with his HB monogram, and few of his later lithographs were coloured. Dorothy George notes that there were conscious imitations of Doyle's work. Most tellingly, the kind of caricature of plebeian or proletarian types shown here is unparalleled elsewhere in Doyle's work.[23] Many other printmakers, including Robert Seymour and William Heath, were being published by McClean at this time. Regardless of its maker, 'The Rival Mag's' confirms the decline of a single plate caricature tradition. It is an awkward, poorly conceived composition, over reliant on written labels in spite of all its stylistic attempts to re-invoke the energy of Gillray and Rowlandson. Furthermore, as a large (15in. by 11in.) single caricature plate, 'The Rival Mag's' is by 1832 something of an anomaly. Although Cruikshank's temperance campaigning maintained a single plate tradition from the 1830s on and C.J. Grant continued to produce his idiosyncratic, large-scale political woodcuts on into the 1840s,[24] the single plate caricature tradition had by 1832 largely given way to text related satirical illustrations characterised by *Figaro in London*,[25] by McClean's own *The Looking Glass*,[26] or by the early years of *Punch*.[27] Even this tradition was soon to give way in turn to the etched or engraved plates which accompanied the early novels of W.H. Ainsworth and Dickens, and filled the illustration pages of the new fiction based middle class monthly periodicals like *Bentley's Miscellany*, *Ainsworth's Magazine*, or *The New Monthly Magazine*.[28] In expressing a reactionary view of the growth of mass literacy, 'The Rival Mag's' underlines its conservative social perspectives, and those of its well off and sophisticated purchasers, in its form and mode as a large single plate hand-coloured caricature. Even though the chosen medium is the relatively recent one of lithography rather than traditional copper engraving or etching, the print remains anachronistic in its style and form.

The print shows a midden or night soil cart at the centre (though a very clean one – it is a matter of relish to imagine the steaming ordure that Gillray might have depicted) driven by a figure deeply engaged in reading 'The Penny Magazine patronised by those who know no better'. The cart is almost running down a sweep's boy, with his soot bag on his back, who has dropped his brush to read 'The Saturday Magazine especially patronised by the clergy'. This caption is in fact a complex pun, as sweeps' boys (presumably because of the parodic resemblance between their sooty clothes and clergymen's black suits) were often known as 'clergy' during the eighteenth century.[29] So the print manages, for all its shortcomings, a brief moment of almost Blakean energy, a compacted play on the evangelicism of *The Saturday Magazine* (often cited by its critics) and on the presumed commonness of the *Saturday*'s readership. The 'clergy', of whatever kind, blacken *The Saturday* by their association with it.

Behind the cart a procession of ragged proletarian grotesques, rendered with the savage deformities and bestial characteristics of Gillray's proletarians (though without Gillray's skill), carries banners emblazoned with the names of various penny genres – 'The Penny Cyclopaedia', 'The Penny Shakespeare', and so on.[30] Each banner carrier is trampling on representative volumes from what might be called the high cultural version of each placard – 'The Penny Novelist' tramples Scott and Smollett, 'The Penny English Essayist' Addison and Steele, 'The Penny Dictionary' Johnson. Of the periodicals, 'The Penny Entertaining Magazine' kicks 'The Evangelical Magazine' and 'The New Evangelical Magazine'. The aim of the print is, of course, the rather smug one of denouncing cheap serial publications as exemplifying a vulgar and presumptuous aspiration within working class culture. But beyond the cultural assumptions of the print lie obvious political ones – by using the iconography of the political procession to represent cultural challenge,[31] the artist deliberately politicises the whole issue of literacy. The power of knowledge is associated with the power of the mob at an imagistic level, even if the representation of that mob is more pathetic or grotesque than threatening. In maintaining the representational code of Gillray's 'London Corresponding Society' print, the artist here inevitably links cultural progress with proletarian unrest.[32]

The nature of this linking is worth a moment's thought because it invokes an important socio-political literary and visual trope of the time – the trope of neglect. At a literal level, such neglect seems relatively harmless – becoming so involved with your reading that you don't look where you are going or attend properly to the task in hand. Yet emblematically this trope can easily become politicised. In seeking self-improvement, social change, or large-scale reform, the reader neglects the here-and-now demands of small-scale responsibility. The classic Victorian exposition of this theme appears in the form of the Jellaby household in *Bleak House* where, in pursuit of a distanced, idealistic, and possibly irresponsible, reformist impulse, Mrs Jellaby neglects her infant family.[33] The result is one of Dickens's most powerful expositions of anarchy, disorder, and muddle. But the trope resurfaces again and again in caricature as well as fiction. Here, for example, is a description of a c. 1829 print by 'Sharpshooter' called 'The March of Intellect': 'A street scene. A woman plays the harp, standing on a pebbled road, two children by her side play the violin and the guitar. The little girl, in a long dress, holds out a collecting box. A man reading a book walks over a baby. A bricklayer holding another book. A wooden structure is plastered with book advertisements …'.[34] The message is clear – 'a man reading a book walks over a baby'. The use of this motif of neglect of the here-and-now is underlined by part of Dorothy George's description of a 'March of Mind' street scene which she dates at around 1828: 'A coachman, absorbed in "An account of the Road, Literary, Historical … &c …" treads heavily on a screaming child'[8].[35] Another directly comparable image can be found in William Heath's 1828 four image plate 'The March of Intellect'[6].[36] In one image of the four, a coachman, walking along utterly engrossed in his reading, allows his horses to bolt and his coach to capsize behind his back without even noticing. The pursuit of knowledge or the march of intellect in these prints are heedless, irresponsible forms of locomotion in which neglect of duty leads to a literal as well as a metaphorical trampling of the helpless. The range of clichés brought into play here is suggestive: 'not looking where you are going', 'not knowing your place', 'headlong pursuit', and so on. The repeated motifs accumulate into a coherent argument: if you neglect immediate responsibility or duty (your 'place') for the distant possibility of improvement or cultural advancement, you will create through neglect an anarchy in which the helpless are trampled underfoot without due regard. Such an argument is really an extension of conservative eighteenth-century ideas of proportion and disruption, in which common-sense responsibilities and obligations could be overturned by the disproportionate or the obsessional.

These notions of 'trampling' must have been particularly power-ful ones in the early 1830s because of the widespread dissemination of images of the Peterloo massacre, in which the yeomanry are depicted trampling helpless, unarmed citizens.[37] Thirteen years after Peterloo, ideas of trampling and civil disobedience must have still been power-fully interconnected in popular consciousness. This interrelatedness was further developed by the central theme in Peterloo image making, which was to show the application of military methods to civil events. This demonstration of coercive, rather than hegemonic, civil author-ity brought together the civic and the military in a deeply disturbing way, which could easily be extended to other forms of cultural negotia-tion.[38] Thus it is not surprising that the act of reading could be represented in prints as an anarchic one which made the reader neglectful of ordinary human and social responsibilities. However, such a perception of reading as neglect was also turned, in an alterna-tive set of narratives, to a more heroic possibility. As many reminiscences and biographies of artisans suggest, the heroic pursuit of knowledge, with time snatched for reading from an arduous life of manual labour, sometimes by propping an open book on a loom or other machine, could be read not so much as neglect as 'progress'.[39] Pulling out the pocket volume of Thompson while the flock or herd strayed into the corn might not have pleased the farmer, but did repre-sent a brief and powerful narrative of 'the pursuit of knowledge under difficulties'. The competing narratives are obvious – 'neglect' as a form of social insubordination against 'neglect' as a form of heroic self-real-isation. Such complex disputes about book learning among the proletariat and the artisans clearly go deep into the social fears and anxieties of a newly emergent middle class consciousness. It is there-fore hardly surprising to find images of the 'educated dustman' carrying this freight of competing values.

Given the pressing contemporaneousness of this debate in the 1830s, it is perhaps surprising to find 'The Rival Mag's' drawing heavily on eighteenth-century caricature traditions more usually applied to personal caricatures of politicians than to the less grotesque, more naturalistic political drawings of Doyle and Seymour. The repre-sentation of proletarian figures in this print are especially dependent on precedent. The protruding forehead, snub nose, flabby mouth and receding chin of the left-hand figure follows traditions of ridicule and contempt defined by Gillray, while the flexed knees and sloping postures of the figures are traditionally suggestive of animalesque social inferiority. The syphilitic noselessness of the 'Penny Evangelical

Magazine' is a pointedly direct juxtaposition of the pure and the corrupt. 'Penny Ancient History' and 'Penny Grammar' represent not so much proletarian figures as half-crazed pedants and antiquarians who have lost contact with everyday social relationships. The overall contempt for proletarian aspirations to culture is heightened by the emphasis on rags and tatters (another traditional device), and by the relentless depiction of figures occupied by the lowest possible trades. The degree of scorn shown here recalls Cruikshank's Gillray-like caricatures of radicals at the time of Peterloo. It is a tempting possibility to assert that these dismissive stereotypes recur at moments of great political tension – 1789, 1819, 1832.

Just to underline the conservative allusions here to eighteenth-century caricature, even the 'trampling on books' motif is sanctioned by long usage, though generally it had been previously used to represent either political corruption or the follies of fashion. While some of the new penny serials described on the banners may have actually existed, much was invented for satirical purposes. By October 1832 *The Penny Magazine* and *The Saturday Magazine* were well established, *The Penny Novelist* was a few months old, and *The Penny Cyclopaedia* had begun to follow *The Penny Magazine* from Charles Knight as the publisher for the Society for the Diffusion of Useful Knowledge.[40] Among the twenty-odd 'penny' titles listed by Joel Wiener in his bibliography of unstamped British periodicals 1830–36 are *The Penny Schoolbook*, *A Penny Universal Biography*, and *A Penny Shakespeare*, all available to the public before this print was published.[41] So the artist had an easy, if topical, target, and needed only feeble powers of invention where reality failed him. The unfairness of this critique of proletarian 'penny culture' is easy to demonstrate. In truth, the course of reading undertaken by many artisans was demanding, ambitious, and culturally alert. Here, for example, is an admittedly poeticised account of the reading of one artisan described in a poem itself written by a Manchester plasterer:

> From the 'Free Library' lo! Johnson, Blair,
> Rollins, Macaulay, Robertson appear,
> Boyle, Newton, Bacon, Tillotson, and Hume,
> With all the classic minds of Greece and Rome;
> While Bulwer, Ainsworth, Lever, Boz and Scott
> Recite their thousand tales in social chat.[42]

The fears expressed by 'The Rival Mag's' over the cheapening and degrading of culture through its usurpation by the proletariat seem laughable given the rigour and ambition of this course of 'leisure' reading. Interestingly enough, four of the authors being trampled in the print appear in the poem as the chosen reading of artisans – Johnson, Rollins, Scott, and Hume. Far from heralding the end of culture, the popularising and cheapening of mass reading matter, for many proletarian readers at least, resulted in access to the literary culture of the educated middle classes rather than a schooling in revolutionary or dissident politics.

Any interpretation of 'The Rival Mag's' needs to take into account its mode (a single plate lithograph produced at a time when single plate caricature was rapidly becoming outmoded), its conservative evocation of mob politics in relation to social change, and its dependence on oppositions or 'rivalries' as a mode of social perception. What exactly is the rivalry predicated by 'the *rival* mag's'? Is the rivalry between a vast array of copycat ventures in penny culture? Or one between penny culture itself and the polite world represented here by Blackwood, Scott, Murray, Johnson, and their fellow authors? Given the print's malicious, if conventional, representation of common people, it seems that the latter is the more likely. The march of literature as constructed in this print is not a triumphant procession of popular cultural attainment, but rather a shambling array of barely human grotesques. The artist must have expected his audience to be conscious enough of a shared caricature tradition to read off this reactionary meaning even from this enfeebled and poorly drawn image.

In a cruder, less attenuated but more demotic mode, many of the conservative assumptions of 'The Rival Mag's' re-appear in an undated print by J.L. Marks called 'The March of Interlect' (illustration 14), although in this print it is the vulgar aspiration to high fashion and social status rather than to learning which provides the source of the satire. In this vigorous but crudely drawn image, a dustman, accoutred in his version of Sunday finery, leads his over-dressed wife and daughter on a 'fashionable' Sunday promenade. Unfortunately, the promenade is not down the Steyne in Brighton (an allusion sanctioned through the allusion to the Royal Pavilion created by the Chinese Gothick form of the parasol carried by Mrs Dustman) but down a dirt track between a neglected cottage and a dust heap. A large pig is standing on the dust heap in full pride of possession. The form and colour of the pig are echoed in the fat lap dog carried by the dustman's daughter.

The immediate visual impact of the print is dependent upon the travesty of fashionable dress displayed proudly by the family – in generic terms the print is a ghastly echo of a fashion plate. The

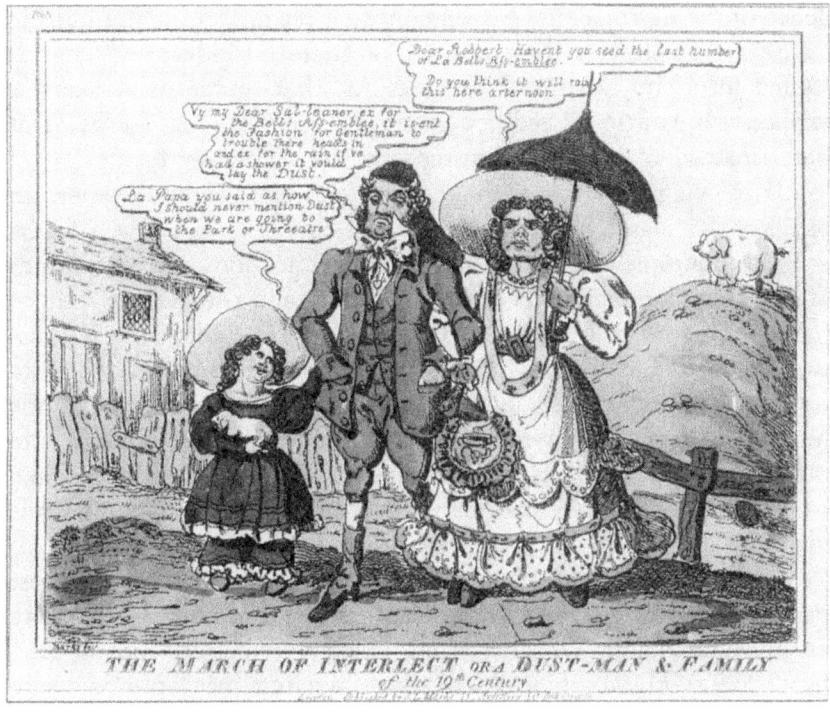

14 J.L. Marks. Hand-colouring engraving. 'The March of the Interlect or A Dustman and Family of the 19th Century.' (J.L. Marks), no date.

dustman's huge floppy bow and hessian boots are ludicrously at odds with his hat, retained from his working dress and, with its extended neck and shoulder cover, emblematically characteristic of his trade. Wife and daughter both wear vastly overtrimmed and exaggerated versions of contemporary fashions – mutton chop sleeves, huge cart-wheel hats, fussy layers of trimming. Mrs Dustman is vastly over-equipped for a stroll with both hat and parasol and an enormous gaudy elaborate reticule which rebuffs any possibility of daintiness or gentility. Thus the print offers an immediate visual joke concerning the unsuccessful efforts of the irredeemably vulgar to appropriate fashionable dress and manners, a joke emphasised by the coarse faces which are placed on the elaborate setting of their clothes.

But there is also, as so often in caricatures of this date, a more complex linguistic dimension. The conversation, appended in speech bubbles, and which has to be read from right to left, offers a range of commentary on the central figures. One strand of the conversation – 'Do you think it will rain here this afternoon' – laughs at the dustfolk's 'mastery' of polite and fatuous chit-chat. Another mocks the dependence of the dustman and his wife on their reading of the fashionable *La Belle Assemblé* for their notions of genteel conduct – a copy is stuffed into Mrs Dustman's reticule. Another source of mockery is explicitly linguistic – 'seed' for 'seen', 'vy' for 'why', 'ex' for 'as', 'this here' instead of 'this', 've' instead of 'we'. This representation of 'cockney' vulgarity of speech – which appears widely elsewhere in prints of the 'march of intellect' as well as, famously, in *Pickwick Papers* – is put alongside attempts at fashionable inflections and affectations of speech – 'La papa', 'my dear Sal-leaner', and the various stabs at pronouncing *La Belle Assemblé*. One further joke links the conversation together. In his attempts to offer only polite chit-chat, which in no sense reveals his trade, Mr Dustman, pursuing the apparently neutral subject of the weather, is trapped by his own politesse into saying the word 'dust'. He is immediately picked up by his daughter, who has been carefully instructed in how to deny her origins while visiting the 'Park or Threeatre'.

The argument of the print is that the association between these people and dirt, dust, and vulgarity is visually, and therefore socially, entirely undeniable. Vulgarity is only made more vulgar, more obvious, by its denial. The coarseness of the faces, the linguistic lapses, the ludicrous dress, the emblematic hats all condemn the dustman's family to irredeemable dustmanhood. 'The March of Interlect' is thus nothing to do with education, literacy, or learning but rather entirely concerned with foolish social pretention. Fortunately, there were more robust and energetic accounts of the same cultural issues available elsewhere within the competing discourses of popular printmaking, and it is to these images that we can now turn.

'A Specimen of the Reading Public' – Crowquill's 'Political Dustman' (1826)

This print of 'Four Specimens of the Reading Public' (illustration 15) is the earliest graphic version of the educated dustman to be cited in this chapter. Unsurprisingly, given its date, the print comprises a large single plate engraved caricature, dependent, like 'The Rival Mag's', on eighteenth-century conventions of humorous representation. But Crowquill's image here is a more accommodating one which, while making specific acknowledgement of the political context already described, none the less positions the 'political dustman' more as a comic than an entirely threatening figure. Much of the print's meaning is to do with its form, in which four comic stereotype figures are

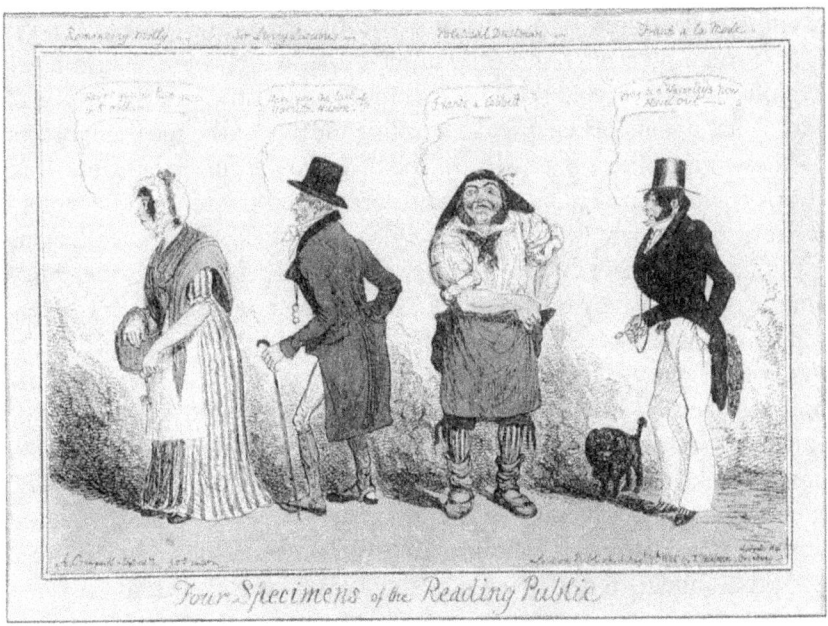

15 'A. Crowquill' (real name A. Forrester). Hand-coloured engraving. 'Four Specimens of the Reading Public' (J. Fairburn), 7 August 1826.

arranged in a simple frieze, related more to each other by the picture plane than any more complex form of compositional unity. The lack of any form of personal interaction between the figures is evident, and each is isolated from his or her social context in order that the amused scrutiny of the viewer should not be interrupted by explanatory detail or narrative possibilities. The print is essentially a simple one, but none the less is revealingly characteristic of the nature of late single plate caricatures and the ways in which they prefigure the vigorous arrival of the woodcut vignette as a major representational mode.

'A. Crowquill' was in fact the working name of two engravers, the brothers Forrester, or, as some sources suggest, Forrestier.[43] However, it was Alfred Henry who pursued a sustained career as an engraver and author, and who is the likely draughtsman of this print. Like many successful designer/engravers of this period (he was born in 1804 or 1805[44]), Forrester was forced to manage a transition from early copper and steel engraved or etched work into the mass circulation wood engraved image making required by the newly created market in cheap illustrated periodicals and books. Single plate caricatures like 'Specimens of the Reading Public' were products of his early years, and soon gave way to a career compounded from work derived from several emergent illustrated traditions. Early in his career, he worked for the small format illustrated monthly miscellanies which were beginning to exploit vignette or end grain wood engraved illustration as a means of addressing a mass readership. In working for two of the most important of these magazines, *The Mirror* and *The Hive*, Forrester came into contact with John Timbs, a key entrepreneurial figure in the development of these early illustrated miscellanies into *The Illustrated London News* and the other broadsheet periodicals which became the staple employer of so many of the new London based generation of illustrators and engravers in the 1840s.[45] Forrester himself worked for *The Illustrated London News* as well as for other periodicals managed and underwritten by Henry Vizetelly, and thus was in the mainstream of early Victorian image making. He drew extensively for illustrated children's books and, in Houfe's judgement, his work shows 'charm and incisiveness' and 'an element of fantasy at a time when grotesqueness was more usual'.[46] Such a move away from the grotesque might be read as further evidence of the waning of the caricature tradition.

Comic illustration was another of Forrester's chosen interests. Despite, if Spielmann is to be believed,[47] an abbreviated and relatively unsuccessful stint at *Punch*, Forrester excelled in putting together the comic miscellanies and sketchbooks also favoured by Cruikshank, and which furthered the development of the comic illustrative tradition from single images into the more extended thematic meditations and narratives which underpin the development of the Victorian illustrated novel.[48] Of particular interest here is the parallel development in artists like Cruikshank, Seymour, and Forrester of the sketchbook format into less miscellaneous, more sustained social commentaries which have certain narrative elements within them. As we shall see, Seymour's *Sketches*,[49] for which Forrester wrote the linking text, offered the most sustained and developed analysis of the idea of the educated dustman available in the nineteenth century at least until Dickens's meditation on wealth, dust, and education as exemplified by Mr Boffin in *Our Mutual Friend* (1864–5). No illustrator of Forrester's generation could have been unaware of the increasingly close relationship between image and narrative exemplified by Dickens's early work, a relationship which was as important for the development of visual as of literary codes in the 1830s and 1840s. The vividness of Forrester's awareness of the interdependence of text and image in early Dickens is shown by the artist's hasty production of a set of extra illustrations for *Pickwick Papers*, in which rapid interpretation of the serialised published text was essential.[50]

Forrester was unusual among the many versatile and adaptable early Victorian illustrators in also being a well established writer. Nor can all his writing be contained within the facetious and miscellaneous occasional jobbing articles which might be required to extend or embellish his drawings. While little of this biographical account of Forrester's later career has direct bearing on a reading of 'Four Specimens of the Reading Public', it is important in relation to the more extended arguments in this chapter about the emergence of image making from the single plate caricatures of the eighteenth century into a new relationship between image, text, mass public, and new modes of reproduction in the early Victorian period. It was the ability of artists like Forrester to adapt to the new mass market that made these changes possible, and it is therefore important to situate this print not only in its specific context but also in the wider narrative of the changes occurring in comic draughtsmanship in the 1830s and 1840s.

'Four Specimens of the Reading Public' is dated 7 August 1826, so it was engraved while Forrester was in his early twenties. While the work of a startlingly young artist in modern terms, caricatures by 'Crowquill' had been appearing in comic journals and printsellers' catalogues for a number of years. The basic target for Forrester's humour in this print is the low level of literary taste exemplified by the demands of the reading public together with the comic discrepancy between social status and literary pretentions, both in an upward and a downward direction. In the print, an elderly rake ('Sir Larry Luscious') asks for a lascivious Harriet Wilson novel, and a young dandy ('Frank a la Mode') enquires about the availability of a new romantic adventure tale by Scott. Both show tastes incompatible with their social status, and additionally suggest somewhat venal natures. On the other hand, a youngish housekeeper out shopping ('Romancing Molly') diverts herself long enough from her duties to ask for a lengthy romance. The comic discrepancy here is between day-dreaming and duty, between fantasy and daily chores. All three of these 'characters', shown in caricature profiles which are emblematically angular, curvaceous, and buxom in turn, seem to be directing their requests for reading matter to an accommodating bookseller just off the print to the left.

The fourth reader, the 'political dustman', is represented in an interestingly different way. For a start, he 'vants' a Cobbett, a demand rather than a request. Furthermore, he demands in the cockney way, like the Wellers in *Pickwick Papers*, substituting 'v' for 'w' in order to show his proletarian assertiveness. As with 'Romancing Molly', the comic alignment of poor grammar and idiomatic speech with literary ambition is deliberately mocking here. Further aggression is shown by posture. Alone of the four readers depicted here, the political dustman is shown full face, confronting the reader in a direct and muscular way. The ham like forearms, carefully displayed by the chosen pose, are given further emphasis by the rolled shirtsleeves. The round, not unfriendly, visage is given greater weight by the extensive mutton chop whiskers and the framing hat-cum-neckpiece which was the immediate means of identifying dustmen and coal-heavers in prints from this period. All the other picturesque garments – neckerchief, apron, gaiters, and overshoes – contribute to the overall effect of considerable physical presence. The assertiveness of the dustman is underlined by his choice of reading. Cobbett's Tory/radical literary output contained a number of strands not all of which were evidently proletarian. But he did seek a wide-ranging re-definition of the audience for both political and practical information, in order to address artisans and workpeople in ways which would enable them to discuss and define their own social roles. It is interesting which Cobbett it is that the dustman 'vants'. Forrester, doubtless, would think the dustman needed Cobbett's *Grammar*, but the dustman himself might find more use in either the practicalities of the *Cottage Economy* or the political information of *The Political Register* and *Twopenny Trash*.[51] The invocation of Cobbett here, in whatever form, crucially brings into play a central argument concerning the relationship between cultural advance and political knowledge within the urban working classes. Cobbett's work, along with that of Paine, was central to the notion that access to cultural and literary discourses and access to knowledge were essential pre-requisites for the proper development of working people. In describing his dustman as explicitly 'political' Forrester acknowledged the troubling relationship between the cultural and the political which is explored by all the prints studied in this chapter.

To sum up, 'Crowquill's' 'Four Specimens' is a characteristic early nineteenth-century single plate caricature drawn and engraved by a young artist at an early point in his career. It follows eighteenth-century precedent in the frieze format (four separate caricatures arranged across the picture plane without any linking compositional elements), the extensive use of captions, the delight in stereotyping, and the use of comic discrepancy as the basis for its humour. Mockery of the tastes of readers and their inability to discriminate between romance and reality had informed humour as diverse as Jane Austen's

Northanger Abbey (1818) and Gillray's 'Tales of Wonder' (1802),[52] in which four women sit round a table terrifying themselves by reading from one of Monk Lewis's Gothic romances. What is new in 'Four Specimens' however is the emergence, possibly even the irruption, of the political into the cultural. Forrester's engraving makes the nature of that irruption, which combines the physical, the political, and the cultural, quite explicit. His dustman is a brawny, aggressive, demanding, and reading one who confronts the viewer head on. However, he is also contained within the democratising conventions of eighteenth-century caricature, where all human foibles and vanities are equally available for mockery. In this print, potential threat can be accommodated within the levelling process of caricature representation without using the denunciatory vocabulary of the diseased and the disgusting (it is tempting to say the 'revolting') which appeared a few years later in 'The Rival Mag's'. In this sense, 'Crowquill's' 'Four Specimens of the Reading Public' sets the tone, if not the representational codes, through which the image of the educated dustman is mediated into early Victorian culture.

Robert Seymour and his dustmen

Robert Seymour (1798–1836) is an important artist and engraver in the context of this chapter because of the recurrent interest he shows in his *Sketches* in the image of the educated dustman as a cultural symbol (illustrations 16, 17 and 18).[53] Seymour's *Sketches* were first published by Richard Carlile as five series of etched plates between 1834 and 1836 but then reprinted in volume form in 1841 after Seymour's death with a prose and verse commentary written, as already described, by fellow artist/engraver and dustman enthusiast Alfred Forrester under his working name of 'Crowquill'. Forrester's prose and verse text is described on Bohn's title page as 'illustration' to Seymour's comic etchings, an interesting reversal of ordinary logic where a text would be 'illustrated' by images. However, the description proves to be a fair one, because Forrester's text is often little more than a literal description of Seymour's plates larded with weak puns and facetious word play. The volume publication of the Seymour plates necessitated a linking text to appeal to the mass readership opened up by Dickens's dramatic exploitation of text against image, but both Bohn and Forrester seem to have agreed that Seymour's plates needed to remain the focus of attention. In much of the second volume of the *Sketches*, the text abandons all links with the plates and pursues an entirely

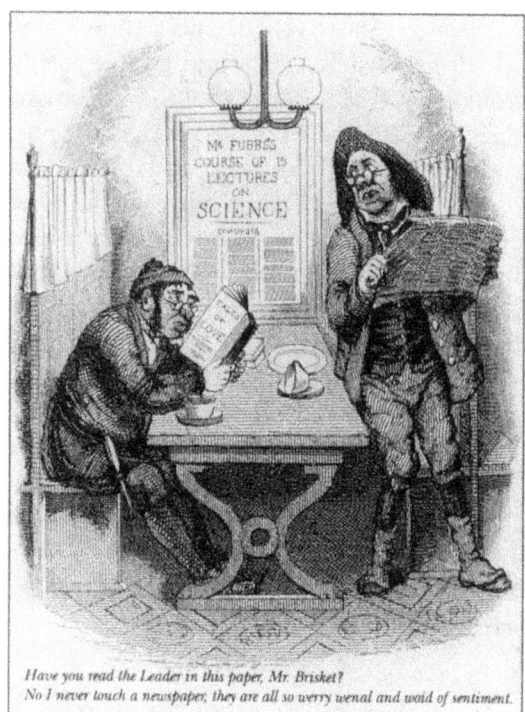

16 R. Seymour. Etching.
'Have you read the leader in
this paper, Mr. Brisket?',
from *Sketches by Seymour*
with a text by Alfred
Crowquill.

Have you read the Leader in this paper, Mr. Brisket?
No I never touch a newspaper, they are all so werry wenal and woid of sentiment.

independent narrative strand of its own. Thus, much of Forrester's
commentary can be read as a tribute to his fellow artist than as a
serious attempt to develop the *Sketches* into the kind of coherent
comic whole represented by *The Pickwick Papers*.

But as well as discussing Seymour's specific representations of
educated dustmen in this chapter, he is important to the overall argument of this book as a representative, potentially even an emblematic,
figure in the development of popular image making in the transitional
period between 1813 (when the lithograph was invented) and 1837
(when *The Pickwick Papers* was published in volume format without
Seymour and Buss's original plates). Houfe offers some key comments
on Seymour, regarding him as 'a somewhat inadequate draughtsman',[54]
who, having failed as a pattern designer and history painter, turned to
caricature in an attempt to emulate Cruikshank. Houfe notes that 'he
learnt the art of copper engraving about 1827 and used lithography in
the 1830s',[55] but makes no mention of his significant work in wood
engraving, especially his vignette caricatures for the extremely important satirical magazine *Figaro in London* edited by Gilbert à Beckett
and subsequently Henry Mayhew,[56] or his pioneering work for *Bell's*

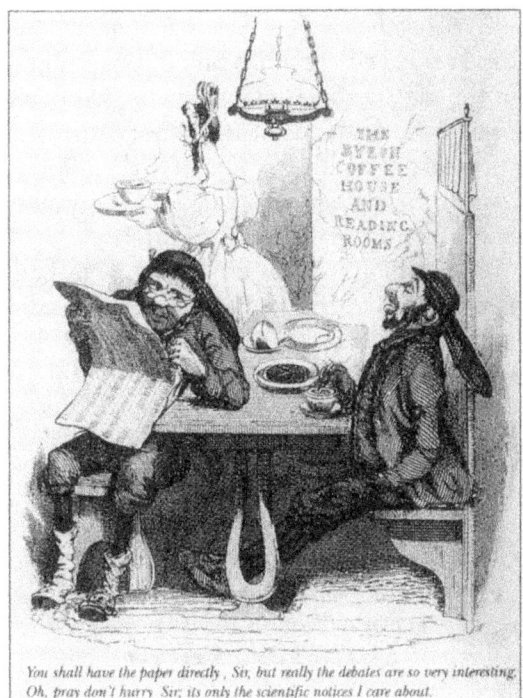

17 R. Seymour. Etching. 'You shall have the paper directly, sir', from *Sketches by Seymour*, vol. 1.

You shall have the paper directly , Sir, but really the debates are so very interesting. Oh, pray don't hurry Sir; its only the scientific notices I care about.

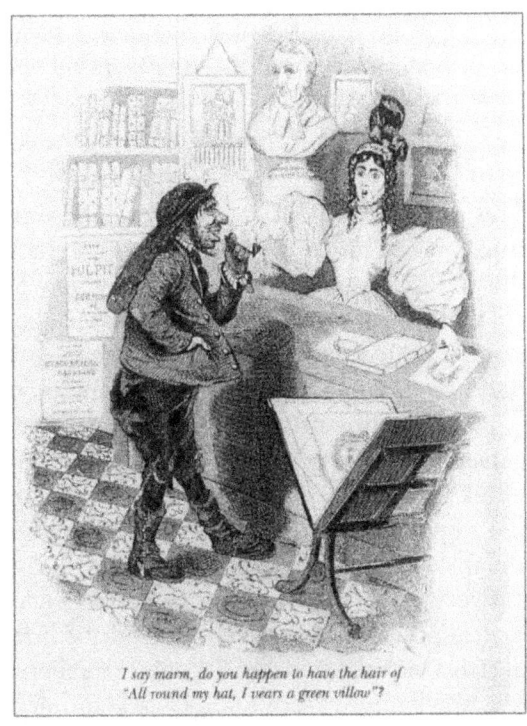

18 R. Seymour. Etching. 'I say marm', from *Sketches by Seymour*, vol. 5.

I say marm, do you happen to have the hair of "All round my hat, I vears a green villow"?

Life in London.[57] For *Figaro in London* Seymour drew sophisticated wood engraved vignettes on political subjects. He was also responsible for the masthead design of a barber stropping his razor among a shop of wigmakers' dummies bearing the features of contemporary politicians. In working for the group of bohemian radicals who ran *Figaro in London*, Seymour had moved a long way from his roots in the eighteenth-century caricature tradition.

Seymour's work for *Bell's Life in London* so precisely emblematises the rise of the vignette wood engraving into emergent narrative modes, that it is worth using Kunzle's description of the magazine's development:

> In 1824 Pierce Egan exploited the success of his *Tom and Jerry* with a raffish newspaper called *Pierce Egan's Life in London* ... The paper remained basically unillustrated until 1826, when a number of cuts by George Cruikshank were introduced as headers to regular features. Then, suddenly, in a radical break from tradition, on August 26, 1827, the now somewhat smaller and less expensive paper was filled with vignettes unconnected with any great news event. Circulation soared, and Egan sold the paper very profitably to Robert Bell ... Bell then launched his own novel pictorial programme, ... [which] had a a magical effect on sales ... The cuts, though usually unsigned, are occasionally initialed [sic] or otherwise identifiable as the designs of the best caricaturists of the age, including Robert Cruikshank, Robert Seymour, the newcomer Kenny Meadows, and the very young ... John Leech. Most are grouped into series, and many into a form of narrative, as their Hogarthian titles testify.[58]

The association of this generation of artists, all of them versed in single plate caricature, with the emergent wood engraved vignette illustration of proto-narratives shows how rapidly the marketplace was changing. It also suggests how crucial Dickens's influence was in securing the predominance of the text as the major medium for extended narrative rather than extended graphic or visual forms.

It is difficult to assess whether Seymour ever, even in his early career, belonged to that group of jobbing caricaturists like Gillray and Cruikshank whose political affiliations are indecipherable beneath their opportunist response to the demands of the marketplace. Given the instabilities of a jobbing culture, it is risky to make the connection between Seymour's work for *Figaro in London* and any consistent ideological position elsewhere in his prints. If the dustman prints from the *Sketches* lack the derision for common people which might be found in, say, Rowlandson's 'Love and Dust', neither do they show any particular democratic tendencies of affection for the labouring populace. Indeed, despite Seymour's relatively genial account of the educated dustman figure, he did manage to produce a caricature (a single plate lithograph at that, drawn as part of McClean's 'Monthly Sheet of Caricatures') which offered a savage critique of *The Penny Magazine* and all the works of The Society for the Diffusion of Useful Knowledge. 'The Penny Patent Knowledge Mill' shows pious liberals dropping 'froth' into a grinding mill to emerge as 'twaddle' through the consumer's outlet pipe and as a gushing stream of pennies from the proprietor's equivalent. Of particular interest here is the 'mashing vat' on the left of the mill, where 'illustrative woodblocks' of 'wondrous condescention and affability' are being stirred into the *Penny* mixture. Clearly, Seymour's connections with progressives and radicals did not stop him from drawing fiercely conservative images when the occasion demanded.[59]

In short, the relative ideological consistency which underlies Victorian wood engraved printmaking has not become apparent in the work of men like Seymour working in the 1830s. Seymour seems still to have drawn for the marketplace rather than in pursuit of any particular ideological or moral conviction. Nor does he draw in pursuit of the lofty, anonymous detachment sought by Doyle. In undertaking a major shift in technique away from metal engraving and lithography into the more vernacular medium of the wood engraving, Seymour, like Cruikshank, does not obviously reject the unaligned, jobbing mentality of eighteenth-century engraving in order to represent the increasingly close connection between wood engraving and bourgeois values shown in early Victorian culture.

Seymour's greatest contemporary reputation, however, was not gained for his wood engraving but for his sporting prints, especially those, to quote from Houfe, 'creating the routine of comic sportsmen from London having adventures in the countryside'.[60] Houfe also makes the important comment that 'much of his work was in the form of folios of prints with little or no text'.[61] Given this preference for the unannotated etched plate, it is ironic that Seymour's greatest claim to lasting notice was as the first illustrator of *The Pickwick Papers*, an irony made all the more poignant by Dickens's determined subjugation of the graphic origins of the book into its predominantly verbal outcome. The process by which commissioned plates by a well known sporting draughtsman of Seymour's stature became secondary to what began as a series of extended captions by an aspiring young journalist called Dickens has gained notoriety as a contributory cause of

Seymour's suicide in 1836. He had drawn and engraved only four plates for *Pickwick* at the time of his death. In then employing Robert Buss (who had to teach himself new techniques and buy new tools only to be replaced after producing a handful of plates) and then the young and relatively diffident Hablôt Browne ('Phiz'), Dickens almost emblematically changes graphic codes from eighteenth-century ones (caricature, exaggeration, the grotesque, sporting jokes, etching and copper engraving) to more obviously Victorian modes dependent on narrative, naturalistic characterisation, and more gently mocking humour.[62] The domination of early Victorian literary forms by the illustrated serial novel involved major changes to the role and form of the graphic image, and Seymour is a characteristic figure in these changes. Because of the various strands and contradictions within his career, it is almost impossible to locate Seymour's career within a clear context of beliefs and values. His images of educated dustmen show an interesting freedom from ideological positioning which may itself reflect the range of his commissions and audiences.

Much of Seymour's etched work is built out of a relatively simple notion of comic difference – town against country, innocence against knowingness, vulgar against genteel. It is the latter dualism which informs most of the educated dustmen images, in which the vulgar, the dirty, and the street invade the genteel interior – the shop, the coffee house, and the drawing room. Such an irruption of the vulgar into the world of elegant restraint might have been a political metaphor for working men who were getting above their place in ways which threatened social stability, but in most of Seymour's prints the refinement and pretentiousness of genteel culture are equally available for satire. The absolute dismay of the prim evangelical shopkeeper in 'I say marm' (illustration 18) on being confronted with a stereotypical dustman asking for the popular ballad 'All Around My Hat' is as much satirised as the dustman who does not recognise his own incongruity. The parodied coffee shop gentility of 'Have you read this leader?' (illustration 16) and 'You shall have the paper directly' (illustration 17) are as sharply critical of the ritualised good manners of polite social life as they are of the intellectual presumptuousness of dustmen. If a society's intellectual aspirations can be satisfied by newspapers, scientific public lectures, and popular romances, what hope is there for true learning or social development? Indeed, the balance of sympathy in these images seems to lie with the 'educated' dustmen. In addition to pointing out the inappropriateness of cultural ambitions in the working classes, the prints also ask why 'culture' should belong exclusively to a pretentious and essentially philistine minority. In satirising the appearance of cultural ambitions in the decaying and squalid environment of the dustman's cottage [14], Seymour is laughing at absurd parental ambitions for their children as much as at lower class aspirations beyond its station.

The goodwill and evenhandedness of Seymour's dustman prints are furthered by their relatively naturalistic representation of the main figures. Seymour may have been (to repeat Houfe's phrase) 'a somewhat inadequate draughtsman', but it is possible to observe the formulation of an increasingly naturalistic mode of representing figures, especially working class figures, emerging from the exaggerations and emblems of caricature in his etched work. Certainly the dustman in 'I say marm' [14] is authentically dirty and dressed with an accurate eye for detail. In this sense Seymour is looking towards novelistic illustration in these later plates, which are in an octavo format unlike the larger oblong shape of many of his earlier sporting prints. The personae of these prints, too (the London sportsman adrift in the country, the educated dustman, the knowing rural clodhopper) begin to emerge from caricature stereotype into something approaching individuality. While Seymour's *Sketches* remain locked into grotesque traditions of caricature representation (many of his figures tend to be either obese or grotesquely thin, for example, and prone to gluttony, greed, or other bestial characteristics at every turn of the situation), the dustmen, at least, do begin to display some recognisably human characteristics. Their dress is rendered with some interest and attention to detail, even if their long-brimmed hats are exaggerated into grotesque protruberances.[63] While Seymour's *Sketches* (like his fascinating few plates for the first issues of *Pickwick*) do not yet belong to the naturalistic tradition of the Victorian wood engraving, they are equally far removed from the remorseless exaggeration and exuberant contempt of the eighteenth-century caricature tradition.

'The Literary Dustman': a woodcut from W.T. Moncrieff's *Songbook* (1834)

This image (illustration 19) from Moncrieff's *Songbook* of a 'literary' dustman reading *The Penny Magazine* and smoking a cigar while reclining on a chaise longue in a genteel drawing room, offers far more than just a jovial, easy-going alternative to the ideologically charged prints examined so far in this chapter. Indeed, the interpretation of this particular image requires an extended journey into the historical

THE LITERARY DUSTMAN.

19 Anonymous woodcut. Text by W.T. Moncrieff.
'The Literary Dustman', from Moncrieff's *Songbook* (1834).

origins of popular stereotypes, in this case tracing the 'literary dustman' back to sources in both popular fiction and the popular theatre. As with Collings's Albion Mill engraving, the interplay between the theatre and graphic image making is of particular importance here. 'The Literary Dustman' arrives in the Moncrieff *Songbook* via a number of transformations from popular fiction to the stage, from the stage on to pottery figures, from the theatre into songs, from songs into graphic images. Nothing could show more clearly how deeply graphic images are embedded in the surrounding culture.

The genesis of the 'educated dustman' stereotype as a popular myth, still accessible through Alfred Doolittle in the musical *My Fair Lady*, has a complex but historically precise origin. Moving the stereotype beyond the relatively exclusive discourse of sophisticated printmaking already examined into more general consciousness initially depended on the publication of Pierce Egan's immensely successful novel *Life in London* in 1821.[64] J.C. Reid's study of Egan[65] offers a detailed account of the novel and its astonishing ability to establish a whole range of popular stereotypes and motifs which cut deep into Regency and Victorian popular culture, and which were particularly important in establishing images of the poorer classes. As Reid notes, *Life in London* was itself dependent for its form, mode of publication, and subject matter on a whole range of preceding literature which exploited the double, if contradictory, focus of moral indignation at, and simultaneous prurient celebration of, low life society in London. The novel was in serial form, and contained both text and illustration within each issue. While this format was not entirely new, *Life in London* was, Reid argues, the 'first work of prose fiction to be so published and certainly the most widely read and imitated.'[66] The relation between plates and texts is not an entirely collaborative one, and suggests the same kind of struggle for precedence between Egan and his illustrator George Cruikshank as that already described between Dickens, Seymour, Buss, and Browne in formulating the format of *The Pickwick Papers*.[67] But perhaps the key element of the book was concerned with its representation of class. It marks the beginning of a sustained literary and visual endeavour to establish ways in which social activities which involved cross class contact might be represented not as aspects of social conflict but rather as a genial recognition of difference and variety within society. This endeavour manifests itself within the Victorian period in many interesting ways – in the crowd paintings of Frith and O'Neill for example[68] – and stands in direct opposition to prints like 'The Rival Mag's' which, using eighteenth-century caricature precendent, sought to represent working people through the iconography of difference and dismissal. In contrast, Egan's 'Invocation' to the novel displays a generous delight in social difference:

> The EXTREMES, in every point of view, are daily to be met with in the Metropolis; from the most rigid, persevering, never-tiring industry, down to laziness. ... The most bare-faced villains, swindlers, and thieves, walk about the streets in the day-time, committing their various depredations, with as much confidence as men of unblemished reputation and honesty ... Yet ... there are some of the worthiest, most tender-hearted, liberal minds, and charitable dispositions, which ornament London, and render it the delight and happiness of society.[69]

Egan's picaresque strategies, including the central narrative device of the idle aristocrat and the street-wise plebeian as joint centres of consciousness, are all aimed at elucidating this variety which is inclusive and warm in its recognition of 'difference' not as an aspect of class, but rather as an aspect of human diversity. Although, as Reid notes 'little space is given to the working class',[70] the social hierarchy of the novel (while clearly established) is based on an acknowl-edgement of the contribution of even the most humble or undeserving to the pleasures and social structures of Regency England.

Reid's fascinating chapter 'The Life in London Furore' gives a sense of how deeply this novel entered popular consciousness. In his 1869 novel *Finish to the Adventures of Tom, Jerry, and Logic*, Egan listed 'over sixty derivations, including books, dramatisations, newspapers, song-books, games, street ballads, drinks, [and] printed tea-trays'.[71] Reid goes on to add snuff-boxes, painted fire screens, shawls, handker-chiefs, fans, cushions, and clothes to the list. Writing in 1971 Reid can only find Walt Disney as a parallel marketing campaign based on mass popular appeal: to the television age of Paddington Bear, Postman Pat, and Mutant Hero Ninja Turtles, the success of Tom and Jerry as popular icons may seem less surprising, although the imaginative effort required to understand how this could have happened before the development of mass electronic communications is considerable. Reid's listings of sequels, piracies, and translations of *Life in London* occupy several pages,[72] ranging from forgotten Regency hacks to substantial Victorian figures like James Grant whose 1868 *Sketches in London* was itself a popular success. Forty years after the publication of *Life in London*, allusions to its form, literary method, and, indeed its popularity could still be widely acknowledged.

It is, however, in the two related forms of the drama and the song-book that Egan's original ideas become most effectively devel-oped into popular consciousness. *Life in London* was an immediate opportunity for stage managers and theatrical entrepreneurs, who, despite the licensing laws which restricted legitimate drama to two London theatres, none the less capitalised on topicality and popular crazes through the medium of 'musical entertainments'. The first adap-tation of *Life in London*, W. Barrymore's 'entirely New, Whimsical, Local, Melo-Dramatic, Pantomimical Drama', was sanctioned by Egan, and opened on Monday, 17 September 1821 at the Royal Amphi-theatre. Dibdin's version of the novel followed less than a month later at the Olympic Theatre, to be followed by many other versions in rapid succession. Reid lists five separate versions in 1822 and 1823 alone.[73] Louis James prints a poster advertising a performance of *Life in Liverpool* in 1835, which describes the translation of Egan's original idea into a provincial setting (which could doubtless be altered as appropriate).[74]

It was, however, W.T. Moncrieff's version of the novel which was to prove the most enduring and the most influential of the theatrical versions of the original novel. Moncrieff's notorious career was built on popular theatrical piracies and he was later to become well known for his adaptations (or travesties) of Dickens and Bulwer Lytton. He was particularly influential, Reid notes, in establishing a tradition of 'roguery in the theatre'.[75] *Tom and Jerry* opened at the Adelphi on 26 November 1821, and its popular success (a run of 300 nights) established the theatre's fortunes. The play remained a resource for theatre companies for the next forty years at least. In his listing of 'Significant Productions on the London Stage, 1837–1901', Donald Mullin notes productions of the play at Covent Garden in 1837, at Sadlers Wells in the same year, at the Victoria in 1842, and at the Grecian in 1863.[76] Edwin Fagg notices additionally an early production at the Coburg, with a revival at the same theatre in 1827.[77] When the 'insignificant' productions and all those before 1837 are added to this list, the astonishing popularity of the play can be at least glimpsed.

Reid gives a clear account of how Moncrieff's dramatic adaptation alters and extends Egan's original text:

> he drew heavily on Egan's text for plot, character, and dialogue. It follows the main line of Egan's narrative, plunders the text wholesale for speeches, and uses all its major scenes. On the other hand, Moncrieff stiffens the plot by giving Logic a female companion, Jane, identifying Kate, Sue, and Jane with the Misses Trifle, and making the pursuit of the young men by the young women a major element in the play. Also, from a mere hint in Egan, he introduces the London gull, Jemmy Green, and makes into colourful, lively characters Little Jemmy, Dusty Bob, and African Sal, whom Egan only names. The roles of Corinthian Tom and Jerry made the reputations of Wrench and Reeve, Bob Keeley was a terrific hit as Jemmy Green, but the public's affections fastened on Walbourn as Dusty Bob and Sanders as African Sal, and their comic pas de deux was one of the major attractions of the piece. When Walbourn retired to take over a public house at Battle bridge, George Cruikshank painted an inn-sign for him showing Walbourn in his Dusty Bob character.[78]

Reid does not mention that in the original novel the dustman was described as 'Nasty Bob' rather than 'Dusty Bob', and was a coal porter rather than a dustman. Bob's ultimate trade, as well as his literary leanings, were the product of Moncrieff rather than Egan, though it might be more plausible to argue that the entire character was more the product of the popular will than any specific author or dramatist.

The development of the genial 'Dusty Bob' stage figure is a key moment in the production of the popular stereotype of the educated dustman, a stereotype which becomes a commonplace within the graphic discourses of the 1830s and 1840s. As I want to go on to show, the 'Dusty Bob' figure was carried in the popular imagination through stage performances, illustrated play texts, and songbooks over several decades. At this historical juncture, the stock figure of the comic dustman with cultural pretentions, constructed in the genial discourses of Regency comic theatre and fiction, intersects with political debates about class, education, and proletarian potential already described at the beginning of this chapter. The outcome of this intersection is a contest within the graphic representations of 'literary dustmen' over the cultural importance and meaning of this stereotypical figure. As we have seen from 'The Rival Mag's', he could be represented through the savage reactionary ridicule and dismissal of the eighteenth-century caricature tradition. But, as the Moncrieff illustration suggests, he might also be constructed as a figure of comic geniality seen with a kind of Dickensian liberality.

The theatre may have been the main mode through which this stereotype was constructed, but other forms of transmission were also significant, if only because they depended on graphic representation rather than ephemeral performance. One important medium was the songbook, which combined song-texts drawn from theatrical performances with other more miscellaneous lyrics. Often the songbooks included illustrations, and Moncrieff's *Songbook* (1834) provides one of the images of Dusty Bob which I wish to examine in more detail.[79] (illustration 19). The image depends on an accompanying text, which is printed in full below. The text itself was drawn from the Moncrieff productions, and was the product of the changed and developed characterisation of Dusty Bob described above. Indeed, the original Egan text had already been subject to a decade of attention by dramatists, entrepreneurs, and popularists. That Moncrieff's exploitation of the Dusty Bob character through associating him with popular song was not exceptional is shown by Reid's list of a range of songbooks all deriving in some form from Egan's original novel or its later dramatisations. He lists *The Corinthians' Song Book, Tom and Jerry's Collection of Songs, Bob Logic's Memoranda, An Original Budget of Staves*, and *The New Harp Songbook*.[80] The most interesting venture in turning dramatisation into popular texts, however, was Catnach's strip cartoon version of the novel derived from some of the original Cruikshank plates and which Reid derides as 'wretched plagiarism'.[81] The borderline between enterprising popularisation and wretched plagiarism may be a relatively fine one in practice. Whatever value judgements are attached to such kinds of commercial exploitation of Egan's original ideas, there is no doubt that broadsheet or chapbook versions of this kind maintained popular stereotypes and stock jokes in the popular consciousness, both visually and verbally, in extremely effective ways.

Beyond the popular press and its various textual interpretations of performance and current popular stereotypes, some other versions of the 'Dusty Bob' character should be noted here. One appears as a Staffordshire porcelain figure, one part of a pair also comprising a figure of 'African Sal'. The two figures were produced some time between 1834 and 1850 by the Staffordshire firm of John and Rebecca Lloyd. Popular Staffordshire figures of this kind are notoriously difficult to date and annotate, and it is fortunate that an article by Delia Napier[82] gives a fairly detailed sense of the context out of which these figures were produced. Napier notes that the African Sal figure is sometimes paired with figures of Billy Waters, a black, one-legged street cadger whom Moncrieff had introduced into *Tom and Jerry*, but she also found references to pairings with Dusty Bob, although unfortunately none seems to be available for study. In researching her article, Napier turned to theatrical prints and found a version of the 'celebrated' Sal and Bob performing a kind of rustic two-step[5]. Napier claims that the print formed a source for the modelling of the Lloyd figures, but, given the range and availability of images of Bob and Sal, a precise source seems unlikely.

The point at issue here, however, is to establish that there was an extremely highly developed market for theatrical texts in the early nineteenth century and that these cheap reprints (often extended into long series or gathered into volume formats by publishers like Duncombe) nearly always included woodcuts 'taken from performance'.[83] The ubiquitous Cruikshank brothers were certainly extremely active in providing these images, which are significant for the way in which they extend the caricature tradition on into the 1830s in the new format of the wood engraved vignette. There is no doubt that a huge variety of representations of 'Dusty Bob' as a stage figure were available in the 1820s and 1830s, and that these did have the effect of sustaining an already widely available stereotypical figure (the educated dustman) on long past its original popularity.

Such a complex process of transmission and transformation of an original stereotype within popular culture is directly acknowledged in the wood engraving taken from Moncrieff's *Songbook*. This acknowledgement is not solely contained in the central foregrounded figure of the educated dustman. The back wall of the room in which the dustman lounges discloses an elaborately framed portrait of African Sal and Dusty Bob. The portrait is presumably intended as a parody of the family portrait gallery in aristocratic houses. In a further comment on the presumptuous aping of the aristocracy, Sal and Bob's portrait is situated next to one of the king in full regalia, holding an orb and sceptre, and mounted on a plinth or pedestal. This specific allusion to Sal and Bob, and their history as popular symbols, is buried in the swags, sconces, and other paraphernalia of a Regency drawing room (decanters, wine coolers, monteiths, and a forte piano). Yet the allusion is a significant one, invoking an impressive (if subversive) pedigree within the genres and modes of popular culture. The assumption, in this relatively unsophisticated image, that the history of Bob and Sal, constructed and sustained as it was within diverse modes and genres, would be known to its audience, is an important one which reasserts the power of vernacular image making in whatever form it is manifested.

With this history of the popular image of the literary dustman in mind, it is now possible to try to decode the image from Moncrieff's *Songbook*. The constituent elements of the image have already been largely identified: the lounging dustman with a copy of the talismanic *Penny Magazine* dangling from one hand and a cigar in the other, at evident ease in a genteel drawing room furnished in high Regency taste with circular gilded mirrors, ample drapes, and a rococo carpet. On the left of the image another dustman, in his dustman's hat, bawls away to his own forte piano accompaniment. He is playing music entitled 'Puritany', an allusion to the hypocrisies of the genteel world of indulgence which the dustmen aspire to join. The song-text printed underneath the image explains that the pianist is in fact the literary dustman's son, and is receiving his nightly music lesson from his complacent father, a motif already used by Seymour in [14]. The backdrop of fantastically framed portraits has already been described.

The image is, as already noted, accompanied by a song-text drawn from Moncrieff's stage adaptation of the original Pierce Egan text. The full text of the song is printed here in a note.[84] The song is essentially a comic attack on the failings of the 'liberal education' enjoyed by the upper classes, except that the dilettante smatterings of culture are transposed from drawing room to dust heap. An emergent idea in the song is that of 'the university of life' and 'the school of hard knocks'. Adam Bell, as the dustman is called here, defends his education both from the picturesque dust-heap and 'all the Peri-o-di-calls'.

At the end of the song, however, there is an interesting transition from a comic attack on cultural pretentiousness to a more explicitly political issue:

> Yes, vhen I sits in Parli'ment,
> In old Sin Stephen's College,
> I means to take, 'tis my intent,
> The 'Taxes off o' knowledge.'

Although understated, this closing remark does bring the entire political and cultural context of mass proletarian education into the poem, and therefore into the accompanying woodcut image. This context is one which is deeply inscribed in all the images discussed in this chapter.

Enough should have been said to support a reading of this image from Moncrieff's *Songbook* as an essentially genial and celebratory one, which, while not denying socio/political meanings and anxieties, none the less finds strategies for regarding the educated dustman as a comic (but not absurd) stereotype which could contain and possibly even resolve the potentially competing social meanings within the image. The constituent elements of this comic view are explicable. First, the print recognises *difference* as a source of comic meanings and takes delight in the discrepancies between gentility and vulgarity. The pivot of the humour is the comic negotiation between pretentious gentility and vulgar aspiration. This negotiation is essentially a two-way process, as it is in interpreting Seymour's images of dustmen in the *Sketches*. The print neither simply denounces the aspirations of working people to culture as an aspect of a new and dangerous political coherence within the labouring classes (as happens in 'The Rival Mag's') nor does it accept the 'cultured' life of the genteel drawing room as a cultural ideal. Indeed, the print is in the eighteenth-century mode of satirising the vacuity, philistinism, and emptiness of aristocratic or genteel cultural ambitions. In acknowledging that cultural pretention characterises the gentility as much as plebeians, the print accepts social difference in an open-handed way.

Second, as we have seen, the *Songbook* print assimilates a whole series of complex socio/cultural issues and debates into the form of popular stereotype. This stereotype – the literary dustman – is derived from popular culture by means of a long series of transmissions and transpositions in genre and mode – the picaresque novel, the popular theatre, transfer printed pottery, songbooks, and popular theatre texts with vignette illustrations. In the course of these transitions, much of the controversial potential of the image of the educated dustman has been subsumed into a comic stereotype, to be greeted with both affection and derision as an acceptable simplification or shorthand version of an initially complex social perception. This is not to say that the 'Dusty Bob' stereotype is entirely without complexity, but rather that any potentially disruptive social meanings have been assimilated into the comic clichés of a predictable cartoon figure. The analogy might be with contemporary television situation comedy.

Third, the *Songbook* print is in its mode a crude woodcut. At a time when lithography, steel engraving, and wood engraving were all widely available as modes of book illustration, the use of the popular vernacular medium of woodcut is a significant one. The Moncrieff *Songbook* is in this sense deliberately regressive, and is consciously invoking a vernacular, broadside, and popular narrative tradition rather than the more sophisticated possibilities of wood engraved illustration of the kind demonstrated in, for example, George and Robert Cruikshank's version of the popular songbook in *The Universal Songster* (1825–7). It is worth noting that many other popular songbooks of this period used highly elaborate steel or copper plate engraved frontispieces even when the text was shabbily produced. In aligning itself with the vernacular energy and street culture of broadside, chapbook, and tract, the Moncrieff *Songbook* image invokes the world of bawdy ballads and rustic swains rather than the tensions of class conflict and division. In every sense – the clumsy framing, the addition of a sustained text, the discrepancy between the crude linear technique of the print and its genteel subject – this image rejects the sophisticated visual discourses of Seymour, Doyle, and the new illustrators of the bourgeois novel who dominate our perception of image making in the 1830s and 1840s. In technique and mode, this print belongs more to Dusty Bob and oral vernacular culture than it does to the increasingly sophisticated world of middle class image making. Despite its sophisticated acknowledgement of cultural stereotype and of polite caricature discourses, in form and technique, this print asserts the energy and vitality of its labouring class subjects even as it satirises their aspirations and pretentions.

Conclusion

The relationship between the images of the 'educated dustmen' studied in this chapter and a variety of social anxieties should by now be clear. But what should be equally clear is that there was not a unified or coherent interpretation of the figure within the various versions offered by popular prints. If the most firmly held line of interpretation seems to be that of assimilating the potential threat of educated working men into a comic, accommodating visual and literary stereotype, there none the less remain more anxious, more retributive images beyond the comforting simplifications of the theatre, the music hall, and the clumsy humorous woodcut. Many of these more fretful images are expressed in the declining media of genteel caricature – the etching, the metal engraving, and the lithograph – presumably to an audience and readership well versed in the graphic codes of Gillray, Rowlandson, and their contemporaries. But by the 1830s, or certainly the 1840s, middle class image making had begun to depend not on retaining the single plate engraving as its dominant medium but rather on appropriating and adapting the vernacular traditions of woodcut and wood engraving to its own ideological purpose. Seymour's attempts to work in etched, lithographed, and wood engraved media to meet the conflicting demands of the print trade at a time of confusion and transition seems almost emblematic, as does Cruikshank's double conversion to wood engraving and temperance. The decline of the caricature tradition, with its ideological instability, opportunism, and cult of the personal, and the rise of wood engraving to dominance as a graphic medium, coincides closely with the emergence of the middle classes as a coherent social force. So it is to traditions of wood engraving, and the ideologies which these traditions reveal, that we should now turn.

List of images cited

[1] 'The March of Literature or The Rival Mag's' (illustration **13**)
Anonymous hand-coloured lithograph (by W. Heath, R. Seymour, J. Doyle?).
(Thomas McClean), 25 October 1832.

[2] 'Four Specimens of the Reading Public' (illustration **15**)
Coloured engraving by 'A. Crowquill' (A. Forrester).
(J. Fairburn), 7 August 1826.

[3] 'March of Intellect among the Black-Diamond Carriers'
Coloured engraving by Isaac Robert Cruikshank.
(J. Fairburn), 1 September 1828.

[4] 'The March of Interlect or a Dustman and Family of the 19th Century'.
(illustration **14**)
Anonymous coloured engraving. (J.L. Marks), undated.

[5] 'The Celebrated Dusty Bob and African Sal'
Anonymous engraving; undated.

A print in the Theatre Museum, London, cited by Delia Napier in *The Antique Collector*, October 1989.

[6] 'The March of Intellect'
Engraving by William Heath.
Thomas McClean, 1829.
Cited by M.D. George, *From Hogarth to Cruikshank – Social Change in Graphic Satire* (London, Viking 1967), illustration 163.

[7] 'The March of Intellect'
Engraving by W. Heath; Undated.
George, *From Hogarth to Cruikshank*, illustration 164.

[8] 'The March of Mind'
Anonymous engraving; undated.
George, *From Hogarth to Cruikshank*, p. 181.

[9] 'The March of Intellect'
Coloured engraving by 'Sharpshooter'.
Description cited from a Finbarr McDonnell catalogue 1989.

[10] 'The Literary Dustman' (illustration **19**)
Anonymous woodcut, with text by W.T. Moncrieff, from Moncrieff's *Songbook* (1834).
Song related to Moncrieff's dramatisation of *Tom and Jerry* (1821), based on Pierce Egan's novel *Life in London* (1821).

[11] 'Have you read this leader in this paper, Mr. Brisket?' (illustration **16**)
Etching by Robert Seymour in *Sketches by Seymour* (London, R. Carlile, 5 vols, 1834).

[12] 'You shall have the paper directly, sir'. (illustration **17**)
Etching by Robert Seymour in *Sketches by Seymour*, as above.
See also [15] below.

[13] 'I say marm' (illustration **18**)
Etching by Robert Seymour in *Sketches by Seymour*, as above.

[14] 'Look Papa'
Etching by Robert Seymour in *Sketches by Seymour*, as above.

[15] 'I say, Bob …'
Pen and ink sketch by Robert Browning senior.
This sketch, which is in the Gordon Collection in the Victoria and Albert Museum, London, may well have been the source for [12]. Two working men are seated in a tavern or coffee shop alcove, smoking pipes. One is reading *The Times*. The first man says 'I say, Bob, what do you think of Bobby Peel's speech, Eh?' The second replies 'Why Jim I never bother my head 'bout sich low wulger stuff as politics I attends lectures on 'stronomy.' Clearly jokes such as these were commonplaces of the new journalism of the 1830s.

Notes

1 M.D. George, *From Hogarth to Cruikshank – Social Change in Graphic Satire* (London, Viking 1967).

2 C. Fox, *Graphic Journalism in England During the 1830s and 1840s* (New York,

Greenwood 1988). Reprint of an Oxford doctoral thesis submitted in 1974. See also P. Anderson, *The Printed Image and the Transformation of Popular Culture 1790–1860* (Oxford, Clarendon Press 1991).

3   For the rise of lithography see: M. Twyman, *Lithography 1800–1850* (Oxford, Oxford University Press 1970). The use of lithography as a medium for caricature, most notably used in Britain by John Doyle, has been much more widely studied in France because it was the favoured medium used by Daumier, Gavarni, and other famous French satirical artists. The distinctiveness of the French lithographical tradition can be partially gleaned from G.N. Ray, *The Art of the French Illustrated Book 1700 to 1914* (New York, Dover Publications 1986). See note 21 below for Doyle.

4   It is hard to get a single narrative history of the rise of the wood engraving, but see: S. Houfe, *The Dictionary of British Book Illustrators and Caricaturists 1800–1914* (Woodbridge, Antique Collectors' Club revised edn, 1981); Anderson, *The Printed Image*; and E. de Maré, *The Victorian Woodblock Illustrators* (London, Gordon Fraser 1980).

5   See, for discussions of the emergence of mass illustrated journals, R.D. Altick, *The English Common Reader* (Chicago, University of Chicago Press 1957); Anderson, *The Printed Image*; and Fox, *Graphic Journalism in England*. B.E. Maidment's essay *Into the 1830s – Some Origins of Victorian Illustrated Journalism* (Manchester Polytechnic 1992), gives some account of the use of illustration in popular magazines of the 1820s.

6   M.H. Spielmann, *The History of Punch* (London, Cassell 1895) is the standard account, but see also R.G.G. Price *A History of Punch* (London, Collins 1957), Houfe's Introduction, the several books on Richard Doyle listed below, and many other sources.

7   J.R. Harvey, *Victorian Novels and Their Illustrators* (London Sidgwick and Jackson 1970) remains the most useful introduction.

8   See, for an interesting account of Dickens's use of vignette illustration in *Master Humphrey's Clock* against his usual practice of separate single plate etchings or engravings, J. Cohen, *Dickens and his Original Illustrators*.

9   See R.L. Patten, *Charles Dickens and his Publishers* (Oxford, Clarendon Press 1978), and Cohen for Dickens's relationships with Seymour. See also notes 53–63 below.

10   C. Rosen and H. Zerner have a fascinating chapter on the Romantic vignette as a distinct genre in *Romanticism and Realism* (London, Faber and Faber 1984).

11   N. Bryson, *Vision and Painting – The Logic of the Gaze* (London, Macmillan 1983), 134.

12   Bryson, *Vision and Painting*, 134.

13   George, *From Hogarth to Cruikshank*, 177–82.

14   Fox, *Graphic Journalism*, 131–57.

15   See, for an account of these developments, Altick, *English Common Reader*, and R.K. Webb, *The British Working Class Reader 1790–1848* (New York, A.M. Kelley 1971, reprint of original 1955 edition).

16   It would be impossible here to give a detailed reading list for accounts of the development of class consciousness and ideas of hegemony in the early period. I have drawn on the following among many others: Raymond Williams, *Culture and Society 1780–1950* (London, Chatto and Windus 1958); Raymond Williams, *Keywords* (London, Fontana 1976), see especially 'Hegemony' and

'Class'; T. Bennett, G. Martin, C. Mercer and J. Woollacott (eds), *Culture, Ideology and Social Process* (London, Open University Press 1981), especially Section 4 on 'Class, Culture, and Hegemony'; F. Jameson *The Political Unconscious: Narrative as a Socially Symbolic Act* (London, Methuen 1981); and A. Gramsci *Selections from Cultural Writings* (London, Lawrence and Wishart 1985).

17   George, *From Hogarth to Cruikshank*, 177.

18   *Ibid.*, 177–182.

19   BMC, no. 15757.

20   George, *From Hogarth to Cruikshank*, 181.

21   For an account of Doyle's political caricatures see G.M. Trevelyan, *The Seven Years of William IV* (London 1952). Engen describes the reasons for Doyle's pursuit of anonymity in the following terms: 'To preserve his objectivity, and maintain what he regarded as essential artistic distance from his subjects, he refused to sign his drawings with his name. Instead he adopted the signature "HB", a combination of two js and two ds placed above each other, and jealously guarded his anonymity until his retirement in 1851', R. Engen, *Richard Doyle* (Stroud, Catalpa Press 1983), 13. The interesting issue here is the notion that a caricaturist should be 'objective'. For the eighteenth-century caricaturists, the partiality of their images depended not on any political integrity, but on the demands of a particular commission or the likely tastes and opportunities of the market place. In this respect, as in many others, Doyle's career signals a shift towards Victorian gentility away from the volatile values and attitudes found in the work of eighteenth-century caricaturists.

22   See, for example, I. Mackenzie *British Prints: Dictionary and Price Guide* (Woodbridge, Antique Collectors' Club 1987), 104 ('his images are much inferior in imagery and execution compared with the earlier masters'); W. Feaver, *Masters of Caricature* (London, Weidenfeld and Nicolson 1981), 69 ('The mild humour of his satires met with approval, as public taste veered to constraint and decorum'); and D. Hambourg *Richard Doyle* (London, Art and Technics 1948), 10 ('The visual gusto, the robust merriment of a Gillray or a Rowlandson were alien to the temperament of this quiet Irish gentleman, who introduced a new note of polite and urbane irony'). This critical insistence on Doyle's gentility (Thackeray talks of smiling in a 'quiet gentlemanly kind of way' at Doyle's images), while it insists on a major shift in the market for caricatures, should not be allowed to conceal the deeply felt conservatism of images like 'The Rival Mag's'. Nor should it allow us to assume that early Victorian caricaturists were necessarily personally committed to the opinions which they constructed in their published works. More detailed accounts of Doyle's life and character can be found in Engen, *Richard Doyle*, 11–17, the same author's *Richard Doyle and his Family* (London Victoria and Albert Museum 1983), 6–9, and Hambourg, *Richard Doyle*, 9–11.

23   See, for example, Rowlandson's famous related image 'Love and Dust' in which both a male and female dust sifter are ridiculed, with considerable energy, through their bouyant and unapologetic lasciviousness rather than through their poverty. The image is reproduced by George, *From Hogarth to Cruikshank*, 73.

24   Grant is to my mind an extremely underrated caricaturist who maintained a crucial link between the broad, even crude, lines of the woodcut and political outspokenness. His work receives some appreciation in Fox and in Louis

James's *Fiction for the Working Man* (Oxford, Oxford University Press 1962), but the continuing association of vernacular idiom and energy with the political radicalism expressed in his work has never been fully acknowledged.

25 *Figaro in London*, which ran weekly from 1831 to 1839 under various editors, was a topical political journal edited for some time by Gilbert à Beckett who sought to represent the opinions of the radical metropolitan bohemian circles which nurtured the young Dickens. The graphic significance of the journal lies in its pioneering use of wood engraved satirical illustrations which were incorporated into the text as vignettes, thus translating the visual energy of the Hone/Cruikshank pamphlets into a serialised form. The main artist was Robert Seymour (see below). *Figaro in London* imported into Britain a satirical format from France which was more famously exploited by *Punch*, but it is an important journal in its own right both for its outspoken political views and for the development of a satirical tradition in illustration in the vignette form. See D. Kunzle, *The History of the Comic Strip: The Nineteenth Century* (Berkeley, University of California Press 1990), 21–3.

26 Thomas McClean's *The Looking Glass* represented an attempt to order the old single plate caricature tradition into a commercial serial format. This chapter offers further discussion of precisely these kinds of shifts towards a text laden serial format as part of the emergence of a distinctively early Victorian discourse.

27 *Punch* was founded in 1841 and rapidly became a national institution. Notwithstanding, the early radicalism of its views, derived from exactly the same sources of man-about-town bohemianism as *Figaro in London*, should not be underestimated.

28 *Bentley's Miscellany* ran from January 1837 until 1868, when it merged with *Temple Bar*. Cruikshank and Leech were among its famous illustrators, while the fiction contributors included W.H. Ainsworth, Dickens, Samuel Lover, and James Fenimore Cooper. A serialised novel, with separate full plate illustrations, was a feature of each monthly issue. *Ainsworth's Magazine* (1842 to 1854) was best known for its fictional collaborations between Ainsworth and Cruikshank, but Ainsworth also used an interesting range of other illustrators, including the French artist Tony Johannot and 'Phiz', who must take much credit for the success of the magazine. *The New Monthly Magazine* was a survivor, in various changed formats, from a previous era, having been founded in 1814 as a general topical review. As a literary periodical in the 1830s and 1840s it was edited by S.C. Hall, Bulwer Lytton, Theodore Hook, Thomas Hood, and Harrison Ainsworth. The dependence of these magazines on serialised fiction illustrated by separated out and sophisticated humorous images etched or engraved on steel, established the experimental formats of Dickens's early works into a norm used by the majority of mass circulation fictions aimed at middle class readers. While cheap popular fiction remained more dependent on the wood engraved vignette assimilated into the text, most of the major novelists – even Thackeray who continued to engrave his own vignette capitals, chapter headings, and tailpieces for many of his serialised novels – used a separate page for most of their illustrations. See J. Harvey, *Victorian Novels and their Illustrators* for an account of Ainsworth, Dickens, and Thackeray. For descriptions of the significance of the above periodicals see A. Sullivan (ed.), *British Literary Magazines: The Victorian and Edwardian Age, 1837–1913* (New York, Greenwood Press 1984).

29   George, *From Hogarth to Cruikshank*, 72–3.

30   For an account of the developing tradition of the representation of proletarian figures within the caricature tradition see J. Brewer, *The Common People and Politics 1750–1790s* (Cambridge, Chadwyck-Healey 1986).

31   George and Brewer both give many examples of 'procession' prints ranging from Hogarth's famous 'March to Finchley' to Rowlandson's 1784 'Procession to the Hustings after a Successful Canvass' (Brewer, *Common People and Politics*, 72). See also H.M. Atherton, 'The Mob in Eighteenth Century Caricature', in *Eighteenth Century Studies*, vol. 12, no. 1, 1978.

32   Printed by Brewer, *Common People and Politics*, plate 91.

33   Charles Dickens, *Bleak House* (1852–53), chapter IV. The novel is of course full of images of disorder used as metaphors or metonyms for social chaos. The illustration entitled 'A Visit to the Bricklayers' shows a similar vision of disarray in a domestic interior.

34   This description of the 'Sharpshooter' caricature, which does not seem to be in BMC, is taken from a 1989 catalogue issued by the London printseller Finbar McDonnell.

35   George, *From Hogarth to Cruikshank*, 181.

36   BMC, 15604 (23 January 1828).

37   See D. Donald 'The Power of Print: Graphic Images of Peterloo' in *Manchester Region History Review*, vol. III, no. 1, Spring/Summer 1989, 21–30. The whole of this issue of the *Review* is devoted to Peterloo, and contains a wealth of graphic material relevant to the discussion here.

38   Donald, 'The Power of Print', *passim*.

39   See D. Vincent, *Bread, Knowledge and Freedom: A Study of Nineteenth-Century Working Class Autobiography* (London, Europa 1981) for many examples.

40   Webb, *The British Working Class Reader*.

41   J. Wiener, *Unstamped British Periodicals 1830–1836* (London, The Bibliographical Society 1970).

42   B. Maidment, *The Poorhouse Fugitives* (Manchester, Carcanet Press 1987), 154.

43   I have drawn my basic information on Forrester from Houfe, *Dictionary of British Book Illustrators and Caricaturists*; R. Engen, *Dictionary of Victorian Wood Engravers* (Cambridge, Chadwyck-Healey 1985); Spielmann, *The History of Punch*; and R.L. Patten, *George Cruikshank's Life, Times, and Art* (London, Lutterworth Press, vol. 1 1992).

44   Both dates are given by various sources. Forrester's name, too, is subject to variation, with Houfe giving 'Forrestier' rather than 'Forrester'.

45   See Maidment, *Into the 1830s*.

46   Houfe, *Dictionary of British Book Illustrators and Caricaturists*, 273.

47   Spielmann, *The History of Punch*, 15 and 449–50. Spielmann's summary judgement of Forrester is worth reprinting: 'Although a versatile man, using his pen and pencil with equal facility and ability – the former, perhaps, more successfully than the latter – Forrester ... was but an indifferent humourist. He was of those who thought that fun could be imparted to a drawing by the simple expedient of grotesque exaggeration of expression; and as a great admirer of Seymour's "Cockney Humour", he was frequently pointless and stilted. Personally he was highly popular with the Staff, for he was philosophically happy and jovial, and sang good songs, and was, moreover, greatly sought after at a time when comic artists were few ... when he left, in 1844, his place was easily and advantageously filled' (449–50).

48 Kunzle, *History of the Comic Strip*, offers the best account of these issues. Kunzle's opening pages on Hogarth, Cruikshank, Seymour, and the development of sustained graphic narratives repay careful reading. They are immensely suggestive of the remarkable transformations taking place within image making during the 1820s and 1830s.

49 See the section on Seymour below.

50 The *Cambridge Bibliography of English Literature* entry on Dickens provides a comprehensive list of Pickwick extra illustration. Forrester's set of plates was called *Pickwickian Papers*.

51 The standard biographical study of Cobbett is George Spater's *William Cobbett: The Poor Man's Friend* (Cambridge, Cambridge University Press, 2 vols, 1982).

52 Gillray's 'Tales of Wonder' is reproduced by George as colour plate XI in *From Hogarth to Cruikshank*.

53 Seymour's *Sketches* contain many other images of street labourers, who form one of his favourite subjects.

54 Houfe, *Dictionary of British Book Illustrators and Caricaturists*, 449.

55 *Ibid.*, 449.

56 Engen, *Dictionary of Victorian Wood Engravers*, 233. Engen makes the important point that Seymour drew for *Figaro in London* on two separate occasions punctuated by his withdrawal from the magazine in protest over the poor quality and carelessness with which his drawings were engraved.

57 Kunzle, *History of the Comic Strip*, 20–2.

58 *Ibid.*, 20–1.

59 R. Seymour, 'Penny Patent Knowledge Mill', BMC 17267 (1 October 1832).

60 Houfe, *Dictionary of British Book Illustrators and Caricaturists*, 449. Engen's phrase for the same area of Seymour's work is 'comic drawings of inept sportsmen from London out in the countryside' (Engen, *Dictionary of Victorian Wood Engravers*, 234).

61 Houfe, *Dictionary of British Book Illustrators and Caricaturists*, 449.

62 Both *The Pickwick Papers* and *Life in London* offer examples of notorious disputes over their originators, with both author and illustrator claiming to be the predominant source. These disputes are informative because they suggest the interesting ways in which illustrators were moving towards sustained narrative in their printmaking, and for the bitterness within the contests between image and text which they reveal. Given that Seymour's *Sketches* had an episodic text added to them after the artist's death, the relationship between image and text is even more complex in this case. Discussions of *Pickwick* by Patten, Cohen, and Harvey provide the most detailed case study for these issues.

One interesting and often neglected way of looking at the contests between word and image as forms of narrative in the early Victorian period would be to look at the role of extra illustration, that is those additional sets of plates produced separately to supplement or replace the original illustrations provided by author and publisher. *Pickwick*, because of its own tangled history of illustrators (Seymour was replaced by Buss who gave way to 'Phiz' (H.K. Browne), with the Seymour and Buss plates replaced by ones drawn by Phiz in all reprints) and its immense popularity, is especially interesting. The extra illustrations by Thomas Sibson, for instance, etched in a spidery Gothic mode to eerie effect, make *Pickwick* a very different, much more eighteenth-century novel than the one which uses Phiz's famous plates. Extra illustration is a subject which has never been fully investigated in relation to the emergence of serialised fiction in the early Victorian period.

63 It is worth comparing the depiction of dustmen as comic figures with the picturesque and documentary representations of contemporary printmakers. W.H. Pyne's series of costume plates make an obvious point of reference (see Diane de Marly, *Working Dress* (London, Batsford 1986), 88–9. De Marly's book describes rich visual sources for the study of working clothes. She does not explain, however, how to make an easy distinction between a dustman and a coal heaver. I wish she had.

64 The publishing history of *Life in London* and its sequels is a complicated one, largely because of the novel's success. The first book edition was published in 1821 with thirty-six etched single page plates by Isaac and George Cruikshank, although the work had been serialised in monthly parts between October 1820 and June 1821. The most sustained and informative account of the novel's genesis and publication is that provided by R.L. Patten in *George Cruikshank's Life, Times, and Art*, 221–31. Patten also provides a further list of imitations and derivations from the book to add to Reid's, cited below.

65 J.C. Reid *Bucks and Bruisers* (London, Routledge and Kegan Paul 1971). This section of my book is heavily indebted to Reid's account of *Life in London* and its influence.

66 Reid, *Bucks and Bruisers*, 52.

67 See note 62 above.

68 See, for example, E.D.H. Johnson, *Paintings of the British Social Scene* (London, Weidenfeld and Nicolson 1986); Christopher Wood, *Victorian Panorama – Paintings of Victorian Life* (London, Faber and Faber 1976).

69 Preface to 1821 edition of *Life in London*.

70 Reid, *Bucks and Bruisers*, 68.

71 *Ibid.*, 74.

72 *Ibid.*, 74–7.

73 *Ibid.*, 79.

74 Louis James, *Print and the People 1819–1851* (London, Allen Lane 1976), 148.

75 Reid, *Bucks and Bruisers*, 79.

76 D. Mullin, *Victorian Plays – A Record of Significant Productions on the London Stage, 1837–1901* (New York, Greenwood Press 1976), 378. See also Patten, *George Cruikshank's Life*.

77 E. Fagg, *The Old 'Old Vic'* (London 1936), 40–2. Fagg's useful summary of the *Tom and Jerry* phenomenon notes the dependence of later versions on 'Dusty Bob' as a comic turn.

78 Reid, *Bucks and Bruisers*, 79–80.

79 The image and its related song text are to be found reprinted in James, *Print and the People*, 149–50.

80 Reid, *Bucks and Bruisers*, 76–7.

81 *Ibid.*, 76.

82 Delia Napier, 'John Lloyd of Shelton' in *The Antique Collector*, vol. 60, no. 10, October 1989, 48–53. Napier reproduces the print from The Theatre Museum.

83 The relationship between the popular theatre and the print trade is a complicated one. I am not clear how the many series of play texts would have been used by their readers, nor why there is such an insistence that the accompanying illustrations (usually wood engraved vignettes) are 'authentic' renditions

of performances. Did the readers re-enact the plays from these texts? Or imagine the theatre experience? There is no doubt as to the extent and popularity of series of popular play texts, nor of the importance in these texts of the relationship between text and illustration. In several of the discussions in this book, the importance of theatrically derived imagery has been asserted – Samuel Collings drew for a theatre orientated magazine, and his prints seem always to reflect theatrical gestures, groupings, and stage sets: Boucicault's melodrama *After Dark* provides one of the narratives of self-destruction, illustrated by a wood engraved vignette, described in chapter 5; and in this discussion I have stressed how the transmission of the 'Dusty Bob' stereotype depends as much on theatrical prints and illustrations as on stage versions. However, I do not feel I know enough to be any clearer about the way in which representations of stage characters mediated between performance and associated text.

84 Song-text drawn from Moncrieff's stage adaptation of the original Pierce Egan text.

The Literary Dustman
Some folks may boast of sense, egad;
Vot holds a lofty station;
But tho' a dustman, I have had
A lib'ral *hedication*,
And tho'f I never vent to school,
Like many of my betters,
A turnpike man, vot varn't no fool,
He larnt me all my letters.
They calls me Adam Bell, 'tis clear,
As Adam vos the fust man,
And, by a co in-side-ance queer,
Vy, I'm the fust of Dustmen,
Vy, I'm the fust of Dustmen!

At sartin schools they make boys write,
Their alphabet on sand, sir,
So, I thought dust vould do as vell,
And larnt it out of hand, sirs;
Took in the 'Penny Magazine',
And Johnson's *Dixionary*;
And all the Peri-o-di-calls,
To make me *literary*.
                  They calls, & c.

My dawning genus fust did peep,
Near Battle-bridge 'tis plain, sirs;
You recollect the cinder heap,
Vot stood in Gray's-Inn Lane, sirs,
'Twas there I studies pic-turesque,
Vhile I my bread was yearnin';
And there inhalin' the fresh breeze'
I *sifted out my larnin!*
                  They calls, & c.

Then Mrs. Bell 'twixt you and I,
Vould melt a heart of stone, sirr;
To hear her pussy's wittals cry,
In such a *barrow-tone*, sirs;
My darters all take arter her,
In grace and figure easy;
They larns to sing, and as they're fat,
I has 'em taught by *Grisi!*
They calls, & c.

Ve dines at four, and arter that,
I smokes a mild *Awanna*;
Or gives a lesson to the lad,
Upon the grand *pianna*.
Or vith the gals valk a *quod-rille*,
Or takes a cup of cof-ee;
Or, if I feels fatig'd, or ill,
I lounges on the *sophy!*
They calls, & c.

Or arter dinner read a page
Of Valter Scott, or Byron;
Or, Mr. *Shikspur*, on the stage,
Subjects none can tire on.
At night ve toddles to the play,
But not to gallery attic;
Dury-Lane's the time o' day,
And quite *aristocratic!*
They calls & c.

I means to buy my eldest son
A commission in the Lancers,
And make my darters every one,
Accomplished Hopra dancers.
Great sculptors all conwarse wi' me,
And call my taste, diwine, sirs,
King george *statty* at King's cross
Vas built from my design, sirs;
They calls & c.

And ven I'm made a member on,
For that I means to try, sirs,
Mr. Gully fought his vay,
And verefore shouldn't I, sirs?
Yes, vhen I sits in Parli'ment,
In old Sin Stephen's College,
I means to take, 'tis my intent,
The 'Taxes off o' knowledge.'
They calls me Aadam Bell, 'tis true,
'Cause Adam vos the fust man,
I'm sure it's wery plain to you,
I'm a *literary dustman!*

CHAPTER 4

Coming through the cottage door:

WORK, LEISURE, FAMILY, AND GENDER IN ARTISAN INTERIORS

Returning workmen and their critics

This chapter centres on a discussion of images of workmen returning home at evening from their labours to the families who await them within the cottage interior. The particular images studied here focus on the cottage doorway as a transitional or liminal space between outside and in, work and leisure, men and families, men and women. They are largely images produced within the propagandising elements of the concerned middle classes in an attempt to interpret, some would say justify, the oppositions described above to those working people (more specifically respectable, literate, and possibly socially ambitious artisans) whose daily experience would encompass the events described or imagined by these images.

In looking largely at images offered specifically to artisans by a culturally active, socially concerned middle class, my interest in 'returning workmen' is significantly different from those many accounts of the same narrative discussed by feminist art historians and literary critics, who have mainly concerned themselves with oil paintings of the scene.[1] These paintings sought to establish meanings within a middle class discourse about gender ideology, a discourse which through its commercial and social manifestations and iconographical tradition specifically excluded artisans. Such a determined focus on middle class ideology as manifested through one of its characteristic and exclusive genres has been underpinned by a general assumption that these are images essentially concerned with *gender*, and especially

with maintaining and disseminating the cultural authority of a definition of gender roles based on 'separate spheres' for men and women.

In this context I have been particularly interested by a recent
exchange between two excellent feminist art historians which
provides a useful and important context for the chapter which follows.
In a review article,[2] Lindsay Smith has engaged in a discussion of
Deborah Cherry's book *Painting Women*.[3] One of Cherry's chapters is
entitled 'Difference and Domesticity', and it contains, among much
else of interest, a detailed reading of a number of paintings of women
awaiting the return from work of the male worker, who is usually
absent from, but immanent to, the painting.[4] Cherry asserts the
centrality of the hearth, with all its allusions to 'domestic felicity', in
these images, and characterises a painting called 'Preparing Tea' by
Jane Bowker in the following terms:

> The contrast between the room with its landscape painting and the
> view out of the window to a distant city and approaching train, works
> with the slippers, empty chair and depictions of the preparations for
> tea to suggest a narrative reading around the immediate arrival of a
> father/husband. The composition organises clearly demarcated spaces
> and identities for masculinity and femininity: femininity is pictori-
> alised as domesticity, dependence and familial service whereas
> masculinity is outside the home and at the same time the pivot for its
> social activities and kinship relations.[5]

For all the intelligence and power of this interpretation of the
painting's organisation of space by gender, it would be equally
possible to build an account of the picture which read the soon-to-
return 'father/husband' in an industrial and urban context rather
than a domestic one. He would become, simply, a 'workman' as well
as a 'father/husband', thus admitting into the painting discourses
about class and city as well as depictions of gender and family. As I
have already suggested, these more inclusive readings become ever
more important when you move away from oil paintings produced
exclusively within middle class discourse to look at those images
which sought to transmit or negotiate images and values between
classes.

Lindsay Smith's critique of Cherry's reliance on a rather crude
notion of Victorian ideas of gender as being built out of a concept of
difference which formulates itself into damagingly distinct 'separate
spheres' for male and female activity, begins with a reading of the same
picture, 'Preparing Tea':

This spell of hearth calls into question Cherry's assertion that 'the composition organises clearly demarcated spaces and identities for masculinity and femininity ...' Cherry, of course, is partially right, yet while the painting brings together an inside and an outside, within the inside things are going on that are not entirely reducible to categories of masculinity and femininity as discrete and entirely knowable. The private is not presented unquestionably as defined by the public. There is a celebration of hearth here ... that cannot be read as complicitous with a patriarchal division of spheres, with a polarity in which one term is invariably and unproblematically privileged over the other.[6]

Smith's caution here is important to the argument of this chapter – the description of this painting in terms of a dialectic of different, competing gendered spaces may not adequately acknowledge the possibility of a more positive, revisionist reading in which women might begin to appropriate the hearth as their own space, a source of independent meanings and pleasures which are not totally constructed by the penetration of the male into the home in order to supply and construct domestic meanings. Smith goes on by arguing in the following terms:

the ideology of separate spheres that underpins the whole of Cherry's argument is not perhaps the most useful model by which to approach the work of nineteenth-century women painters. In itself, their identification of subtle permeations within the domestic realm ... indicates that a discussion of women's painting in the context of its production should not simply begin from the premise of a desire to overthrow the tyranny of the domestic by appearance in public life, or by the aspiration to a civic identity. Instead, it should also re-address the cardinal function of the hearth (as linchpin of separate spheres) in gender politics of the period.[7]

As far as I can tell, the images discussed in this chapter were not produced by women artists or engravers. To some extent, Cherry's and Smith's arguments about how far images of the hearth might either express or contest the dominance of the male, the public, and the civic over the female, the domestic, and the familial are also arguments about women as producers of art. But the debate between Cherry and Smith about how far the male world of urban industrial productivity actually constructs the representation of the family and the domestic interior is a central concern of this chapter, even though the images studied are authored by men in a much more self-consciously class orientated and propagandist context.

While acknowledging the force of the 'separate spheres' argument, which remains an essential building block for feminist interpretations of Victorian culture, my concern is a slightly different one. If the narrative of returning workmen is about gender, to my mind it is also about class and industrialisation. I believe this difference in emphasis can be clearly identified by looking at those images beyond sophisticated oil painting where a less coherent, more polemical, socially interventionist set of images appear. In particular, I am interested in showing how apparently coherent and powerful middle class ideological formulations – the necessary interdependence of work and leisure, the identification of women with home and hearth and men with labour, the family as a consolatory and morally influential presence in the male worker's consciousness – begin to break down under the pressure of empirical evidence of the brutalising actualities of mass industrial production.

It may seem that these kinds of discussions merely point to the subjective nature of 'interpretation'. As a feminist art historian Cherry understandably privileges a radical critique of Victorian constructions of gender roles, drawn both from profound scholarly understanding of the subject and from her own ideological identity, over interpretations which depend on class. As a male social historian/literary critic, I prefer readings which foreground class and class relationships against gender. But I hope this chapter shows more than the ideological differences between critics. My argument is that the discourse about the hearth, which Cherry so brilliantly recognises as a central one in Victorian oil paintings by women, is differently interpreted and constructed within popular engravings and mass circulation literature aimed at an artisan readership. The focus, in my view, moves from hearth to door, from rural to urban, from unsustainable idyll to unsettling industrial realities.

'The Family Economist' and its discourses

The title page of *The Family Economist* (illustrations 20 and 21) has been widely used for illustrative purposes by recent scholars and picture editors, to the point where it has almost reached iconic status. It is used, for example, to illustrate the improving 'mission to the home' of the Victorian middle classes in Irene Dancyger's *A World of Women*, where *The Family Economist* is identified, wrongly to my mind, as a women's magazine.[8] It is used for similar purposes in Jenni Calder's *The Victorian Home*.[9] J.F.C. Harrison has pointed out the ways in which mottoes were used as part of the title page design in his study of adult literacy and education.[10] In all three commentaries, the title page is read as being ideologically transparent, as directly transmitting conservative values of domesticity, of gender roles, and of respectability from an entrepreneurial middle class to an artisan readership through the medium of a cheap (1d a month), mass circulation magazine.[11] Additionally, the three discussions all centre on the original 1848 title page, with its vignette of a male working in the fields seen through a rustic cottage window while his family work and play together round the cottage hearth (illustration 20). Yet, in the 1850 volume of *The Family Economist* (illustration 21), this apparently settled image is replaced by a much more ambiguous one in which the window on to the scene of steadfast rural labour has been blocked off, and the tidy cottage dresser replaced by a half open door which frames a standing male figure.

Such a radical change to the original image throws in doubt the ideological consistency and certainty which Calder, Dancyger, and Harrison identify in *The Family Economist*, especially as there seems no obvious good reason to re-draw the 1848 vignette given that magazines tend to depend on a familiar, easily recognised title page configuration. Accordingly, it may be necessary to acknowledge that the title pages to *The Family Economist* comprise a more complex verbal and visual formulation than immediately apparent, especially when taken together. An interpretation of these title pages requires acknowledgement of a range of component structures – visual, verbal, narrative, and graphic – which together constructs its ideological statement. In trying to give proper weight to this range of possibilities, I should like first to discuss the idea of the 'cottage' artisan magazine as a literary genre; second, the motto and saying as a typographical and cultural event in the Victorian period; third, the traditional narrative of the returning artisan arriving home at eventide from the ardours of the day's labour; and, finally, the ideological vision which sustained this narrative of cottage contentment despite obvious empirical evidence to the contrary.

The discourses of the 'cottage' magazine

The values which *The Family Economist* sought to represent might to some extent be read off from its title, which brings together notions of domesticity and thrift into a single phrase. The implied or intended readership is also made clear through the magazine's title page – the

BEGIN WELL IF YOU MEAN TO END WELL.

THE

FAMILY ECONOMIST;

A Penny Monthly Magazine,

DEVOTED TO THE MORAL, PHYSICAL, AND DOMESTIC IMPROVEMENT
OF THE INDUSTRIOUS CLASSES.

VOLUME FIRST.

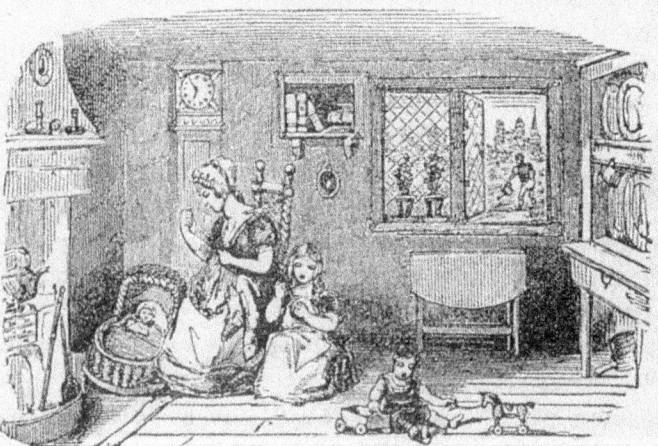

The Cottage Homes of England
    By thousands on her plains,
They are smiling o'er the silvery brook,
    And round the hamlet fanes :
Through glowing orchards forth they peep,
    Each from its nook of leaves :
And fearless there the lowly sleep,
    As the bird beneath their eaves.

The free fair homes of England !
    Long, long in hut and hall
May hearts of native proof be reared
    To guard each hallowed wall.
And green for ever be the groves,
    And bright the flowery sod,
Where first the child's glad spirit loves
    Its country and its God.

LONDON:
GROOMBRIDGE & SONS, PATERNOSTER ROW.
AND SOLD BY ALL BOOKSELLERS.
1848.

EDUCATION IS A SECOND NATURE.

LABOUR RIDS US OF THREE GREAT EVILS, IRKSOMENESS, VICE, AND POVERTY.

A GOOD TEMPER IS ONE OF THE PRINCIPAL INGREDIENTS OF HAPPINESS.

20 Anonymous wood engraved vignette. *The Family Economist*, vol. 1, 1848.

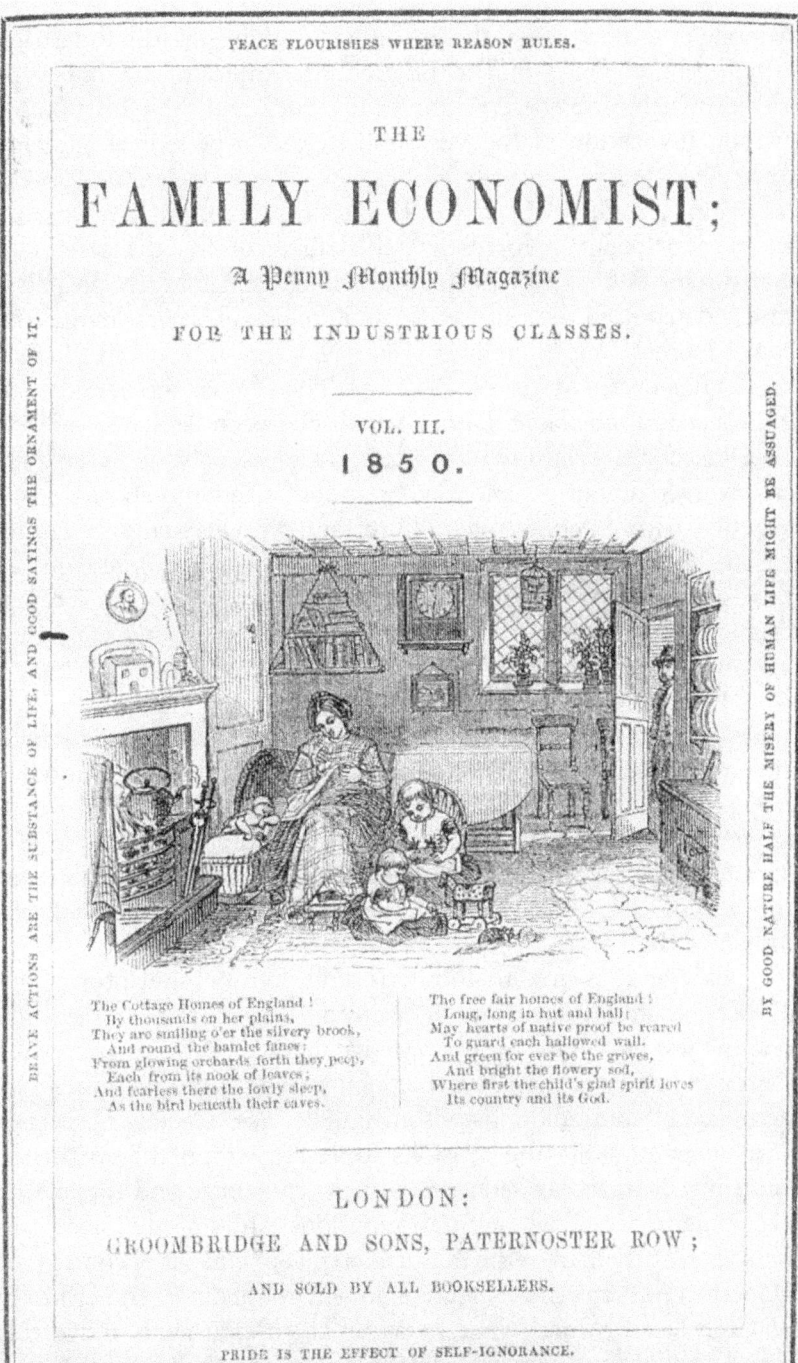

21 Anonymous wood engraved vignette. *The Family Economist*, vol. 3, 1850.

low price of the magazine, the unequivocal address to 'the industrious classes', the vignette of the tidy cottage interior, the improving mottoes which form the typographical border, and the Christianised, patriotic invocation of the verses all suggest a periodical explicitly directed to a respectable, ambitious, but socially deferential artisan readership. *The Family Economist* belongs to the second generation of magazines of popular progress which flourished after the collapse of Chartism in 1848. The first generation of magazines aimed specially at artisans dated from the early 1840s and included *Howitt's Journal*, *The People's Journal*, *Douglas Jerrold's Shilling Magazine*, *Eliza Cook's Journal*, and *The Illuminated Magazine*, all of which had grown out of, and modified, *Chambers' Edinburgh Journal* which had been launched in 1832. These magazines sought to offer a cultural, philosophical, literary, and possibly even a political and ideological alliance between progressive elements within bourgeois culture and intellectually ambitious sections of the artisan class.[12] Projected by liberal entrepreneurs and 'friends of the people', these magazines gave artisan readers access to ideas (*Howitt's Journal*, for example, offered the best and most thoroughgoing account of French socialist thought available in Britain in the 1840s) and even, on a limited basis, to print. An underlying ideological purpose – that of constructing an alliance which would merge evident economic and class interests into shared cultural and intellectual values – differentiates these periodicals from political or specifically Chartist journals, which worked through the rhetoric of difference and opposition. Yet there are many similarities of interest, tone, and indeed, format between the artisan and the radical Chartist journals in the 1840s.

Easy as it is now to turn this ambitious cultural project into another manifestation of subtle bourgeois hegemonic impulses, it is none the less important to acknowledge that the magazines of popular progress dating from the 1840s did publicise with startling honesty the fractures and contradictions within middle class ideology. Especially conspicuous now are the tensions expressed within the writings of liberal intellectuals between the wish to encourage and support the development of artisan cultural ambitions while at the same time disassociating them from the political arena. To cite out of context one of George Gilfillan's more memorable remarks about Ebenezer Elliott, the 'Corn Law Rhymer' 'when he writes about corn-fields' rather than 'Corn Laws', 'what a pleasant companion does he then become'.

After 1848, the need for a specifically cultural alliance between liberal intellectuals and ambitious artisans was less pressing, and *The*

Family Economist makes it clear even on its title page that this is a magazine directed at artisans from above, perhaps largely as a commercial or entrepreneurial undertaking. The contents were largely aimed at reflecting the assumed interests of the readers rather than at ostentatiously shaping or constructing artisan self-images. Yet this distinction may prove to be a false one, as the notion that commercialism disproves or denies ideological purposes can scarcely be seriously maintained.

The *Family Economist* was published by Groombridge & Sons, one of the new publishing houses of the 1840s which specialised in developing the mass literate or just literate readership. The educational, cultural, and economic progress of the artisan classes had, by the 1830s, been sufficient to define artisans as a potential mass market for literature, especially periodicals. Other firms which exploited similar readership in comparable genres during the 1840s and 1850s were William Tweedie, Partridge and Oakey, and Cassell, whose post-Chartist *Working Man's Friend* offers a direct comparison with *The Family Economist*.[13] Underpinning these rapid developments lay the outstanding success of huge projects undertaken by the Chambers brothers in Edinburgh – not just the rather earnest and formidable unillustrated *Chambers' Edinburgh Journal*, but also the cheap series of *Popular Information* and *Papers for the People*. Although essentially entrepreneurs, the Chambers brothers were themselves from an artisan background, and were genuinely committed to a vision of a calm cultural progress within the working classes. A generation later than *The Family Economist*, firms like Nelson and Warne, which specialised in chromolithography, moved the mass popular market on to another stage, this time away from self improvement towards a more diversionary and entertaining kind of literature. All these firms understood the crucial role of illustration, especially the use of the vernacular woodcut tradition adapted for the mass market, in selling their books and satisfying the needs of their artisan readers. In this respect *Chambers' Journal*, which was unillustrated, was an isolated phenomenon. The publications of a firm like Groombridge, while ostensibly directed at an artisan readership, none the less located their books a notch higher in the cultural scale than another group of mass literature entrepreneurs, the provincial firms of Milner and Sowerby from Halifax, Nicholson of Wakefield, and J.S. Pratt of Stokesley who produced cheap 'cottage library' literature sold in the streets like broadsides, and catering for a variety of tastes in a glittering but shoddy format.[14] By making these fine distinctions it is possible as a first step to locate *The*

Family Economist in a wave of entrepreneurial publishing ventures of the late 1840s and 1850s which sought to exploit an artisan readership in commercial terms while offering simultaneous encouragement to its cultural aspirations.

Central to this endeavour was the translation of separate popular and vernacular literary and graphic genres into a collective serialised form. The contents of *The Family Economist* suggest exactly such a drawing together of established popular modes. The magazine comprises short improving narratives (derived from tract literature), recipes and advice on thrifty housekeeping (drawn, interestingly enough, from precedents in Chartist periodicals like *The Reformer's Almanac* as much as from Mrs Trimmer and eighteenth-century improving periodicals), calendars of gardening tasks or events of popular interest (invoking the almanac and calendar vernacular tradition so brilliantly exploited in the 1820s by William Hone's *Table Book* and *Everyday Book* and in the 1860s by Chambers' *Book of Days*),[15] factual information of the kind popularised in the 1830s by *The Penny Magazine* and *The Saturday Magazine*, direct moral homily (again derived from the tracts), and poetry by the likes of Thomas Hood and Eliza Cook of an exhortatory and elevating kind commonplace in the magazines of popular progress. The textual illustrations in *The Family Economist* are essentially explicatory and demonstrative woodcuts in the *Penny* and *Saturday* tradition. It is important to suggest precedents for all these elements, as the eclectic gathering of popular genres here shows how determinedly *The Family Economist* draws on established forms in order to press its claim on artisan attention. An assessment of the extent to which these sources are re-formulated both generically and ideologically in their transition to the commercial artisan literary discourses of the 1850s is one reason for attempting a close reading of this text.

Eclecticism, then, is a keynote of this particular title page. The immediate impression is of a crowded, complex design which seeks, with some success, to integrate a wide variety of elements: a long, explanatory title; a woodcut vignette; exhortatory verses; four mottoes; and the publishing details. The clever use of rules makes the page possible, dividing up the various components with delicate lines, while, through the use of the motto-lined border, providing an overall unity of effect. A similar dialogue between the component elements and the whole page is provided by the typography. A wide variety of sizes is used, but the same typeface is maintained apart from the Gothic sub-title, a consistency which again provides unity. Overall, despite a secular insistence on the practical, thrifty, respectable discourses of artisan self-help, the most direct visual analogy for this title page is to be found in tract literature (see [8]). This analogy is an interesting one given that *The Family Economist* foregrounds secular usefulness against the Christianised knowledge so central to, for example, *The Penny* or *The Saturday*. Of the complex range of popular genres brought together and unified in this title page, the most startling is, however, the visually arresting use of the motto. It is worth saying a little more about the motto as it constituted an important discourse in Victorian Britain.

The motto

In his discussion of 'the literature of success' in *Learning and Living*, J.F.C. Harrison draws attention to the saying within this literary mode; 'the social devices and conveniences of the age acquired the compulsion of moral, even religious, virtues. They were popularised in many forms, but particularly as proverbs and aphorisms.'[16] Harrison cites *The Family Economist* as part of his evidence, and goes on to suggest the reliance of two of the most widely read Victorian conduct manuals, Smiles's *Self Help* and Tupper's *Proverbial Philosophy*, on the epigrammatic method. He might have mentioned Ruskin as a further example, notably in later editions of his works where he differentiated his more memorable statements as aphorisms by printing them in different typefaces, or even colours. Certainly Harrison's contention that the widespread popularity of the aphorism was caused by its ability to reduce complex moral choices to simple memorable rules of conduct seems fully borne out by the practice of another widely read popular biographer and ideologue of popular progress, Edwin Paxton Hood.[17] In one of his most interesting books, *The Uses of Biography*, Hood's usual accumulative mode of exposition is continually cut across by typographically distinct comments which attempted to summarize the arguments in simple proverbial formulations such as 'Biography Forms the Museum of Life'.[18] Another book of the same period, *The Mental and Moral Philosophy of Laughter* (1852), italicises a similar sequence of proverbial wisdom: 'The sources of laughter then lie in incongruity'; 'Wonderful is the detective power of ridicule and mirth'; 'Humour the Teacher, but Wit the Scourge'.[19] This apophthegmatic mode was a deliberate attempt to retain an important element of orality in Hood's work. Through this means, a vast reservoir of effortless cliché wisdom and proverbial anodyne was available as a shared mode to both artisan and middle class reader. Other sources for the motto as a mode of discourse include the embroidered sampler, a tremendously widely used ornamental form in artisan and middle class homes,[20] the widespread use of sayings as chapter headings in novels (drawn from many sources or even made up if an appropriate motto did not come to mind), and above all, tract and devotional literature. So once again this *Family Economist* title page depends on the exploitation of widely used and diverse traditions of discourse all of which sought to translate popular forms into an expression of middle class values. The annexing of vernacular traditions for ideological purposes is one of the crucial symptoms of the purposefulness and unity of middle class ideology in the mid-Victorian period.

The visual integration of mottoes into complex or eclectic texts, so obviously a feature of *The Family Economist* title page, and pioneered by samplers, is well illustrated in the pages of another artisan periodical *The British Workman*, which was published in the mid 1850s.[21] The aim of *The British Workman* was to retain the visual impact and appeal of the handbill and sampler into a typeset page. *The Family Economist* follows *The British Workman* in once again drawing a variety of popular modes, secular and devotional, visual and typographical, vernacular and relatively polite, into a single integrated image. The mottoes in *The Family Economist* are interestingly secular – while there is nothing in them which would contradict conventional Christianity, the stress is on social conduct rather than on individual spiritual self-examination. One, indeed, offers the motto genre itself a moment of self-congratulation: 'Brave actions are the substance of life and good sayings are the ornament of it'. The mottoes here are 'ornamental' in two ways, both as a feature of a pleasing typographical lay-out, and as a gloss on, or an epigrammatic summary of, a well-lived life.

At the centre of this title page, however, is the dominating wood-engraved image of a cottage interior. It is to this vignette that I now wish to turn.

The artisan's homecoming

The pastoral trope of the evening return of the agricultural labourer to his family can be traced back to the harmonised Georgic pastoral mode of Theocritus or Virgil.[22] However, a more selective account of this tradition should provide an adequate context here, and the obvious place to start is the evening vision of Gray's 'Elegy', with its famous opening invocation of the 'homeward way' of the 'weary ploughman' whose arrival home occupies a later elegiac stanza:

For them no more the blazing hearth shall burn,
Or busy housewife ply her evening care:
No children run to lisp their sire's return
Or climb his knee the envied kiss to share.[23]

Gray's poem is, of course, a self-proclaimed elegy, a recognition of the difficulty of sustaining the Georgic vision of nature improved and rendered full of economic and moral meaning through human and social presence on into an age of rapid rural and agricultural change. In this stanza, Gray laments one specific instance of the failure of the heroicising eighteenth-century pastoral vision: the loss of the inter-penetration of work and home in a dialectic of rural contentment. What Gray sees as a necessary and 'natural' interconnection between labour and domesticity is here celebrated just at the moment when the separation of leisure from toil began to become an increasingly power-ful economic and social reality.

Gray's works, and especially 'The Elegy', became standard texts for illustrated editions, especially in the latter half of the nineteenth century. Most of these editions were in an untroubled, celebratory pastoral mode, many with engravings by, or in the manner of, Birket Foster's fussily idyllic country scenes.[24] Few of these editions use the domestic or figurative themes in 'The Elegy' as a source of subjects for engraving, but it is none the less possible to find popular engravings of the scene of the artisan's evening return described in the quoted stanza. One such vignette [3] from an edition of 'The Elegy' exactly contemporary with *The Family Economist* title page, although the orig-inal drawing was made fifteen years previously,[25] locates the scene of the return outside the cottage door, but uses the circular form of the vignette to emphasise the unity, fecundity, and vigour of the family group, which spirals round the central male figure, relegating the be-cowled wife to the periphery. The image is sculptural and heroicising, despite the gaping, apparently doorless, cottage doorway which tells of poverty and cold. My point here, is not entirely to do with the specific formulation of this image but rather with a recognition that Gray's work must have been widely known to a relatively large readership in the mid-nineteenth century through a succession of illustrated editions. In some cases, as in this one, there were representations of the scene of the artisan's return which re-affirmed Gray's attempts to formulate a heroic pastoral vision in which work, family, and leisure were elided into a single ideological statement.

Gray's poem was also important because it served as the source for another powerful formulation of the same narrative, Robert Burns's

'The Cotter's Saturday Night', first published in 1784/85. Burns's poem, despite its vernacular subject and diction, alluded to the sophisticated or learned pastoral tradition in a number of ways, notably through the use of an epigraph from Gray's poem and by using a quotation from Pope's 'Windsor Forest'. Burns translated Gray's artisan homecoming into more homely terms, and furnished it with elements crucial to Victorian versions of the theme – the cottage, the hearth, the wife, cleanliness, thrift, order:

> The toil-worn COTTER frae his labour goes,
> This night his weekly moil is at an end,
> Collects his spades, his mattocks and his hoes,
> Hoping the morn in ease and rest to spend,
> And weary, o'er the muir, his course does hameward bend.
>
> At length his Lonely Cot appears in view,
> Beneath the shelter of an aged tree;
> Th' expectant wee-things, toddlan', stacher thro'
> To meet their Dad, wi' flicterin noise and glee.
> His wee-bit ingle, blinkin bonilie,
> His clean hearth-stane, his thriftie Wifie's smile.
> The lisping infant, prattling on his knee,
> Does a' his weary kiaugh and care beguile,
> And makes him quite forget his labour and his toil.[26]

Subversively, this description resolves into a distinction, perhaps even an opposition between 'cares', labour, and 'toil' on the one hand, and the virtues of a domestic family Saturday night, gathered round the hearth, on the other. Burns is claiming the narrative of the returning artisan for a version of agricultural labour which stressed the domestic virtues of respectability, piety, humility and family loyalty. Like Gray's 'Elegy', 'The Cotter's Saturday Night' was a famous poem, widely known at all levels of society, and rendered even more famous by Burns's early Victorian status as a biographical model for artisan or self-taught writers. His writing career, if not his private life, offered an early and obvious example of the 'pursuit of knowledge under difficulties' and had been widely used in middle class propagandist accounts of artisan cultural development.

Burns's poem, like Gray's, appeared in many illustrated editions, often published by provincial publishers catering for a local, but not entirely unsophisticated, readership.[27] The most famous and enduring of these provincial editions was the Catnach and Davison edition published in Alnwick in 1808 with numerous wood engravings drawn by Thurston and engraved by Thomas Bewick (or at least by members of his workshop). Volume 1 of this edition contains a superb vignette of the artisan's homecoming (illustration 22), in which a single sturdy toddler greets her returning father, watched by her mother from a distant cottage doorway.[28] This particular image mediates a quite sophisticated rural narrative back into vernacular terms, but avoids the crudities usually associated with a vernacular visual code. The lack of the heroic here is striking – the artisan's spade and sack, balanced on a thick stave, are given a weight acknowledged, but not celebrated, in the bent form and painful gait of the cotter. The child's pose is sturdy and natural but again without idealisation. By all these means the image is stripped of its moralising and heroicising codes and becomes a 'simple' naturalistic narrative of family affection. Thurston's drawing also denies the central presence of the domestic in this version of the narrative – the outside/inside divide is represented through a chain of receding figures which smoothes the transition from work to the domestic hearth.

The extent to which Bewick and Thurston deny the heroicising impulse in their subject can be gauged through a comparison with a very similar, if cruder wood engraving published in 1824 in the 2d weekly periodical *Saturday Night* along with Burns's poem.[29] [4] The placing of many of the visual elements in this print is directly comparable to that

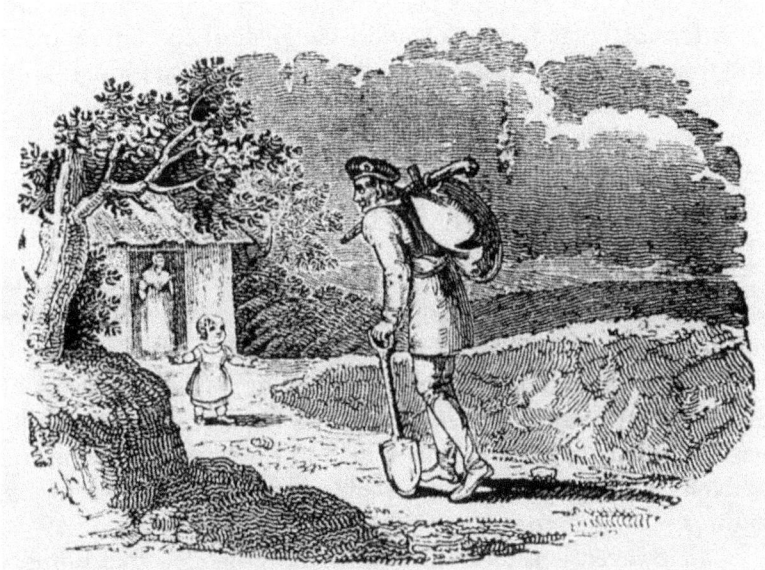

22 Wood engraved illustration to 'The Cotter's Saturday Night'. Drawn by Thurston; engraved by Bewick, for *The Poetical Works of Robert Burns*.

in Bewick's print – the male figure, sack over shoulder and spade in hand, surveys a distant cottage overhung with trees, with wife and child emerging to greet the returning labourer. But here the male figure dominates the scene, towering over and diminishing the cottage. The distance between home and figure has grown enormously, again asserting the centrality of the labourer, who is sturdier and less obviously burdened than Bewick's workman despite the complexity of his tackle. Set against a marine landscape, and with the pilaster effect of the cottage window mullions, this scene seems closer to Arcadia than Arbroath. Even the floppy brimmed hat in the anonymous print lacks the solidity of the discharged soldier's bonnet in Bewick and Thurston's image. The celebratory impulse of the *Saturday Night* print checks the naturalism in the detail of the main figure, so that Bewick's clarity, as well as his focus on the family, are lost. How important or well known these images may have been by 1850 is hard to evaluate, but they certainly serve as another useful reference point in trying to decode the title page of the 1850 *Family Economist*.

Beginning this discussion of the returning artisan motif with Gray and Burns in this context is not solely a matter of iconographic significance. Gray's poem was extremely influential on the artisan and self-taught poets who were beginning to find their way into print in the 1830s and 1840s.[30] That these writers should turn to the neo-classical couplet of Pope or the academic and self-conscious lyric forms of Gray for poetic models is not surprising given their cultural insecurity and their need to prove their intellectual power and formal skill, even if these models ultimately inhibited the potential range of their work. Burns's simple lyrics were also frequently put forward as models for working men writers by sophisticated and powerful critics like Kingsley and Carlyle, with Kingsley's essay 'Burns and his School' providing a central definition of the arguments.[31]

However, as already suggested, it was Burns's life rather than his work which was most influential, despite middle class anxiety about his morals. Burns appeared to self-taught writers as an example of the way in which cultural achievement might be linked to social and economic success. The combination of sophisticated literary knowledge and vernacular lyric skill shown in his work also vindicated the ambiguous cultural aspirations found in much poetry by working men authors.

However, it is clear that in imitating models like Burns, Gray, and Pope, self-taught authors often borrowed not just their language and forms but also whole ideological structures as well. Accordingly, it is not unexpected to find a Manchester self-taught artisan poet, the reed-maker John Critchley Prince, concluding an ostensibly celebratory poem (unlike the elegiac 'Elegy') called 'The Poet's Sabbath' with precisely Gray and Burns's trope of the artisan's homecoming. The poem was first published in volume form in 1843:

> Shadows are round me as I tread the floor
> Of balmy breathing fields; my weary feet
> Bear me right onward to my cottage door;
> I cross the threshold – take my accustomed seat.
> And feel, as I have always felt, that home is sweet!
> My wife receives me with a quiet smile,
> Gentle and kind as wife should ever be;
> My joyous little ones press round the while,
> And take their wonted places on my knee:
> Now with my chosen friends, sincere and free,
> I pass the remnant of the night away ...[32]

It is noticeable that the fluency of Gray and Burns's lyric forms has here given way to a more anxious and fractured verse form. Prince's resolution of the narrative, as one might expect from an urban artisan whose trade had been destroyed by the technological developments of the industrial revolution, modified the pastoral harmonies of Gray's elegiac vision by calling into the poem the oppositional elements from Burns's poem:

> And wish that human life were one long Sabbath-day.

At this moment the previously absent fact of week-day labour is brought back disruptively into the poem's argument. Prince's cottage vision, unlike Gray's, is built out of a tacit antithesis between home and labour, and even between the reconciling necessity of repose and work. Gray's consoling elision between agricultural labour and domestic repose cannot survive without challenge the obvious divisions between work and home predicated by the new kinds of industrial culture established in the 1830s and 1840s.

Another poem by an artisan writer, despite being published ten years after *The Family Economist* title page, exploits exactly the same narrative trope, and reveals even more clearly than Prince both the persistence of Gray's influence and the consequent shift in meanings brought about by major social change. Philip Connell's 'A Winter Night in Manchester' opens with a direct imitation of Gray and Goldsmith but modulates through a stanza describing street activities into the now familiar trope of the cottage hearth:

Far other scenes now bless the workman's night,
In slippers easy, chair, and shirt sleeves white,
With hair to one side comb'd and well-wash'd face
Radiant with happiness – while in her place
The very cat enjoys her evening nap.
Purring her grateful anthems in his lap.
And ever as he casts around his eyes
A look meets his, beaming with hopes and joys,
And quiet happiness – his own dear Bess
Nursing their baby boy in fond caress,
His vermil' lips around the nipple press'd
And half his cheek hid in her milkwhite breast:
There sits the workman in his happy home,
The fire fair blazing round the cheerful room,
The carpet brush'd, the grate and fender bright,
The polish'd table glancing to the light,
The hearth pure white, the chimneypiece array'd
With dogs and shepherds nestling in the shade;
The simple shelves with glass and china bright,
The busy bare-faced clock not always right;
The baywood bookcase, full, select, but small,
Curtain'd with crimson, pendant on the wall,
And hung around – the lovely, good, and wise
Look from their maple frames, with living eyes.[33]

Connell's entire poem is a prolonged meditation on the question of what constitutes suitable leisure activity for a sensitive and cultured urban artisan. The poet rehearses a series of possibilities – loitering on Victoria Bridge to consider the aesthetic potential of a November night in Manchester; the urban and gregarious pursuits of pub, prostitutes, and the theatre (all rejected as vulgar and demeaning); domestic pleasure; reading; introspection. Thus the poem describes, in neo-classic couplets, a phrased retreat from contemplation of industrial reality via urban alienation and family life into terminal introversion. Such a retreat is not just a personal failure but also represents a defeat for those poetic strategies which might have controlled or structured a resistance to urban anxiety. The poem forms an interesting gloss on one of its obvious poetic sources, Gray's 'Elegy'. In Gray's poem the poetic fluency remains uninterrupted despite growing intellectual tensions within the speaker's perception of the countryside. In Connell's version of the 'returning artisan' (or here the 'just returned artisan') narrative, which occupies the central section of the poem, the verse enacts, probably unconsciously, the failure of poetry as a means of confronting the distresses caused by urban industrial life. The section of the poem quoted above is an almost obsessional attempt to use the ordering precision of the couplet to construct a vision of domestic order by means of locating even the 'very cat' in an exact place in the scene. The result is over-stated, but moving in its compulsion to seek order, domestic repose, and emblematic tidiness as a means of coping with factory life.

The correlations between Connell's poetic description of a cottage interior in 'A Winter Night in Manchester' and the graphic representation of the same scene in the 1848 and 1850 *Family Economist* title pages are striking, even allowing for the probability that the two vignettes depict rural rather than urban dwellings. The blazing fire, the gleaming table top, the ornamental chimneypiece, the simple shelves, the hanging bookcase, the ostentatious clock are all prominent components of both scenes. These similarities of representation might be further extended through comparisons with other versions of artisan interiors in contemporary fiction. *Mary Barton* and *North and South*, both novels which assert documentary realism as part of their fictional strategies, offer obvious examples of comparably emblematic and ideological coded accounts of artisan domestic scenes. One obvious explanation for these marked similarities might be that all these descriptions were an accurate version of empirical reality. But more persuasive still are the arguments which suggest that these detailed descriptions are structured more by shared ideological expectations than by any coherent factual basis. These cottage interiors seem to me emblematic and value laden rather than intentionally naturalistic.

A further useful contrast with *The Family Economist*, and indeed with Connell's poem, can be found in John Gilbert's engraving for a poem about work by Gerald Massey. [6] Here one can see a confident middle class annexation of the 'returning artisan' trope for a coherent mid-Victorian celebration of the united stoical working class family. This engraving appeared in a showy illustrated gift book published by Routledge in 1858 made up of a poetic anthology organised around the theme of *The Home Affections*, edited by Charles Mackay and with illustrations by 'eminent artists' under the direction of the Dalziel brothers.[34] Massey, himself from artisan origins, offers in the poem both a bleak and a heroicised version of the work/home antithesis, balancing two stanzas of denunciation of the struggle of urban labour ('I have fought, I have vanquisht, the dragon of Toil') against two which celebrate home and family. Yet even in the attack on toil,

Massey defends the self-reliance, energy and manliness of labour. Gilbert's engraving thus follows the poem by acknowledging the realities of urban poverty, positioning a single candle against the gloomy shadows which form a backdrop to the scene. But Gilbert centres his image on precisely the same sculptural family shape, both monument and dynamic spiral, as his American namesake, if in reverse, with the women occupying the periphery of the scene. The heroic endurance of the workman is emphasised by the strong vertical of the stand chair in the right foreground, itself a monumental piece of furniture. The artist here shows every confidence that a combination of celebration and pathos can hold the image together as a sympathetic representation of industrial family life which would gratify both the social concern and the family vision of a middle class readership.

An additional detail offers an interesting gloss on Gilbert's illustration. In 1861 Routledge published a cheap, single volume *Poetical Works* of Gerald Massey, something of an achievement for a writer from an artisan background and with professed radical views.[35] Aimed at a slightly different, culturally more ambitious, but financially less competent readership than *The Home Affections*, and certainly more meanly produced, Massey's *Work* included a cut down version of Gilbert's plate (illustration 23). In cramming this quite large and impressively scaled illustration into a small octavo page, the candle and the chair on the right-hand side have been cut away, which brings the focus exclusively on to the family group. By these means this powerfully heroicising image was given renewed or expanded currency with a potentially wider readership. As a clear example of how plates were re-used as established visual tropes even at quite sophisticated levels of the literary market (and not just in provincial broadsides), this illustration could not be bettered. Having once formulated an image into a block, the widest possible use of that block becomes an economic necessity. The function of such re-use in disseminating and extending the currency of particular images should not be underestimated.[36]

The issues raised by these uses of the 'returning artisan' motif are complex. This narrative trope exercised a powerful and persistent hold on both artisan and middle class perceptions. It would be easy to cite many late Victorian versions of the same theme, the most interesting of which seems to me Arthur Hughes's late painting 'Home From Work' now in the Russell Cotes Gallery in Bournemouth. It is, however, a trope which originates in a Georgic vision of pastoral harmony between work and home, between Labour and Nature, but which shifts by successive transformations in both literary and graphic formulations into a mode of reconciling an implicit conflict between labour and leisure. The use of this new version of the narrative, in which the house becomes an antithetical element to the factory, is a necessary context for reading the 1850 *Family Economist* title page.

Ideology and *The Family Economist*

In trying to read off the ideological formulation constructed by the vignette wood engravings which comprise the varying title pages of *The Family Economist*, it may be best to begin with what is not being said, those meanings which are by implication being excluded from this particular representation. In the 1848 title page (illustration 20), the setting is uninterruptedly rural, with a country scene continuing the fertile, plant-lined theme of the window sill. A male worker, possibly the householder, is framed by the open window, watering plants in his smallholding. Behind his active figure rises a church spire set alongside a row of tall trees. Along the right-hand wall of the cottage is a large dresser displaying rows of plates in an orderly metonym for domestic organisation. Even the bare boards of the cottage floor cannot disrupt this organically composed scene of the interdependence of work, leisure, and family contentment. This formulation of the scene is in direct contrast with the 1850 title page (illustration 21), where the window blots out the world of work rather than celebrating it, and where the emblematic dresser is replaced by a half-open door and a male figure.

But more powerful comparisons in revealing the potential disquiet which underlies an apparently celebratory image are with two illustrations to tract narratives of almost the same date, the first one of the Chambers brothers' secular tracts of 1847 (illustration 24) and the second a slightly later tract narrative published by The Society for Promoting Christian Knowledge in 1853[37] (illustration 25). Both these tracts illustrate narratives which act as direct and unequivocal refutations of the narrative trope of the happy returning artisan learnt from Gray and his successors. Both are from kinds of literature directed specifically at artisan readers with reformist intentions and both interestingly construct the returning artisan in an unheroic and disruptive way in which conventional representation of drunkenness through clothes, posture, and expression is put to use to offer a naturalistic rather than an ideological image. Here the returning artisan is a threatening drunk who creates a stagey but carefully realised panic in the wife and children placed, as usual, in the orderly cottage interior. The two vignettes accompany a similarly direct re-writing of the narrative. In the Chambers brothers' tract a rather restless but fundamentally hard-working and conformist servant marries a local workman without finding out his true character. He takes her small savings and launches into dissipation, returning home only to replenish his funds. He beats his wife, who contracts breast cancer as a result, and undergoes radical surgery. Her husband falls into petty crime, and then more serious trouble. He is apprehended and then sent to Botany Bay. He eventually dies in Australia. Meanwhile his wife struggles to maintain herself and her child. After many tribulations she is rescued through a chance meeting with a prosperous relative, but, interestingly, the narrative acknowledges its own fictive closure by pointing out that few readers will have rich uncles to rescue them from hastily made marriages. Narrative and woodcut alike insist on both the fictive structures of tract literature and on the fundamental naturalism of representation of the brutalised husband.

The tract published by The Society for Promoting Christian

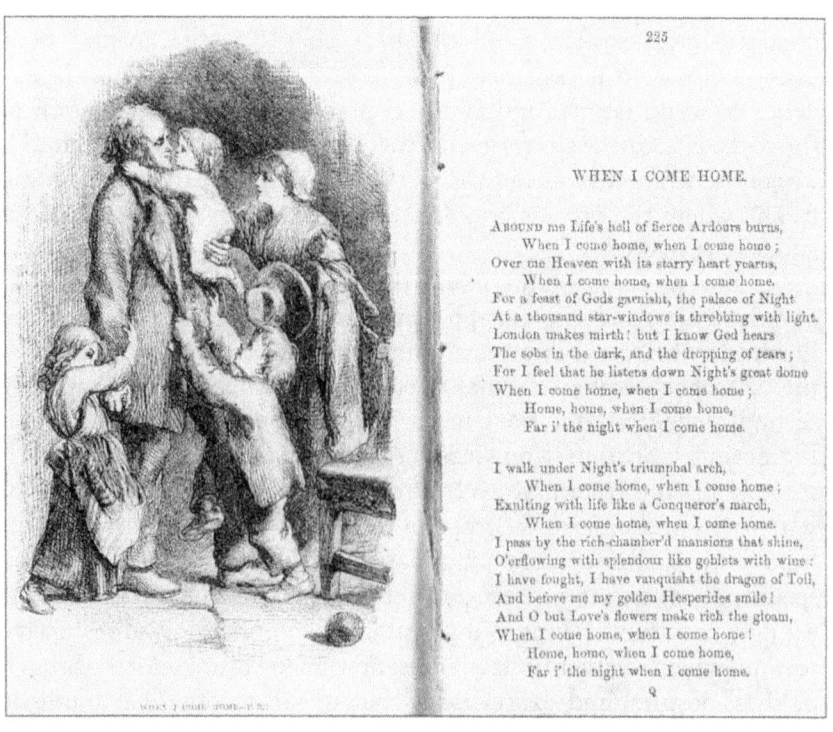

23 Wood engraved illustration to *The Poetical Works of Gerald Massey*. Drawn by John Gilbert.

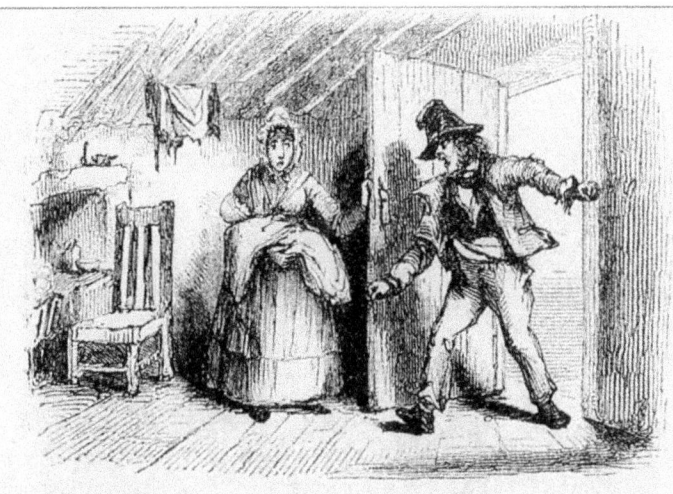

WOMEN'S TRIALS IN HUMBLE LIFE.

STORY OF PEGGY DICKSON.

WHAT a neat-looking girl Peggy Dickson was when we first saw her, a great many years ago: active, sprightly, and obliging, everybody thought well of her, and said she deserved to be happy. Peggy was brought up as a domestic servant from about her twelfth year, when she had the misfortune to lose both her parents, and in the course of time she went through a number of respectable places.

Peggy had received little or no education, but she possessed good principles, and was liked by her employers. In more than one of her situations she might have lived for any length of time in a state of comfort, being kindly treated, and receiving the highest wages that were paid; but, like many others in her class, Peggy was a little too fond of changes. She never liked to stay long in any place; fidgetted about from term to term, always seeking better situations, or leaving those she was in, from the most trifling excuses. In one house she was not allowed to let a number of acquaintances call upon her; in another she was scolded for spending time needlessly when sent on errands; and in a third she was only allowed to have every alternate Sunday evening, not the whole day, to herself. These, and the like of these, she considered sufficient reasons to shift her situation, with a view to bettering her condition. Peggy's fate verified the old proverb, that " an unhappy fish often gets an unhappy bait." By one of these luckless removes, she got into

No. 163.   1

24 Anonymous wood engraved illustration to 'Women's Trials in Humble Life–The Story of Peggy Dickson'. *Chambers' Miscellany of Useful and Entertaining Tracts*

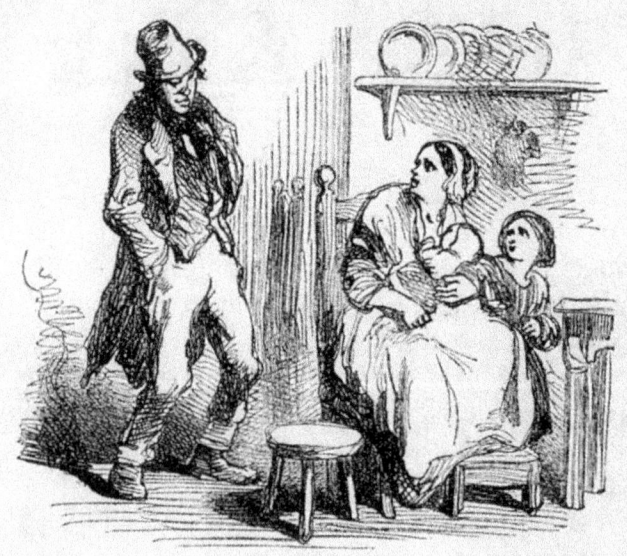

No. XIV

HOME TALES,

FOUNDED ON FACT.

BY THE AUTHOR OF " CHARLIE BURTON," &c.

ROBERT WILSON; or, WILL HE KEEP HIS PROMISE?

PUBLISHED UNDER THE DIRECTION OF
THE COMMITTEE OF GENERAL LITERATURE AND EDUCATION,
APPOINTED BY THE SOCIETY FOR PROMOTING
CHRISTIAN KNOWLEDGE.

LONDON:
Printed for the
SOCIETY FOR PROMOTING CHRISTIAN KNOWLEDGE;
SOLD AT THE DEPOSITORY,
GREAT QUEEN STREET, LINCOLN'S INN FIELDS,
4, ROYAL EXCHANGE, AND 16, HANOVER STREET, HANOVER SQUARE;
AND BY ALL BOOKSELLERS.
1853.
Price 3s. 4d. *per* 100.

25 Anonymous wood engraved illustration to 'Robert Wilson, or Will He Keep His Promise?', from a series *Home Tales Founded on Fact.*

Knowledge offers a similar narrative. An inexperienced and stubborn young woman insists on marrying a known drinker who degenerates into brutality and, consequently, poverty. Her children die, she is finally driven into madness by the coincidental death of her last child and the arrival of the bailiffs. She is taken away, but in her absence her husband finds God and is reformed. Trusted by forgiving neighbours, the husband finds work, his wife recovers, and comes home to replace her lost children with new babies. The structure here of a God who manifests himself by clear social vengeance and reward may be a convenient theological simplification, but the ease with which the 'returning artisan' trope can be appropriated to such an alien purpose suggests the difficulty of continuing to use Gray's narrative for ideological purposes in the mid-Victorian period. In order to succeed in its celebration of artisan domestic contentment, *The Family Economist* engraving has to repress a range of interpretative possibilities which enter the narrative through the social changes consequent upon urbanisation and industrialisation – the returning labourer may be vicious, drunk, out of work, alienated. As the Chambers brothers' and *Home Tales* tracts suggest, family housing conditions or illness may deprive the narrative of its central action, as the artisan may well choose to seek the pub or some other diversion of the kinds rehearsed by Philip Connell rather than the consolations of family and hearth. The social realities of a harsh industrialised culture threaten the celebratory narrative of the artisan's homecoming with all the possibilities of alienated labour.

Bearing these issues in mind, an interpretation of *The Family Economist* 1850 title page thus depends on the significance of the male figure, who is half hidden in the doorway. His pose is the reverse of heroic, indeed is almost slouching, as he gazes at the orderly domestic interior with both mother and the two eldest children absorbed in their separate activities. The unified grouping of the intent mother and children extends the strong triangular shape of the hanging bookshelves, and emphasises the separateness of the domestic group from the world outside the cottage.[38] The figures turn away from the outside world glimpsed through the window, focusing on the hearth rather than the doorway. I think it is hard for contemporary viewers to regard the male figure as anything other than a disruptive intrusion into this scene, as he seems to lurk voyeuristically on what is presumably his own doorstep. Is he pausing to contemplate his own domestic happiness, to savour the quiet, respectable activity round his own fireplace? Or does he pause in full consciousness that his male presence will bring the world of work intrusively into the domestic sphere? The threat the male figure offers to the scene is a powerful combination of his gender and his industrial role. Indeed this vignette might stand as a classic exposition of Ruskin's notorious association of gender with work in a famous passage of *Sesame and Lilies*, first published in 1865:

> We are foolish, and without excuse foolish, in speaking of the 'superiority' of one sex to the other, as if they could be compared in similar things. Each has what the other has not: each completes the other, and is completed by the other: they are in nothing alike, and the happiness and perfection of both depends on each asking and receiving from the other what the other only can give. Now their separate characters are briefly these. The man's power is active, progressive, defensive. He is eminently the doer, the creator, the discoverer, the defender. His intellect is for speculation and invention; his energy for adventure, for war, and for conquest, wherever war is just, wherever conquest necessary. But the woman's power is for rule, not for battle, – and her intellect is not for invention or creation, but for sweet ordering, arrangement, and decision. She sees the qualities of things, their claims, and their places. Her great function is Praise ... The man, in his rough work in the open world, must encounter all peril and trial; – to him, therefore, must be the failure, the offence, the inevitable error: often he must be wounded, or subdued; often misled; and *always* hardened. But he guards the women from all this; within his house, as ruled by her, unless she herself has sought it, need enter no danger, no temptation, no cause of error or offence. This is the true nature of home – it is the place of Peace; the shelter not only from all injury, but from all terror, doubt, and division. In so far as it is not this, it is not home; so far as the anxieties of the outer world allowed by either husband or wife to cross the threshold, it ceases to be home; it is then only part of that outer world which you have roofed over, and lighted fire in.[39]

This passage has, not surprisingly, been identified by feminists from Kate Millett onwards as a crucially conservative but compelling male definition of gender which expressed a dominant Victorian ideology. But it seems to me that even here the superb rhetoric fails to resolve all the contradictions of Ruskin's position in order to present a unified ideology. More powerful even than the argument about home here seems to me Ruskin's tragic definition of the male world of work as inevitably sinful, corrupting, and brutal. As a psychological statement I find here Ruskin's fear of his own inadequate masculinity as prominent as his fear of women.

But the crucial issue is Ruskin's association of the male with the heroic if brutalising world of work and the feminine with the morally sustaining world of home and hearth. In his pursuit of complementary unity, Ruskin works by posing contradictions and differences. *The Family Economist* 1850 title page vignette accepts this formulation built on difference and opposition in its simplest possible terms. The aim of the image is to repress difference into a single vision of the peacefully domestic, an aim reinforced and confirmed by all the other coded messages of respectability, domesticity, and thrift enacted in this title page. But notwithstanding the unity of purpose expressed here, the vignette is finally at odds with the surrounding ideological formulations. Situated directly under the word 'industrious', directly above verses describing the 'free fair homes' of rural cottage dwellings, and surrounded by mottoes celebrating good sense, rationality, and 'good nature', the engraving seeks to assimilate and extend well established tropes of domestic harmony, drawn initially from Gray but transmitted, as we have seen, through many popular or even famous subsequent versions.

Yet the presence of the male workman here seems to me to disrupt what the image seeks to celebrate. Instead of savouring the cleanliness, respectability, warmth, family affection, and 'economy' of the scene, the male figure at the door seems to me an essentially anxious even threatening, presence. Despite the conscious use of much of the conventional iconography of cottage contentment, this illustration ends up allowing in all the disruptive possibilities it seeks to conceal. The heroic artisan of Gilbert's image, the sturdy naturalistic of Bewick and Thurston's engraving, the simple swain of Gray's poem, and the pious family man of Burns's, have here been allowed to slide into a figure precisely antithetical in nature – the threatening drunk of *Home Tales*. Surprisingly, given the complex of allusions and modes through which it is constructed in the 1850 *Family Economist* title page, the consolatory ideology of respectability is haunted here by fear of its implacable enemies; the alienating effects of hard labour, the violence of the brutalised husband, and the false consolations of drink. If it is possible to regard these illustrations as coded versions of ideological positions, then it is obvious that middle class ideology is more fractured, more conscious of its own repressions and fantasies than might be expected. In the overtly ideological formulation of the returning artisan motif, aimed at audiences both within and beyond the middle classes, it can be seen that a great deal of idealisation occurs. The apparent realism of the woodcut mode in fact suppresses empirically identifiable reality in pursuit of a literary or mythic construction of an everyday event as it ought to be rather than as it was. But in some of the images directed more exclu-

essential part of all favourite perfumes: it is a principal ingredient in the renowned old Windsor soap, all sachets, or dry perfumery-bags contain it, few essences or bouquets are without it, and yet this is a perfume that no one likes!

The scents of the ancients were, as far as we know, entirely dry perfumes, such as myrrh, spikenard, frankincense, all gum resins which are still in use by perfumers, and they were used rather to perfume the air than the person, although it was a very old custom to scent the beard. It is a question purely of taste as to whether scent is allowable to the male sex, but among Englishmen, at least, the feeling is against it; the fashion is certainly feminine, and long may it be confined to the ladies, for although it would be a superfluity to paint the lily, we may yet be permitted to perfume the living violet.   A. W.

"HIS HAND UPON THE LATCH."
A YOUNG WIFE'S SONG.

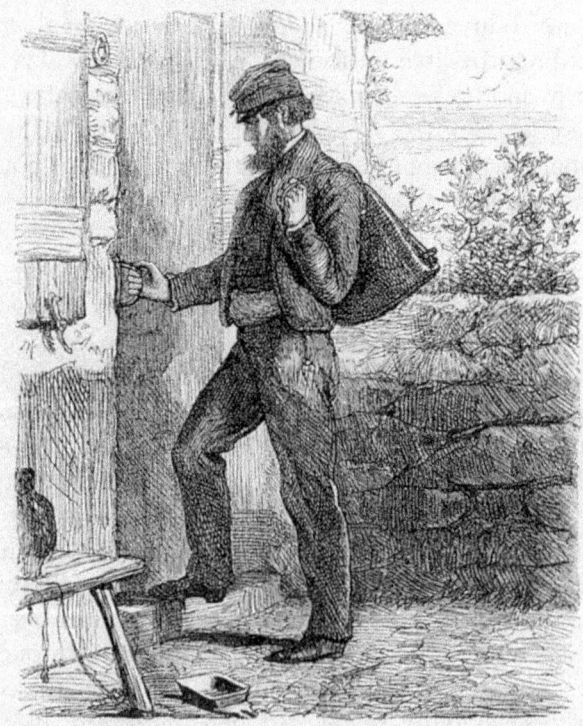

My cottage home is fill'd with light
  The long, long summer day,
But, ah! I dearer love the night,
  And hail the sinking ray,
For eve restores me one whose smile
  Doth more than morning's match,—
And life afresh seems dawning while
  His hand is on the latch!

When autumn fields are thick with sheaves,
  And shadows earlier fall,
And grapes grow purple 'neath the eaves
  Along our trellis'd wall,—
I dreaming sit,—the sleepy bird
  Faint twittering in the thatch,—
To wake to joy when soft is heard
  His hand upon the latch!

In the short winter afternoon
  I throw my work aside,
And through the lattice, whilst the moon
  Shines mistily and wide,
On the dim upland paths I peer
  In vain his form to catch,—
I startle with delight, and hear
  His hand upon the latch!

Yes; I am his in storm and shine;
  For me he toils all day;
And his true heart I know is mine,
  Both near me and away.
And when he leaves our garden gate
  At morn, his steps I watch,—
Then patiently till eve await
  His hand upon the latch!   BEART.

26 Anonymous wood engraved illustration to 'His Hand Upon the Latch – A Young Wife's Song', *Once a Week*, 8 December 1860, 668.

sively at artisan readers distressing mundane truths insist on being represented, so that the heroic artisan seeking the solace of the family hearth becomes the drunken threat embodied in the tract literature. The image then contains, perhaps even expresses, contradictions. While encouraged in the perception that returning workmen offer a vision of domestic contentment, a harmonious alliance between labour and family life, artisan audiences are also reminded that the labourer is potentially brutal and degraded. In looking across this range of images, it is important to recognise the diversity and self-consciousness with which this particular event is constructed in graphic terms. Any notion of the hegemonic power of a unified middle class version of artisan culture needs to be put alongside the evident variety of interpretation available within these images. The struggle to construct a unified meaning out of social perceptions is precisely that – a continuing struggle between competing possibilities, especially between what ought to be and what was.

One can only hope that the narrative closure of *The Family Economist* vignette is that of Bewick and Thurston and not that envisioned by the illustration of *Home Tales Founded on Fact*. Indeed given the confident subsequent use of the same narrative (the family group centre on the mother disturbed by the male presence at the half-open door) in one of the central books of conservative gender definition in the later Victorian period, Mrs Ellis's *The Women of England*, the story ought only to have one happy if non-naturalistic ending.[40] Of such dreams was ideology made, despite the nightmares of observable reality.

Conclusion

In making these links between power, ideology, and acts of representation, I have sought to avoid reductiveness. In particular, it is tempting to make an absolute link between social change (here the attack on leisure and on the family caused by new urban industrial modes of production) and its representation in contemporary popular prints (here characterised by a growing pessimism and realism in the depiction of working men returning to their family homes). As Norman Bryson puts it, in a passage which crucially underpins my argument here, 'coincidence is not yet determination'.[41] He goes on, more expansively, and using Greuze as his example:

> even if ... an unprecedented iconography of the family as a unit in separation from society does in fact appear in tandem with the emergence of a new kind of family life and organisation, still it does not

follow that related economic and political transformation homoge-
nously *cause* the Greuzian family to appear on the surface of the
canvass ... Correspondence of an ultimately uni-directional kind
(from society to image, and not the reverse) may indeed exist, yet
propositions concerning that correspondence remain incoherent until
both the specific place of Greuze's mutation of the general iconographic repertoire of familial representation, and the specific role of
the image in the social formation as a whole, are clarified, or at least
admitted as object of inquiry say.[42]

Translated into the terms of this essay, Bryson is warning
against reading the changing images of returning artisans as necessary
products constructed by new social, economic, or cultural reality.
Rather, he argues, we need to read the new images in terms of all
those available to the artist as a 'repertoire' of possibilities. This is
the reason for my attempt to assemble a range of versions of the same
social event from differing levels of social discourse. But Bryson also
suggests a further level of necessary awareness – attention to 'the
specific role of the image in the social formation as a whole'. In other
words, Bryson is stressing the need to acknowledge that images are
not merely determined by an economic base, but can themselves be
factors in the cultural production of a society, a cultural production
which has as its product the construction of social meanings. In this
essay, I have argued that while the images of artisans returning home
from labour do have a specific role in social formation, that role is
less simply unified than might be expected. Indeed, the images allow
themselves to be read (or even demand to be read) ideologically,
hence acknowledging their central concern with the construction of
specific social meanings. These images are overtly ideological, it
seems to me, and do not attempt to conceal their ideological intention under the guise of 'realism' or an unproblematic representation
of empirical truths. Their appearance in acknowledged discourses of
social instruction, characterised by the generic formulations of
cottage magazine, motto, tract, and exemplary biography, is itself a
recognition of an over-riding ideological intention. Yet, as Bryson
argues, 'correspondence of an ultimately uni-directional kind (from
society to image ...) may indeed exist', and this correspondence is
apparent to some extent in the images discussed in this chapter, especially in the apparent linking of realism as a representational code
with an increasing pessimism in the social meaning constructed by
the image. The happily employed smallholder of the 1848 *Family
Economist* gives way to the disruptive lingerer of a year later, the

awaited family mainstay of Bewick, Burns, Gray gives way to the threatening drunk of the tract literature. 'Coincidence is not yet determination', but it remains coincidence. While it is dangerous to construct an historical 'truth' from popular prints (yet also to suggest how revealing they can be of ideological structures and class positions), it is hard to disregard the slide from overtly ideological idealism towards a self-punishing naturalism in the representation of scenes of artisan homecomings between 1750 and 1850. Whether this slide is to be read as a form of progressive, even subversive, increase in social awareness or as merely another manifestation of the power of middle class ideology to assimilate and accommodate awkward truths, remains a fundamental problem. Certainly the fractures, differences, and self-doubts apparent in these images seem to confirm Bryson's denial that images arise directly and necessarily from social and economic realities.

I have chosen to regard the social and economic realities constructed by these prints as primarily ones concerned with class and industrialisation. Therefore, the line of argument drawn from feminist criticism and described at the beginning of the chapter, which sees images of domestic interiors as primarily coded statements about family, gender, and patriarchy has been relegated to the background. There are good reasons for arguing for this particular focus. The images studied in this chapter are the product of male engravers. The intention of both *The Family Economist* and the tracts, clearly acknowledged in their generic formulations and publishing history, is to offer images conceived by one class to an audience in another, and I think this distinctive intended audience is crucially associated with industrial values and the social order in these images. Finally, I believe it is dangerous to argue out from a firmly defined 'separate spheres' conception of Victorian gender relationships to its inevitable manifestation within visual images. I suspect, much like Lindsay Smith in her account of Deborah Cherry's *Painting Women*, that the relationship between ideology and representation is a less complicit one than this model suggests.

Beyond these areas of debate lies the further issue of whether the simple wood engraved vignette is to be read as a realist or naturalistic mode at all. This is an issue which can be fruitfully carried forward into the discussion of a whole range of other Victorian images, images again concerned with the representation of women's experience as both naturalistic narrative and ideological fantasy.

List of images cited

[1] Anonymous wood engraved vignette (illustration **20**).
The Family Economist vol. 1, 1848.
(London, Groombridge & Sons).

[2] Anonymous wood engraved vignette (illustration **21**).
The Family Economist, vol. 3, 1850. Title page.
(London, Groombridge & Sons).

[3] Wood engraved illustration by K.S. Gilbert to stanza VI (unnumbered pages).
Gray's Elegy
(Philadelphia, G.S. Appleton 1850).

[4] Wood engraved illustration to 'The Cotter's Saturday Night' (illustration **22**)
Drawn by Thurston; engraved by Bewick.
The Poetical Works of Robert Burns (Alnwick, Catnach & Davison 1808, 2 vols), 224.

[5] Anonymous wood engraved illustration to 'The Cotter's Saturday Night'
Saturday Night (London), vol. I, no. I, title page.

[6] Wood engraved illustration to C. Mackay, (ed.) *The Home Affections*
Drawn by John Gilbert
(London, Routledge & Co. 1858), 257.

[7] Wood engraved illustration to *The Poetical Works of Gerald Massey* (illustration **23**)
Drawn by John Gilbert
(London, Routledge, Warne, and Routledge 1861), 225.

[8] Anonymous wood engraved illustration to 'Women's Trials In Humble Life – The Story of Peggy Dickson' (illustration **24**)
Chambers' Miscellany of Useful and Entertaining Tracts
(Edinburgh, William and Robert Chambers), vol. 20, no. 163 (1847).

[9] Anonymous wood engraved illustration to 'Robert Wilson, or Will He Keep His Promise?' (illustration **25**)
in a series *Home Tales Founded on Fact*
(London, Society for Promoting Christian Knowledge, 1853).

[10] Anonymous engraving
Frontispiece to Mrs S. Ellis, *The Women of England*

[11] Anonymous wood engraved illustration to '"His Hand Upon the Latch" – A Young Wife's Song' (illustration **26**)
Once a Week 8 December 1860, 668.

Notes

1 Feminist historians and art critics have contributed much to the discussion of the 'returning artisan' motif. The chapter by L. Davidoff, J.L. 'Esperance and H. Newby in J. Mitchell and A. Oakley (eds), *The Rights and Wrongs of Women* (Harmondsworth, Penguin 1976), 139–75 called 'Landscape with Figures' is a most important discussion of the themes described here, and it should be read alongside Lynda Nead's excellent study *Myths of Sexuality: Representations of Women in Victorian Britain* (Oxford, Blackwell 1988). Nead's discussion of

Joseph Clark's 'The Labourer's Welcome' in her chapter called 'The Norm: Respectable Femininity' sets the agenda taken up by Cherry and Smith and this chapter. See, for the origins of 'separate spheres' debate, K. Millett, *Sexual Politics* (London, Hart-Davis 1970) and some of the essays in M. Vicinus (ed.), *Suffer and Be Still* (London, Indiana University Press 1972).

2   Lindsay Smith 'Polly Put the Kettle On' in *Art History*, vol. 17, no. 3, September 1994, 464–70.

3   Deborah Cherry, *Painting Women – Victorian Women Artists* (London, Routledge 1993).

4   See illustration 26 for a popular wood engraved version of this idea, perceived and interpreted from the point of view of the expectations of the returning workman rather than the waiting woman. None the less, the image forms a powerful statement of Lynda Nead's perceived 'norm' made all the more powerful by the absence of the woman from the image.

5   Cherry, *Painting Women*, 135.

6   Smith, 'Polly Put the Kettle On', 464–5.

7   *Ibid.*, 466.

8   Irene Dancyger, *A World of Women – An Illustrated History of Women's Magazines* (London, Gill & Macmillan 1978), 34.

9   Jennie Calder, *The Victorian Home* (London, Batsford 1977), 110.

10   J.F.C. Harrison, *Learning and Living* (London, Routledge & Kegan Paul 1961), 208.

11   *The Family Economist* was published from 1848 to 1853.

12   See B.E. Maidment, 'Magazines of Popular Progress and the Artisans', *Victorian Periodicals Review*, vol. XVII, no. 3 (Fall 1984), 82–94.

13   Little has been written specifically on these firms and their role in disseminating literature to a new mass readership, but for the general context see V. Neuburg, *Popular Literature: A History and Guide* (Harmondsworth, Penguin 1977) and D. Vincent, *Bread, Knowledge and Freedom* (London, Europa 1981). Examples of the development of these kinds of periodicals might be found in *Cassell's Illustrated Family Paper* (1853–1867), *The British Workman* (Tweedie, Bennett, and Partridge 1855 on), and *The Family Friend* (1848 on – begun as a monthly but weekly after 1852).

14   Some indication of the activities of these firms can be gained from Neuburg, *Popular Literature, passim*.

15   Hone's *Everyday Book* was first published in 1826–7, and *The Table Book* in 1827–8. *The Everyday Book's* sub-title, an 'everlasting calendar of popular amusement', makes clear the popular genres which Hone was re-using. Chambers' *Book of Days* was published in 1862 as a 'Miscellany of popular antiquities', so again the key word 'popular' is given a new currency. William Howitt and Thomas Miller are two other authors who took over and re-drew the almanac and day-book tradition for an increasingly literate and serious-minded artisan readership. See Howitt's *Book of the Seasons* (London, Bentley 1831) and *Year Book of the Country* (London, Colburn 1850). These books are important not only for the way in which they continue to celebrate a tradition of heroic rural labour on into the mid-Victorian period, but also because they suggest in their illustrations a changing representational code for describing the countryside. Howitt's 1831 volume, which was reprinted frequently, has simple vignettes in the Bewick tradition accompanied by verses. The 1850 volume, however, has pretty and crowded Birket Foster vignettes engraved by

Edmund Evans. Miller's *Rural Sketches* (Darton – many undated editions in the 1850s) had comparably pretty illustrations by Branston engraved by Landells and others. Given the wide currency of these kinds of books among artisan readers, it seems possible to infer that these images of the countryside were extremely influential in establishing a representational code for agricultural subject which mapped a shift from the countryside as a site for heroic labour to the countryside as a source of aesthetic and moral values perceived by contemplation rather than toil.

16   Harrison, *Learning and Living*, 208.

17   B.E. Maidment, 'Popular Exemplary Biography in the Nineteenth Century – Edwin Paxton Hood and His Books' *Prose Studies*, vol. 7, no. 2 (September 1984), 148–67.

18   E.P. Hood, *The Uses of Biography* (London, Partridge and Oakey 1852), 11.

19   E.P. Hood, *The Mental and Moral Philosophy of Laughter* (London, Partridge and Oakey 1852), 11, 67, and 73.

20   See R. Parker, *The Subversive Stitch* (London, Virago 1984). Interesting in the context of this essay is Parker's description of a late eighteenth-century tradition of embroidering samplers with designs taken from landscape paintings.

21   *The British Workman* was published by William Tweedie, Partridge & Co., and A.W. Bennett, a consortium of firms all interested in Christianised popular reading.

The use of mottoes within rules to form a decorative border to the page was used quite widely in exemplary literature. In Godfrey Golding's *How to Get On* (London, Cassell n.d.) for example, an anthology of 'good devices' and useful exhortatory sayings, the page layout is managed in a manner very similar to that used by *The Family Economist*, with decorative capitals furthering the ecclesiastical resonance of the textual layout. Noticeable in this instance, however, is the difficulty of finding a coherent way of reading a lengthy 'saying' round the page. Where the quotation or epigram runs round two sides of the page, top is paired with bottom margin, left with right. Such fragmentation can be irritating to the reader.

22   Relevant introductions to the conceptual framework of pastoral can be found in P. Marinelli, *Pastoral* (London, Methuen 1971) and in B. Loughrey (ed.) *The Pastoral Mode* (London, Macmillan 1984). William Empson's *Some Versions of Pastoral*, first published in 1935, is still central to such debates. For British pastoral painting see J. Barrell, *The Dark Side of the Landscape* (Cambridge, Cambridge University Press 1980) and A. Bermingham, *Landscape and Ideology* (London, Thames and Hudson 1987).

I acknowledge, of course, that a full visual history of the 'returning artisan' as a motif in pastoral painting would have to include Gainsborough ('The Woodcutter's Return' (c. 1773) now in Belvoir Castle, offers a good example), Palmer, Morland, Wheatley and many other eighteenth-century landscape painters. Of the many formulations of the image published in print form William Hamilton's 'The Happy Cottagers' (originally a stipple engraved illustration to Macklin's *Poets' Gallery* of 1794) and Francis Wheatley's 'The Fisherman's Return' (engraved by Barney from an oil painting of c. 1790) provide powerfully idealised versions. In reducing such a complex representational tradition to a simple ideological formulation, I am seeking a means of entry into mid-Victorian popular versions of the 'cottage' idea rather than attempting any serious exploration of rural themes in British painting.

Other interesting oil paintings on similar themes would include Arthur Hughes's 'Home from Work' (1861) in the Forbes collection (see Susan P. Casteras, *Victorian Children* (New York, Harry N. Abrams 1986)), and an entirely different re-working of the same theme by Hughes in the Russell Cotes Gallery in Bournemouth.

23 H.W. Starr and J. Henderickson (eds), *The Complete Poems of Thomas Gray* (Oxford, Oxford University Press 1966), 38.

24 A Birket Foster edition of 'The Elegy' was published in 1853. He also illustrated Burns (1846), Bloomfield's *The Farmer's Boy* (1857) and contributed to *The Home Affections* (1858, see note 34). Foster's influence on mid- and late-Victorian wood engraved versions of pastoral was immensely powerful. Houfe describes his art as 'gentle and subtle', 'much of it in a small scale low key, tiny detailed landscapes with pretty vegetation herds of sheep and cows and cottagers at their doors'. (S. Houfe, *The Dictionary of British Book Illustrators and Caricaturists 1800–1914* (Woodbridge, Antique Collectors' Club, revised edn. 1981, 308)). As Houfe suggests, Foster is a key figure in sustaining the confident, untroubled pastoral vision of the eighteenth-century landscapists on into the mass produced era of popular wood engraving.

An extremely conservative formulation of the opening scenes of 'The Elegy' can be found in the Westall/Finden steel engraved vignette in the 'gift book' edition of Gray, printed by Whittingham and published by J. Sharpe in 1826. The cottage is excluded in this image, in which the setting sun irradiates the face and smock of the returning swain, merging his figure into the shadowy dusk. The tonal effects possible in steel engraving allow Westall and Finden to create a unified, if sombre, mood of rural harmony, in which the workman 'naturally' fits. The coherent harmonising tonality of this engraving is not something that can be easily reproduced in wood, however skilfully engraved. Both Bewick and Constable illustrated 'The Elegy' but neither drew this particular scene.

25 *Gray's Elegy* (Philadelphia, G.S. Appleton 1850). With illustrations by K.S. Gilbert. Unnumbered pages, but this illustration accompanies stanza VI.

26 J. Kinsley (ed.) *Burns – Poems and Songs* (Oxford, Standard Authors 1969), 117.

27 See, for example, Mackenzie and Dent's Newcastle edition of 1802 with engraved illustration by W. Davidson. This edition does not have an illustration to 'The Cotter's Saturday Night'. The four volume edition illustrated with Stothard's steel engravings and edited by Currie furthers the metal engraved tradition discussed in note 24. Such engravings are in quite a different graphic mode to the wood engraved illustrations discussed in this essay, and can be situated in a less naturalistic, more placid tradition derived largely from oil painting and mezzotint.

28 *The Poetical Works of Robert Burns with his Life* (Alnwick, Catnach and Davison, 2 vols, 1808), 1, 223.

29 *Saturday Night*, vol. 1, no. 1 (London, Hodgson 1824), 1. This periodical appears to be directed at an artisan readership, but I have been unable to find out much about it. It seems to belong to a whole group of twopenny illustrated magazines, usually weeklies, which pre-figure periodicals like *The Penny Magazine* and *The Saturday Magazine* but which lack the overt didacticism of the new penny journals of the 1830s. Other titles of this kind would include *The Mirror of Literature* and *The Literary World*. This small format twopenny

genre seems to have survived on into the post-penny era in periodicals like *The Literary World*, whose editor went on to become one of the key figures in the development of *The Illustrated London News*. See B.E. Maidment, *Into the 1830s – Some Origins of Victorian Illustrated Journalism* (Manchester, Manchester Polytechnic 1992).

30   See B.E. Maidment, 'Essayists and Artisans – The making of Nineteenth Century Self-Taught Poets', *Literature and History*, vol. IX, no. 1 (Spring 1983), 74–91. For further discussions of these issues see M. Vicinus, *The Industrial Muse* (London, Croom Helm 1974) and B.E. Maidment, *The Poorhouse Fugitives* (Manchester, Carcanet Press 1987).

31   C. Kingsley, 'Burns and his School' in *The North British Review* (1848) and reprinted in Kingsley's *Miscellanies* on many occasions.

32   J. Prince, 'The Poet's Sabbath' in *Hours With The Muses* (Manchester, Abel Heywood, sixth edn 1857), 36–8.

33   P. Connell 'A Winter Night in Manchester' in *Poaching On Parnassus* (Manchester, John Heywood 1865), 29–32.

34   C. Mackay (ed.), *The Home Affections* (London, Routledge 1858). Gilbert's illustration is on p. 257. Gilbert's collaboration with Routledge is important in that it drew the Dalziel brothers into the mainstream of illustrated publishing in 1856 when they engraved Gilbert's drawings for selections from Longfellow. See P.H. Muir, *Victorian Illustrated Books* (London, Batsford, revised edn 1985), 134. The Dalziels' work for *The Home Affections* prefigured their work as art editors for important illustrated family periodicals like *Good Words*, which was founded in 1862. Houfe (*Dictionary of British Book Illustrators and Caricaturists*) has many interesting things to say about Gilbert, arguing that 'his popular appeal cannot be overestimated'. His popularity was based according to Houfe, on his 'majesterial' draughtsmanship, and sense of 'majesty and grandeur on the printed page', specialising in 'lofty sentiments'. Douglas Jerold's notorious remark about Gilbert – 'We don't want Rubens on *Punch*' – takes on an interesting edge when comparing this group from *The Home Affections* with the more modest and naturalistic versions of the scene suggested by the other illustrations in this chapter.

35   *The Poetical Works of Gerald Massey* (London, Routledge, Warne, and Routledge 1861). Gilbert's illustration is on p. 225. The illustrators are not named or acknowledged in this edition.

36   The best known example of this process is the cutting down and re-using of Edmund Evans's blocks for some of William Allingham's fairy tale volumes.

37   'Robert Wilson, or, Will He Keep His Promise?', *Home Tales Founded on Fact*, No. XIV (London, Society for Promoting Christian Knowledge, 1853).

38   This strong triangle, built out of mother and children, is a central feature of a picture by Gainsborough, 'The Cottage Door' (1780), which is persistently relevant to this chapter. In Gainsborough's oil, the elements of tree-cradled cottage, blank open doorway, and family group built into a unifying triangular form are all influential on the 'returning artisan' pictures, especially as, despite the absent father, the painting is usually read as on of Gainsborough's most powerfully harmonious images. E.D.H. Johnson describes it as 'his most satisfactory resolution of the Arcadian vision' in which 'a natural order reigns of which the simple peasant family is just the human manifestation', E.D.H. Johnson, *Paintings of the English Social Scene* (London, Weidenfeld and Nicolson 1986), 118. Johnson ably defends the 'Rubensesque' power of the

inter-related triangles of the compositional elements here, but, after working on this chapter, I still find the absence of the father disturbing. Barrell, *Dark Side of the Landscape*, 65–72, reads Gainsborough's paintings on this topic of the idyllic cottage family group as idylls which are historically challenged by the social realities of rural labour. To me, the discourse of the later Victorian accounts of the same idea centres much more on the family than on labour as the central issue.

While considering the compositional formulation of the returning artisan motif, it is worthwhile mentioning the obvious neo-classical version of the same event. In Greuze's 'Return of the Drunken Father' for instance, the mother and two children are arranged in a supplicatory frieze on the same plane as the returning drunk with their profiles only available to the viewer. The triangular unity of the images discussed in this chapter as a way of empha-sising the protective centrality of the female figure stands in contrast to an Enlightenment equality of supplication, in which the children are as active as the mother. Albert Boime discusses Greuze's picture as a representation of the potentially disastrous misuse of patriarchal authority in *Art in an Age of Revolution 1750–1800* (Chicago, University of Chicago Press 1987), 42. The painting is in The Portland Art Museum, Portland, Oregon.

39 E.T. Cook and A. Wedderburn (eds), *The Works of John Ruskin* (London, George Allen, 39 vols, 1903–1912), vol. XVIII, 121–2. *Sesame and Lilies* was published in 1865.
40 Mrs S. Ellis, *The Women of England* (London n.d.), frontispiece.
41 Norman Bryson, *Vision and Painting: The Logic of the Gaze* (London, Macmillan 1983), 133. Bryson's chapter on 'Image, Discourse, Power' (chapter six) is a powerful and coherent exploration of many of the theoretical issues which underpin this essay.
42 Bryson, *Vision and Painting*, 133–4.

CHAPTER 5

Did she jump or was she pushed?
NARRATIVES OF SOCIAL RESPONSIBILITY AND SUICIDES IN MID-VICTORIAN LONDON

Introduction

At first glance, the project of this chapter – to discuss the popular graphic representation of women and suicide, mainly depicted in wood engravings published in periodicals or as illustrations to fiction – may seem redundant. Many of these images have been extensively studied before – extensively and excellently – by scholars from a wide range of differing academic backgrounds: from social history (Olive Anderson),[1] from literary studies (Barbara Gates),[2] and from feminist art history and cultural studies (Lynda Nead, Linda Nochlin, and Helen Michie among others).[3] In addition, George Cruikshank's famous glyphograph of a woman with billowing skirts and a transcendental expression delineated floating between the balustrade of Westminster Bridge and the murky Thames, which formed the eighth and last plate of a narrative sequence called 'The Drunkard's Children', has been closely annotated by Cruikshank's many commentators (illustration 27). Vogler's edition of *Cruikshanks's Graphic Works* and Hilary and Mary Evans's biographical study contain particularly useful commentaries.[4]

Not only are all these commentaries helpful, but they also focus on precisely the major themes of this book: the relationship between empirically based historical research and the analysis of representation; the ways in which graphic representations form discourses concerned with ideology and power in Victorian culture; and the interconnections between verbal, often literary narratives and their

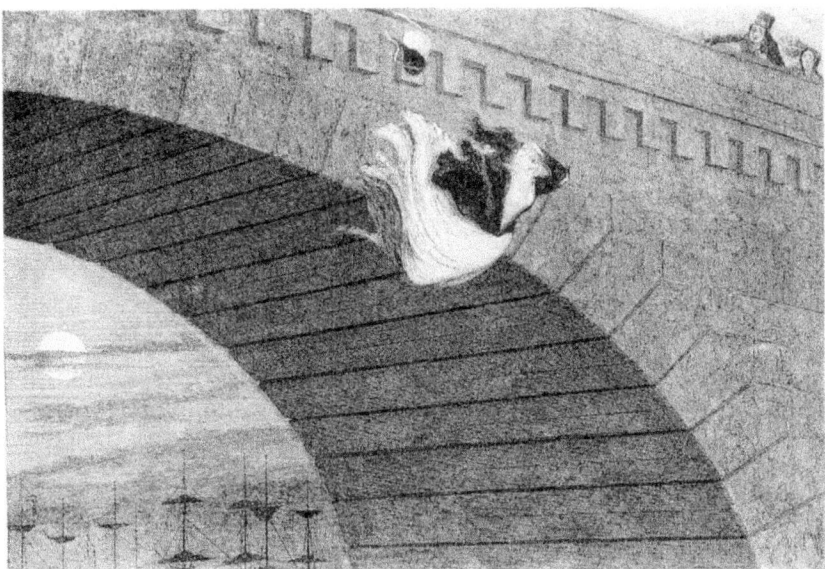

27 G. Cruikshank glyphograph. 'The maniac father ...'. Plate 8 from the sequence 'The Drunkard's Children' published by David Bogue in 1848.

visual counterparts. Yet it may well pay to be suspicious of the unanimity among these scholars in defining the available graphic and literary resources for defining Victorian concepts of suicide. The admittedly powerful illustrations and paintings by Doré (see illustrations 29 and 31) (linked to Hood's poems 'The Bridge of Sighs' and 'The Song of the Shirt'), Cruikshank [7], Watts [14], Augustus Egg [16], and the illustrations to Dickens's novels by Hablôt Browne ('Phiz') [3] and Doyle [2] appear again and again in the scholarly text book discussions of Victorian ideas of gender, drink, social despair, and death.[5] The same images are also standard fare for the picture editors looking for graphic evidence of the underside of Victorian culture – the glistening, sinister Thames, seen through a riverside arch alive with half glimpsed human habitation, confronts the reader from the pages of many an illustrated book.[6] I have tried in this chapter to extend the range of both images and texts available for discussion, looking especially at narrative and non-naturalistic depictions of suicides. Partly, this wish to include a wider range of sources is merely the outcome of empirical research, but it is also a suspicious response to the coherence, indeed the unanimity, of scholarly interpretation of these images.

Despite much attention, then, to this fashionable and fascinating set of images, I believe there are more and more various stories to be told. I have found these in a variety of places, formulated in a similar variety of literary and visual modes: in fiction (especially two of Edward Jenkins's polemical novels *Ginx's Baby* (1870), now virtually unknown but a controversial bestseller in its day, and *The Devil's Chain* (1876);[7] in influential non-fictional magazine contributions by well known serious journalists of the likes of Angus Bethune Reach and G.H. Lewes;[8] in oil painting, especially Thomas Graham's 'Alone in London' [6] in Perth Museum and Art Gallery;[9] and, most particularly, in graphic images drawn from periodicals and magazines, the most startling of which is Kenny Meadows's wood engraved illustration to an article by Reach on suicides published in *The Illuminated Magazine* for July 1844[10] (see illustration 30). The generic variety and interconnectedness of this extended range of sources provides a second reason for my interest. How do these differing discourses inter-relate, and in particular how are we to read together the visual and literary codes for the discussion of women committing suicide? These questions generate further complexities. Within each image, a number of recurrent motifs and tropes have to be accommodated, which together create an extended narrative. How are these various elements to be integrated into a single explanation?

Thus at one level the aim of this chapter is to show how the literary and visual discourses which seek to construct a social explanation or commentary on suicide interpenetrate to a quite remarkable degree. The visual images discussed here are either derived from texts, published together with texts (often in ways where the page layout insists on interconnectedness), or allude to texts in ways which assume a shared knowledge between author, artist, and audience. Such a level of interconnectedness can be easily demonstrated from empirical evidence. Harder to establish are the shared formal, generic, and modal assumptions between texts and images. Documentary realism and the Victorian literary and visual conventions of social concern clearly compete with the formal devices of melodrama, pathos, and narrative closure. Competing generic formulations seem to provide a dynamic in these texts and images which make them complex and compelling.

What were these images intended to do? There are several competing possibilities. The narratives of suicide might be read primarily as a form of socially motivated self-analysis, an extension of the ethos of the statistical society, Government reports ('Blue Books'), and *Morning Chronicle* reportage to a disturbing and widespread field of social anxiety. This would make the narrative essentially a naturalistic

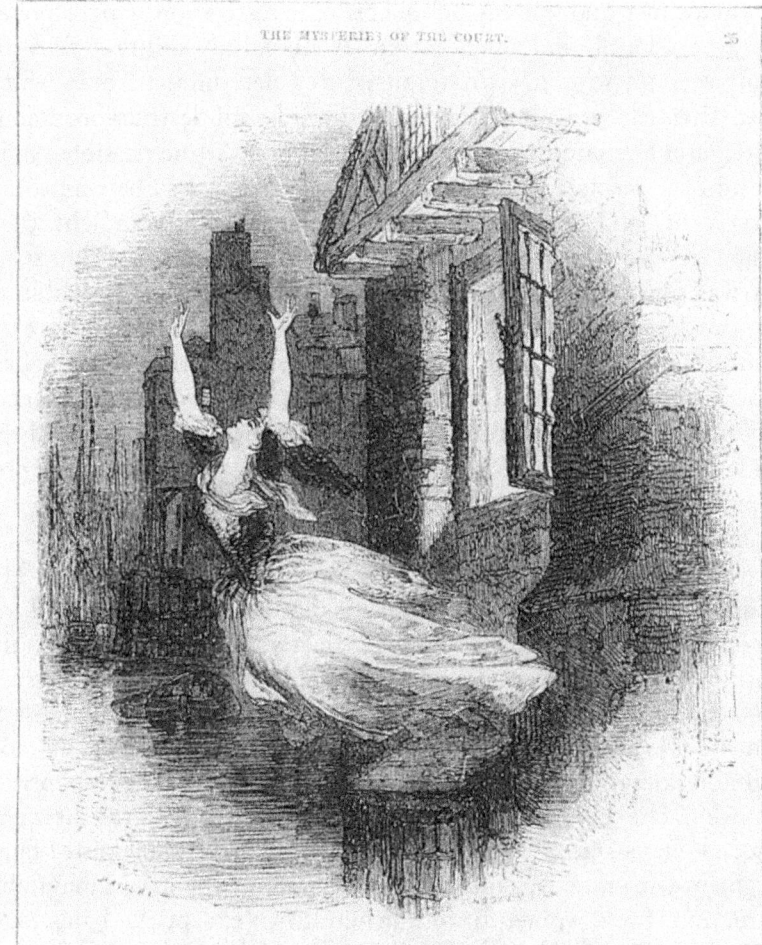

THE MYSTERIES OF THE COURT.

The maiden gave no immediate answer: but she fixed her eyes upon the artist with a mingled expression of reproach and doubt—as if to intimate that it would be cruel of him to trifle with her feelings, and yet that she could scarcely believe him to be capable of such ungenerous conduct.

"Miss Foster, I am serious," he hastened to observe. "Do not wrong me by a suspicion——"

"Oh! pardon me, Mr. Woodfall," she exclaimed: "but I feared lest in your anxiety to serve me, you might be over-rating your ability—or at least that you fancied others to possess hearts as good and generous as your own, and as willing to afford the friendless orphan a home——"

"The Marchioness of Bellenden will receive you with open arms," interrupted Woodfall, with the solemn seriousness of one who was confident in the assertion he was making. "Your misfortunes will endear you to her: and moreover, even before I knew your name—which I only learnt ere now—I have spoken of you to her ladyship——"

"Spoken of me!" exclaimed the orphan, once more throwing upon the artist a look which if not actually laden with suspicion, was at least mistrustful enough to give him pain.

"Oh! now you doubt me again!" he murmured, in a tone of mingled reproach and vexation. "But it is natural—I am a stranger——"

"Once more I beseech you to pardon me," said Rose: and, yielding to the impulse of that ingenuous fervour which made her feel that she was but ill-requiting the young man for all his kindness and disinterested attention towards her, she extended her hand, observing, "I was wrong to doubt you even for a moment: and indeed it was not doubt—but rather amazement and wonder——"

"That I should have ever mentioned you to the Marchioness?" exclaimed Woodfall, taking the fair hand of the orphan and pressing it gently in

56

28 Henry Anelay. Wood engraved illustration for G.W.M. Reynolds's *The Mysteries of the Court of London.*

and a reformist one, an act of collective investigation which looked towards legislation and amelioration. A second possibility is that the narrative is not so much a naturalistic as a deterministic one, which argued that the prevalent tendency towards self-destruction among isolated and alienated young women in London, while possibly symptomatic of a desolate and uncaring urban society, was beyond social intervention and institutional reform. This narrative might then become an essentially consolatory one, in which the middle class spectator was positioned as an appalled but helpless observer, unable to resist the determining social pressures which formulated themselves as a narrative of inevitability. A third possibility takes the aghast (presumably male) spectator even further, away from appalled specularity into outright prurience. As I hope to show, some versions of the suicide narrative acknowledge even as they seek to resist the interpretation of female suicide as a form of sexual spectacle, in which the woman is transfigured but not redeemed by the male gaze.

The distance between these interpretations is a wide one. The pursuit of self-understanding and self-regulation could be regarded as a characteristically heroic Victorian social endeavour. However, the determination to know and explain is unmistakably overlaid in these images by the desire to stand and watch. An apparent willingness to delineate and accept social responsibility seems in these images almost inevitably to imply the possibility of resisting and denying responsibility as well. The discourse of suicide in these prints is both the discourse of social engagement and the discourse of principled laissez-faire. Caught in the carefully constructed narrative of their own inevitable destruction, these women have nowhere to go except the balustrades of Waterloo Bridge. How can the spectator be positioned, or position him or herself, to intervene in this narrative? Or is the spectator too often able to substitute some kind of personal gratification for social responsibility, and discover something pleasurable or even thrilling in these images of self-destruction, an act which transgressed so many taboos of Victorian culture?

Regardless of which interpretation seems the most powerful, I also wish to show that, despite the apparently realist narrative through which the social phenomenon of violent suicide was structured and contained within Victorian culture, there were disruptively non-realist, indeed non-naturalistic, modes available to writers and artists. Hence, the central image in this discussion is Kenny Meadows's emblematic-cum-psychological fantasy version of a cluster of suicide motifs (illustration 30). This chapter does not pretend to add to our

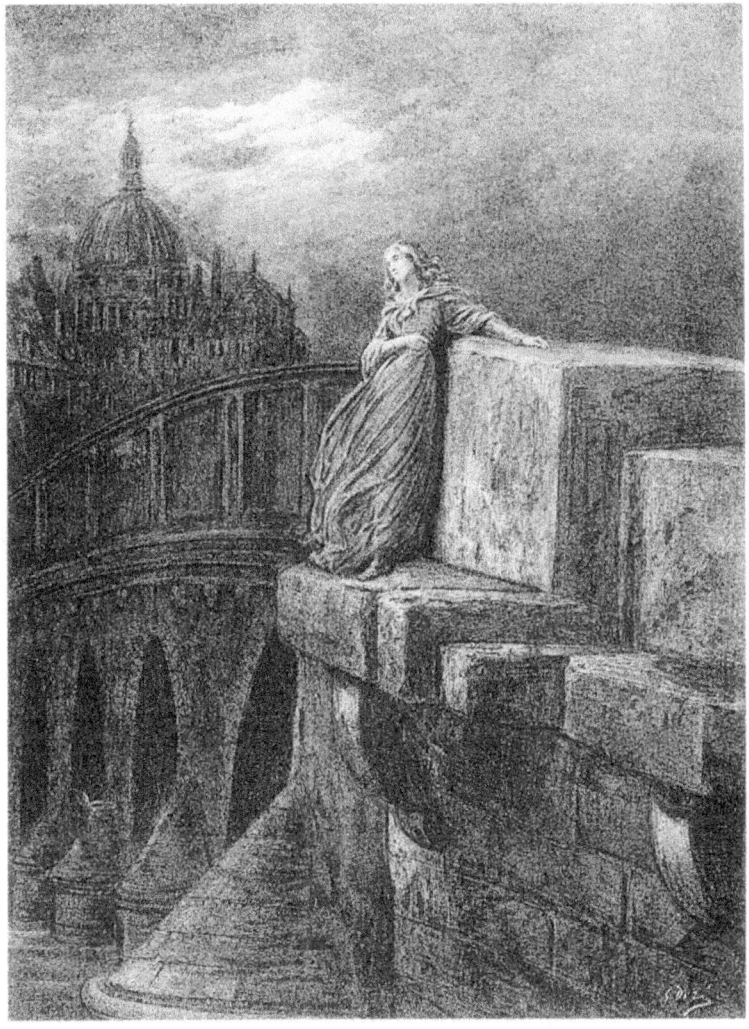

29 Gustave Doré. Wood engraving by L. Stocks. 'The Bridge of Sighs – One More Unfortunate' from Thomas Hood's *Poems*.

empirical knowledge of Victorian suicide, but it is intended to help to unpack the complex structures of belief and values, the hidden ideological and literary assumptions, through which mid-Victorian image makers sought to depict suicide.

Most of the images discussed use the apparently naturalistic medium of the wood engraving. The wood engraving, as widespread in Victorian culture as the coloured photograph in our own, was generally regarded as the most effective graphic method available, for a mass

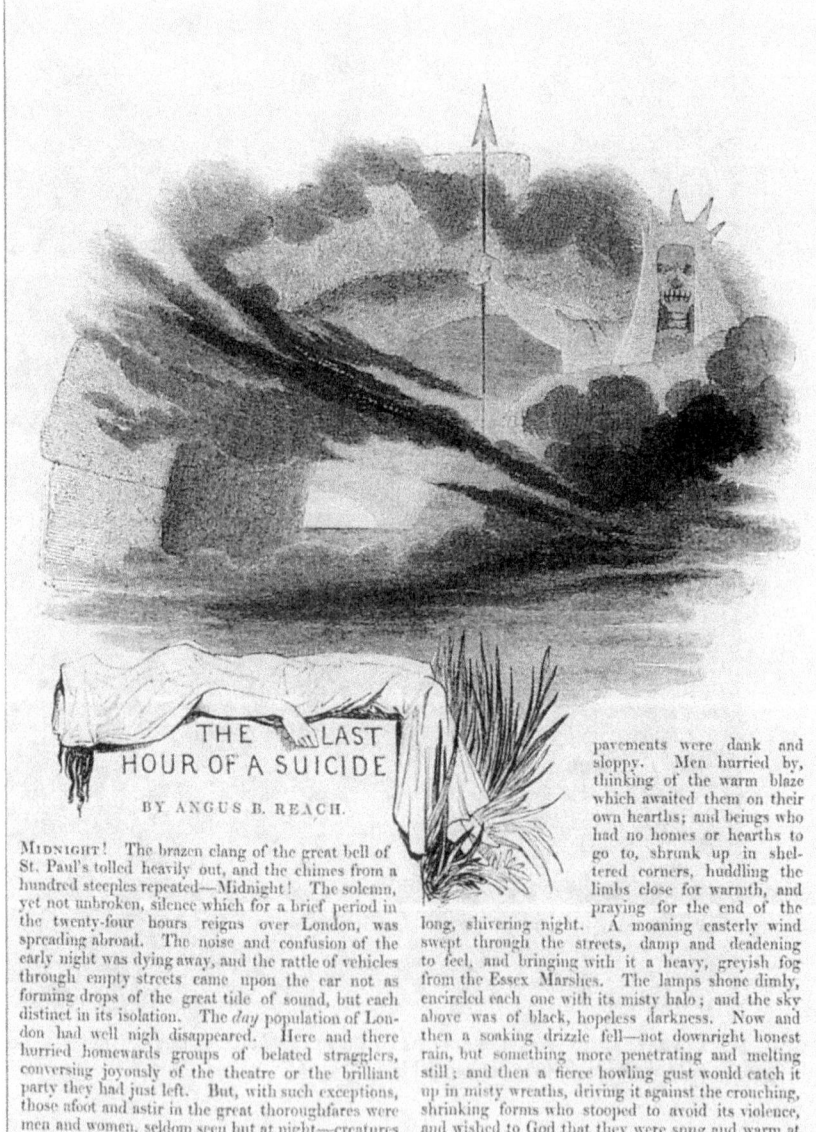

THE LAST
HOUR OF A SUICIDE

BY ANGUS B. REACH.

MIDNIGHT! The brazen clang of the great bell of St. Paul's tolled heavily out, and the chimes from a hundred steeples repeated—Midnight! The solemn, yet not unbroken, silence which for a brief period in the twenty-four hours reigns over London, was spreading abroad. The noise and confusion of the early night was dying away, and the rattle of vehicles through empty streets came upon the ear not as forming drops of the great tide of sound, but each distinct in its isolation. The *day* population of London had well nigh disappeared. Here and there hurried homewards groups of belated stragglers, conversing joyously of the theatre or the brilliant party they had just left. But, with such exceptions, those afoot and astir in the great thoroughfares were men and women, seldom seen but at night—creatures to whom the face of sunshine seems unnatural—who flit by, sometimes muffled up and silently, or clothed in glaring garments of silk and satin and gaudy ornaments, screaming gay songs with a miserable affectation of gaiety, and reeking from the loud, ribald orgies of a night tavern!

It was a cold, damp, clammy, cheerless night—the pavements were dank and sloppy. Men hurried by, thinking of the warm blaze which awaited them on their own hearths; and beings who had no homes or hearths to go to, shrunk up in sheltered corners, huddling the limbs close for warmth, and praying for the end of the long, shivering night. A moaning easterly wind swept through the streets, damp and deadening to feel, and bringing with it a heavy, greyish fog from the Essex Marshes. The lamps shone dimly, encircled each one with its misty halo; and the sky above was of black, hopeless darkness. Now and then a soaking drizzle fell—not downright honest rain, but something more penetrating and melting still; and then a fierce howling gust would catch it up in misty wreaths, driving it against the crouching, shrinking forms who stooped to avoid its violence, and wished to God that they were snug and warm at home.

On the water everything was tenfold more dismal still. The fog careered in long heavy wreaths along the stream—the wind howled most drearily among masts and rigging, and dashed the black muddy water against the piers of bridges and slimy landing places with a chill monotonous splash. No traffic

30 Kenny Meadows. Wood engraved vignette illustration to A.B. Reach, 'The Last Hour of a Suicide' in *The Illuminated Magazine*, vol. 3, July 1844, 161.

audience at least, for a sustained analysis of the morphology and structure of their own world. One purpose of wood engraving is essentially representational, a recognition of the need to describe a newly and ever increasingly complex society with accuracy and precision. This kind of delineation was also widely regarded as an additional form of explanation, maybe even of justification. To delineate was to understand and to control. But the wood engraving also belonged to deep rooted traditions of non-naturalistic representation – it was the medium, as we have seen, of play-text and broadside, Gothic romance and popular fiction. It is worth pausing to consider the divided history of the wood engraving as a medium before moving on to discuss particular images.

The Victorian wood engraving and its uses

The functions of the woodcut and wood engraving in the Victorian period were startlingly diverse given its obvious deficiencies as a representational medium – it is monochrome, linear rather than tonal, and, in the early days of its widescale use at least, small in size. The obvious advantages which it possessed over steel or copper plates or lithography were its ability to be set as part of a traditionally composed page of print, its power to sustain a huge print run without major deterioration in the quality of the image, and cheapness. So on a first reading it looks as if the rise of the wood engraving was a triumph of economic needs over representational limitations.

Crucially, for the Victorians, the wood engraving was a medium of *exposition*, of technical explanation of an increasingly technological society (see illustration 5). To cite obvious examples, two of the key new mass circulation periodicals launched in the 1830s, *The Penny Magazine* and *Chambers' Information for the People*, both prominently serialised descriptions of technological processes which were explained both verbally and visually.[11] The visual explanation of technical process became a staple of illustrated journalism, sustained by the interest generated by the Great Exhibition of 1851 in periodicals like *The Illustrated Exhibitor*.[12] By the 1860s and 1870s general interest magazines like *Good Words* were still making widespread use of explanatory articles called 'A Visit to …' or 'A Day in the Life Of …', a tradition which re-surfaced, for example in the cutaway diagrams in post-war boys' comics like *The Eagle*.[13] In this sustained project of technical explication, wood engravings were taking to themselves the functions which had previously been possible only in the delicate linear effects of copper plate engraving. Although the audience for such explanatory copper plates had been extended considerably in the late eighteenth century by widely popular works like *Barclay's Dictionary* and other popular illustrated encyclopaedias,[14] copper plate engraving remained expensive. As a form of explication, the wood engraving became an essentially representational medium, a means by which the appearance of the world was rendered to an audience eager for knowledge and understanding. The topographical, zoological, botanical, and technological focus of the illustrations to the new mass circulation journals of the 1830s make these representational functions quite clear. For all its evident deficiencies as a mode of description, the wood engraving emerged into mass culture in the 1830s as a realist medium used to depict natural beauty, structural complexity, and technological ingenuity. Such a stress on the naturalism of the wood engraving might be best understood as an ideological one with the wood engraving expressing the need of a sophisticated, propagandising middle class, newly alert to the potential of mass circulation illustrated literature as a means of disseminating a harmonious, Christianised, rational, analytical, expository world view through the appropriation of a medium long associated with popular entertainment.

But if the wood engraving, to middle class eyes at least, could be regarded as an expository and realist mode, its history as a popular medium had depended on quite another set of values. In alliance with broadside songs and ballads (see illustration 1), the wood engraving had had a long association with narrative (and hence with a written text), serving as an essentially fictive medium drawing on fantasy rather than naturalism for its main direction. The central role of the wood engraving in the development of sustained serial issue cheap fiction, in periodicals like *The Penny Novelist*, in reprints of eighteenth-century Gothic texts, in sensational part-issue fiction like G.W.M. Reynolds's novels (see illustration 28), is at least as important a development of the literary market in the 1830s as the emergence of *The Penny Magazine* or *The Saturday Magazine*. The role of woodcut or wood engraved illustration in cheap fiction is complex. At one level the wood engraved illustrations to penny fiction were narrative in function, allowing non-literate or barely literate readers access to the narrative, and offering supporting interpretations of events for more ambitious readers of the text. At another level, such illustrations are diversionary and decorative, giving pleasure both by their qualities as designs and by their evocation of long traditions of broadside and chapbook imagery. At another, even more complicated, level the wood engravings associated with fiction offered the reader tropes, fantasised shorthand clichés for narrative truisms, a simplifed visual vocabulary for horror, fear, despair, passion, betrayal – the whole range of Gothic emotional responses. Wood engravings in this context offer the satisfactions of fantasy, ways of reading off extreme sensations, vicariously experienced by the compulsive reader through the simplified representational codes of popular illustration.

So the wood engraving could be used for complex attempts at rational, documentary social analysis – as in, to take two famous examples, the government reports on child labour in mines (images which were re-used to immense effect in *The Illustrated London News*) or in the illustrations to Mayhew's pseudo-documentary *London Labour and the London Poor*.[15] Equally, though, wood engravings and woodcuts remained important as a medium of popular fantasy, a way of reading the world through Gothic tropes of extremity, disaster, accident, coincidence, and reversal. No wonder that there was a concerted attack led by the liberal intellectuals on behalf of the socially concerned middle classes on the corrupting effects of sensational popular fiction. At a graphic level, this attack manifests itself formally in the very precise format of the middle class serialised novel, in which large wood engraved or etched illustrations are seldom integrated into the text (the failure of Dickens's single attempt at such integration in *Master Humphrey's Clock* is an instructive one) but are rather presented in the single plate tradition on separate pages, facing rather than engaging with the text. These relatively self-contained images are the ones constantly invoked by collectors and scholars as the dominating achievements of Victorian illustration – Millais's *Orley Farm* plates, Phiz's *Bleak House* series of illustrations, the many plates in *Once A Week* or *Good Words*.[16] The wood engraving was reclaimed by Dickens, Thackeray, and Trollope as a genteel medium (see illustration 8), commenting on the text from the safe distance of a separate page, and using the visual language, simplified into linear effectiveness, of the sophisticated oil painting.

But there are inevitably many occasions where there is a collision within single wood engraved images between the attempt to delineate complex social realities and the wish to permit fantasised narratives of emotional extremity and Gothic sublimity. We have already seen this collision precisely demonstrated in the both naturalistic and Gothic wood engraved vignettes in tract literature of drunken workmen returning to their families which were studied in the previous chapter. Within mass circulation illustration, differing cultural levels are frequently acknowledged within a single image. Nor are graphic images, any more than language, free from the ideological battles within a class-divided society over the production of meanings.

This chapter is an attempt to look at one prominent site where visual images drawn from the discourses of social responsibility (debates about the nature and causes of prostitution, about the morality of suicide, about the extent to which poverty determines behaviour) coincide with (or collide against) the discourses of popular fiction (narratives of how broken hearts, despair, and poverty all inevitably lead to sensational resolution in violent acts of self-destruction). The violence of this collision may well explain the prominence of representations of the suicidal moment within Victorian consciousness.

Victorian suicides described and debated

The major discussions of Victorian suicide noted at the beginning of this chapter, however different their conclusions, do create a useful agenda of issues raised by the study of Victorian suicide. It might be possible to summarise these in the following way: i.) as well as the social reality of Victorian suicide, the issue was surrounded by (and its social meaning constructed in) a series of discourses which manifested themselves in literature, painting, engraving, and drama; ii.) these discourses were essentially constructed as narratives, in which the momentum towards suicide was explained in a series of narrative motifs or tropes: isolation in the city, estrangement from family, intemperance, prostitution, self-hatred, suicide; iii.) suicide was essentially a *gendered* phenomenon belonging to women; iv.) within these narratives the issue of responsibility was always left unresolved – while women were held responsible for their own sinfulness and decline into desperation, none the less the narratives acknowledged the social and environmental pressures which affect, and perhaps delimit, conduct; v.) these narratives are highly *deterministic* – once a woman is located by a narrative trope, the outcome of her life in inevitable and logical. What has happened within the literary and graphic construction of suicide at least is that self-murder, with all its taboos and anxieties as a subject, had become knowable, and hence containable. The medium through which this knowledge of suicide is accumulated is that of an explicatory fiction drawn on, alluded to, or re-structured with startling unanimity of purpose within the literary and graphic discourses of the mid-Victorian period. This unanimity of purpose is such that details within the narrative seem to develop into a series of shorthand notes for widely agreed social explanations. The coherence and repetition of this series of notes or images is immediately apparent to anyone trying to study the subject, and I intend to spend some time in examining the emblematic details used again and again in these representations. But before moving on to look at details, it is necessary to look at some of the more sustained narrative versions of Victorian suicide, both literary and visual, narratives which are so well developed in the period that they permit constant abridgement, summary, and shorthand versions of themselves to be formulated which are expressive of the wider assumed narrative however brief or compressed they might be.

In order to suggest both the generic diversity and the ideological coherence of the suicide narrative, I intend to look at four versions, all of them late in the Victorian discussion when agreement over the narrative was well advanced. The first comes from a book of exemplary narratives[17] aimed at artisan readers and published by a firm specialising in Sunday School Prize books and other improving literature, produced with all the attractions of decorated cloth binding, illustrations, and careful page layout. Such care over design and production was entirely characteristic of mid-Victorian middle class perceptions of the kind of Christianised improving fiction best adapted to transmitting ideological messages to working class readers. The second and third come from a sophisticated, even an experimental, novelist who was also a radical MP, and who used the novel as a form of social indignation, exploiting non-realist fictional techniques to confront a patently verifiable set of social problems. The intended readership here is both sophisticated yet aware of the shock effects of popular sensational fiction. The fourth is a late Victorian oil painting, executed perhaps for gallery or public exhibition rather than for hanging in a private house. It is a painting which acts as a compendium of those visual motifs which had by the 1870s clustered around the suicide narrative.

NARRATIVE THE FIRST

George Orme's *Roger Miller or, Heroism in Humble Life* is a biography of a London missionary worker who had himself been converted at a young age from working class dissipation. As well as forming an exemplary biography, the book also offers a survey of urban poverty and sinfulness and a series of biographies of working people or paupers redeemed from their misery and sin by faith. It is worth quoting one of these interpolated 'biographies' in full:

> Fanny – was a native of Tunbridge Wells. She had at an early period gone into domestic service, and had occupied a situation in a respectable house in Brighton, while there, she had been induced to resort to the Theatre, and led to conceive a passion for the stage. By some means she became acquainted with the performers, whom she afterwards accompanied to London. Soon she found her way to 'the street'. She was a tall and remarkably fine-looking young woman, and was distinguished by great energy of feeling and purpose. One vice introduced another, and her entire moral nature went rapidly to decay; extreme drunkeness was added to other forms of the grossest licentiousness, and in all she became singularly bold, shameless, and abandoned. There was no description of wickedness from which she would shrink. Not unfrequently would she steal away at early day with the clothes of the wretched men who she had caught by 'her much fair speech and flattering words,' and pawned them for drink before they arose from their miserable couch of sin and shame. The watchman of Farringdon Street, she fearlessly defied, and more than once felled to the ground. She was, in fact, the terror of the neighbourhood, and even the police, from very fear, abstained from interfering with her, and carefully stood aloof. She continued in this downward course, until at length, in a fit of drunkeness and dissipation, amid the silence and darkness of night, while the mighty mass of London's population were assembled in scenes of pleasure or gathered round their peaceful hearths, this wretched slave of sin had hurried, with dismal and tumultuous thoughts, to Waterloo Bridge, and was in the act of casting herself from its fearful height, when a stranger, passing, arrested and saved her. She was taken to a neighbouring house, and subsequently to Mr. Miller. She was then but twenty two.[18]

This narrative may or may not be, as the text claims, a documentary one, but it collects together a number of conventional tropes which create a series of connections or movements: a predisposition to pleasure leads to a predisposition to sin; a predisposition to both leads to London; London leads to prostitution; prostitution leads to drunkeness; drunkeness leads to violence (particularly shocking in a woman); everything leads to Waterloo Bridge. Of course these connections need not necessarily be read off in this order – indeed they may be best understood as conventionalised acts of rhetorical association as much as documentary explanations. In the case of 'drunkeness' and 'desperation' the connection seems more an alliterative than a socially established one. The woman's isolation is also interestingly insisted on – even the police left her alone to work out her own dialogue with guilt and shame. Freed from the agencies of social control, her career enacts an inevitable chain of degradation which stems from her predisposition to pleasure/sin. Simple as this narrative is in its associative method, it still contains a number of potent images – the crowded, but hidden, dense population of the metropolis; the invocation of the bridge/river by night; 'darkness and silence'; the arbitrariness of survival, demonstrated through the casual intervention of a nameless 'stranger'.

Two other brief comments on this narrative are worth making. Fanny is 'arrested' by a passing stranger. At one level arrested is merely the precise Latinate word for stopping someone in the middle of something. But it is also what the police do, or should do. As the narrative states earlier, 'the police, from very fear, abstained from interfering …'. So the normal agencies of social concern are here replaced by the random kindness of strangers. This is indeed an arresting moment in the narrative. A second comment concerns the function of the anonymous stranger. The narrative intention of the stranger is clear – even individuals as far gone in sin as Fanny can be redeemed by the power of God acting through not society as a whole but rather through individuals of true moral worth. But the stranger, in the casualness and arbitrariness of his presence in the narrative, also serves, in fictional terms to deconstruct the asserted and presumably intended naturalism of the fictional biography. What is supposed to demonstrate the redemptive power of God actually only calls attention to itself as a feebly incredible fictive closure. Randomly redemptive strangers belong more to fiction than to the 'real' world of Victorian prostitution.

NARRATIVE THE SECOND

Even vastly more sophisticated narratives than *Roger Orme* draw on the same sources of imagery and interpretation. Edward Jenkins used suicide as a blatantly popularising element in his fiction in an attempt to pursue his wider polemical purposes, offsetting an almost prurient sensationalism against a perceived seriousness of purpose. His declared seriousness depends on his defence of the documentary truth of his fictive strategies – in the Preface to *The Devil's Chain*, written to counter critical charges of sensationalism, he asserts: 'there is not a single incident in these 276 pages which not only may not happen, but which has not in some form or other repeatedly occurred.'[19]

After this assertion, the opening of the novel itself still provides something of a shock:

> One February afternoon, just as the yellow, dingy thing in London called light was deepening into absolute darkness, and the gas was beginning to flicker in streets and shops, passengers in St. Martin's Lane, about half-way between St. Martin's Place and the cross-ways, were startled by a shriek which came from a window in the third floor of a house on the east side.
>
> A shrill, harrowing shriek it was, that cut and pierced the dismal air, and seemed to make it quiver with horror – the shriek, too, of a woman. Those who, hearing it, at once lifted their eyes to the window whence it came, discerned for a moment, through the dusk, a struggling shadow within the casement, struggling with some unseen hands, struggling only an instant, for the next moment it sprang through the window, with a second shriek more keen and terrible than the first, turned once, struck with its head almost noiselessly on a projecting sill of stone, turned over again and then dropped head-first with a dull thud on the stone pavement. And there it lay, a bundle of clothes and clay.[20]

There are a number of salient features in this unrepentently sensationalist writing. One is clearly the very self-conscious way in which the passage establishes the gender of the suicide. Despite the sustained anonymity of the victim – indeed the rendering of the suicide herself as a 'thing' or 'clay' – the carefully casual association of the shriek with a woman is rhetorically central to this passage. It is the main source of horror. The gendering of this awful death provides the dynamic of the subsequent chapter, in which the bystanders respond with a 'thrill of horror' which seems to be partly sexual in origin, then two or three 'trembling' men pull the suicide's gown and petticoats down 'decently' over a 'woman's feet' which are covered with 'gay shoes and stockings'.[21] ('Gay' here of course links the suicide directly to prostitution.)

A second feature of the passage is the author's insistence on vividly precise and naturalistic rendition of detail which spare none of the reader's feelings. The suicide's fate is revealed by 'drops [of blood] spattered about the flags' and the pavement 'was dinted and split' in a reversal of the expected effect of a collision between a human skull and a paving stone. If the flags were broken, what must her head have looked like? Jenkins's reformist and socially interventionist purposes may well justify his chosen fictional methods here, but his willingness to draw on both an unrelenting naturalism and a prurient, gendered sensationalism at the same time is rather disturbing to my reading of the book, and raises many of the problems posed by the other images and descriptions in this chapter.

After opening his novel in this startling way, Jenkins, by a brilliant narrative manoeuvre, changes direction entirely. The suicide is not pursued as an introduction to a sustained narrative development, but rather as a local device 'to illustrate the dangers of therapeutic drinking. Rather than a central plot device, the suicide merely serves to drive the bystanders in a state of shock into the neighbouring pubs to restore their equanimity through brandy. In particular, one innocent (but corruptible) pretty young female bystander was helped by a young man as far as the nearest bar, where, taking more drink than she was used to, she fell into the clutches of the apparently amiable young man, and 'from that day on for ever, was to know virtue and honour no more'. Bizarrely, neither the name of the suicide nor the reasons for it are ever stated. Yet not so bizarre – this failure to elucidate may not be so much a post-modernist narrative joke, but rather an assumption that the reader can write the full narrative of the leaping suicide for him or herself. The clutching hands, the 'gay' apparel, the despairing shriek, the gathering dusk and gloom are all the clues needed to piece together a coherent narrative. The full pattern of isolation / prostitution / drunkeness / self-loathing / suicide narrative motifs can be easily assembled here from nothing more than a brief shorthand of sensational effects and local details.

NARRATIVE THE THIRD

The Devil's Chain stands in interesting contrast to Jenkins's major analysis of the social causes of suicide, his best known novel *Ginx's Baby* (1870) which concludes, rather than begins, with a suicide. Here, the explanation of the causes of suicide is not constructed through brief emblematic details but rather by the development of a sustained critique of poverty, institutional neglect, and social alienation. Despite the many elaborate fictional games played by the narrative, the overall drive is much more overtly naturalistic than the sensational methods of *The Devil's Chain*. As the penultimate paragraph of the novel states: 'Society ... in the sacred names of Law and Charity ... has at last driven him [Ginx] over the parapet into the greedy waters'.[22] The setting for this suicide is Vauxhall Bridge, in the middle of a dark night, with a recognition of 'the awfulness of the dense, suppressed life that was wrapt within the gloom and calm of the hour.'[23] These qualities – the murkiness of the night; the sense of the presence of hidden but immanent swarms of similar people with similar narratives to tell; the feeble light; the white face against the gloom – all form part of the visual furniture of the graphic representations of suicide, as we shall see. The key points to note here are, firstly, that an author as well informed and serious minded as Jenkins is quite at home in using the sensational vocabulary of popular suicide, and, secondly, that the apparent tension between the realist and melodramatic possibilities in explaining suicides do not cause the author any loss of self-confidence in depicting this complex subject.

NARRATIVE THE FOURTH

The fourth 'classic' exposition of the suicide narrative I would like to consider as an introductory way of decoding the range of available popular graphic images of the same event is an oil painting, 'Alone in London' [6], painted by the Scottish artist Thomas Graham. The painting shows the Embankment at dusk, dominated by massive, sculptural, barely glimmering lights, looking down the river towards St Paul's Cathedral. The cathedral's dome is shown rising above the arches of Waterloo Bridge, which cuts across and dominates the upper third of the picture. In the foreground, but dwarfed by a prominent lamp base, a young woman leans wearily on the balustrade, staring into the middle distance. The narrative is quite obvious from the sequence of emblematic details – isolated in London on arrival from the country, and after experiencing the unvarying narrative events already outlined in previous accounts, the girl will eventually arrive at the balustrade and hurl herself into the waters below. Again the narrative is emblematic as well as representational. The huge, overbearing, sculptural lights that in fact only emit glimmers, the glassy smoothness of the water, the London skyline implying thousands of comparably lonely and desparate lives, the gloomy weather – by now the uniformity and unanimity of the emblematic narrative will be becoming clear.

Yet the narrative of suicide in Graham's painting, whilst evidently present in these emblematic details, is not the only narrative made available to the viewer. As I have already suggested there are underlying tensions within this narrative between a socially concerned, naturalistic reading of the painting and a non-naturalistic interpretation which stresses the emblematic determinism of the narrative, and which forms a narrative construction of ideological meaning. As in Orme's narrative in *Roger Miller*, the possibility of an arrested closure is not entirely withheld from Graham's painting. The girl might be redeemed, might find happiness and righteousness through chance, luck, or the redemptive powers of the passing stranger or sudden appearance of 'rich uncle'. However unlikely these non-naturalistic possibilities are, Graham suggests in 'Alone in London' that they must not be entirely discounted. The title of his work deliberately evokes Hesba Stretton's treacly but famous Religious Tract Society story published under the same title.[24] A huge bestseller in its own day, this illustrated short fiction describes the redemption of exactly the kind of figure which Graham shows leaning against the balustrade. Thus it is important to maintain this sense of narratives riven by competing meanings when reading these depictions of suicide motifs. These competing meanings have to be repressed to maintain that a single unified meaning is constructed in these images, just as suggested in chapter 4 we saw the naturalistic narrative of domestic violence repressed in most of the representations of workmen returning to their cottage homes. No narrative as sustained and complex as that of suicide could exist except as a series of competing and often conflicting possibilities. Through these potentially competing representations, the fractures, anxieties, and contradictions of Victorian middle class ideology become visible.

'Alone in London'

It is worth pausing long enough to see how this 'alone in London' sub-narrative was itself assimilated into Victorian visual and literary preoccupations. The roots of the 'alone in London' narrative lie in both an earlier and a comic tradition: the arrival of an ingenuous country girl in London, beset with immediate dangers from thieves, swindlers, pimps, and brothel keepers was a comic trope used as frequently in restoration comedies as in eighteenth-century caricature, where it was often accompanied by the emblematic breaking of china to signify lost virginity. Clearly, comic formulations of this narrative were less appropriate for Victorian artists and writers, who were more interested in the narrative as a form of social exploration than as a means of laughing at innocence abused by metropolitan corruption. It is informative of the nature of these Victorian social concerns to look at the transitions made by the 'alone in London' motif as it joins the growing stock of Victorian visual tropes.

    G.J. Pinwell's fine illustration to 'The Deserted Village' in *Dalziel's Illustrated Goldsmith* [19] offers an interesting example.[25]

Pinwell offers a fluently dramatic, even melodramatic reading of the section of the poem which comprises a short narrative of sexual ruin in the city:

> Ah! turn thine eye
> Where the poor Houseless shivering female lies.
> She once, perhaps, in village plenty blest,
> Has wept at tales of innocence distrest;
> Her modest looks the cottage might adorn,
> Sweet as the primrose peeps beneath the thorn;
> Now lost to all, her friends, her virtue fled,
> Near her betrayer's door she lies her head,
> And pinch'd with cold, and shrinking from the shower,
> With heavy heart deplores that luckless hour
> When idly first, ambitious of the town,
> She left her wheel and robes of country brown.

Despite the sententiousness of Goldsmith's neatly formulated couplets, the appropriateness of his narrative to Victorian purposes was readily grasped by Pinwell, who disposes the fallen girl in a massive side-lit triangle offset against the caricatured beau-monde lady entering a warmly lit carriage or sedan chair behind. The railings against which the girl leans act as both cage and threat, with the elaborate swirls of the wrought iron stanchion taking on a bestial, snake-like ominousness. The girl herself refers in her pose and setting to Rossetti's famous image 'Found' (another image of the city isolate redeemed),[26] though in Pinwell's engraving the virile, good hearted rescuer is notably absent. Indeed, Pinwell's image is built round the absent (but omni-present) seducer, who belongs to the unnoticing world of wealth and fashion which crosses the backdrop of the illustration in silhouette like some kind of macabre dumb-show. Pinwell's reading of Goldsmith's parable of moral decline is totally Victorian in its technique and structure, yet he has seized on an interesting element in 'The Deserted Village' which allows Goldsmith's focus on rural decline to elide into Victorian narratives of the alienating effects of the city without obvious difficulty.

Equally interesting in signalling a transition from eighteenth-century modes of depiction of the 'ingenue in the city' motif to Victorian bourgeois readings of the same narrative is the early *Pickwick* plate of Mr Pickwick's arrival in London drawn by Robert Seymour [20] (see chapter 3, note 62). The plate did not survive the death of its artist into later editions of the novel, but was speedily replaced by a re-drawn version of the scene executed by 'Phiz' who became the novel's only illustrator. The reasons for the tensions between Dickens and Seymour are immediately obvious from this illustration. Seymour was working in an eighteenth-century caricature tradition in which there were no 'heroes'. According to the caricature code of equal absurdity, the ingenue Pickwick is as ludicrous as the street people who greedily accumulate to exploit his arrival in the city. Indeed, the leering bystanders, including a coal-porter sucking a clay pipe, are in many ways more sympathetically portrayed than the querulous Pickwick, whose bad-tempered demeanour is emphasised by the defensive use he is making of his umbrella. For Dickens, and thus for 'Phiz', too, the picaresque opportunities for humour given by the portrayal of Pickwick as an innocent, suggesting his essential goodness and vulnerability, are more compelling than his grotesque rusticity. The impartially satirical formulations of the codes of eighteenth-century caricature are hardly appropriate for a bourgeois hero staving off a dangerous world largely made up of urban chancers. Ultimately, the author and major illustrator see *The Pickwick Papers* as a novel about human goodness rather than human folly.

This summary of the way in which Victorian artists and writers annexed and transformed the narrative of newly arrived isolates in the city is grotesquely truncated, but it does offer evidence of how, in order to sustain the narrative of suicide, other potentially competing and potentially less pessimistic narratives of the city had to be acknowledged and subsumed. The eighteenth-century literary tradition of describing the urban ruin of innocent country girls through comic narratives was clearly not sustainable into the Victorian period. The tragi-comic ballad, broadside, and theatrical stories of ruined girls which were as powerfully humorous and prurient as they were (or pretended to be) moralistic, had to give way to the more fervent, spiritualised, melodramatic, and (crucially) pessimistic codes through which women alone in London were represented. Accordingly, Graham's painting seems to me to evoke the 'alone in London' narrative idea only to subsume it to a wider, more despairing set of narratives which indicate only self-destruction as a possible closure.

These 'classic' versions of the suicide narrative (Orme, Jenkins, and Graham) come quite late in its history, as they date from the 1870s. By this time, the narrative and its emblematic code has had time to evolve into a stereotypical and determined one made up of elements and motifs which have to some extent lost contact with the empirical social knowledge from which they originally derived. So the next phase in unravelling these graphic narratives of violent suicide must be the attempt to describe and deconstruct the detailed emblematic vocabulary on which these pictures depend, a vocabulary employed again and again with remarkable consistency of representation. My argument will be that in choosing one motif from the available stock permitted by the extended narratives of suicide, the whole narrative and its long history as a form of social explanation is evoked. These allusions to a series of available extended intertexts can be found in the apparently unimportant background motifs, tropes, and visual details which crowd these dramatic images. The ostensible visual focus on the central character in these versions of the suicide moment should not stop the viewer from reading the image as much through detailed allusion as through the melodramatic overall effect.

The graphic narratives of suicide

In the popular prints named in the 'List of images cited' at the end of the chapter, the suicide narrative is evoked through one of three frozen moments within the narrative. These might be called 'On the Brink' [1 to 6] (which is also the carefully chosen title of [2]), 'The Leap' [7–12], and 'Under the Arch' [13–18]. 'On the Brink' images describe the contemplation of suicide, usually from a vertiginous position above water. 'The Leap' images show the suicide in mid air, usually framed by the arch of the bridge from which he or she has just leapt, with his or her face transfigured by a rapturous expression. Women depicted in this way are usually floating on a cloud of billowing skirts of the kind which the Westminster workmen in *The Devil's Chain* took such care to adjust in the cause of decency. 'Under the Arch' images show the corpse coming to land or being lifted out of the river, usually under the threatening arches of a bridge. The persistence and consistency of these formulations within the popular prints has allowed me to use them as the organising mechanism of the following image list.

Yet in describing this variety of representational moments I am arguing not for differing interpretations of the event, but rather that they all evoke the same controlling and determining narrative of suicide. The moment through which the narrative is depicted may vary, but essentially the narrative itself never changes. Within these 'moments', however, a more detailed emblematic code is at work. The central dramatic moment in these images is enacted in front of, or, as the visual plane of these illustrations is often a single one, amidst a network of visual details which comprise something approaching a metonymic system or code. It is easy to list the more obvious of these:

i.) darkness, often containing the looming, shadowy presence of a city skyline, or else offset against a range of feeble, separately articulated street lights; ii.) lights, used either as in (i) or else as huge animalesque, sculptural elements by which the London Embankment is evoked as a metonym for loneliness and despair; iii.) the city skyline, invariably that of London; iv.) the bridge arch, seen either from below (the suicide's view) or above (the city's view); v.) the neo-classical balustrade of the bridge, sometimes displaying the sculptural lamp standards of (ii); vi.) the tomb-like slab, which is also the mortuary slab, on which the rescued body is laid. At one level, all these details are apparently naturalistic. The scene is almost always set in a place that is recognisably London. Often a particular London bridge is rendered with some degree of documentary accuracy – often, as the literary narratives make clear, a precise bridge is named. The distinctive lamp standards of the London Embankment are usually drawn with due attention to their distinctive shape and presence. The skyline is demonstrably that of the Thames. The instantly recognisable dome of St Paul's Cathedral is almost always present. And of course, as the secondary literature already cited makes abundantly clear, the London bridges were a common site for Victorian suicides. Yet the naturalism of these details is less striking than their constant reiteration as metonyms or symbols, their obvious function as a narrative code rather than as a recognition of a social reality.

Furthermore, several of these visual details belong to a number of competing graphic discourses which might be expected to disrupt the unity of the suicide narrative with less pessimistic picturesque possibilities – some of which have already been glimpsed in, for example, Pugin and Rowlandson's aquatint celebration of the fire at the Albion Mill (see chapter 2). Two of these visual motifs are most obviously open to contradictory readings – the bridge arch and the London skyline. The bridge arch belongs both to a picturesque topographical tradition running from Canaletto to Henry Pether and to a tradition of Victorian social realism which includes both painting (Augustus Egg [16], Gustave Doré (illustrations 29 and 31), and Abraham Solomon [17]), and fiction, with Dickens and Wilkie Collins forming the most obvious examples. The London skyline, similarly, could be used to represent heroic industrial and imperial meanings, but was also capable of rendering isolation and despair.

The bridge arch motif has its origins in the development of picturesque townscape painting.[27] The dominating presence here was Canaletto whose celebratory images of the river compared London

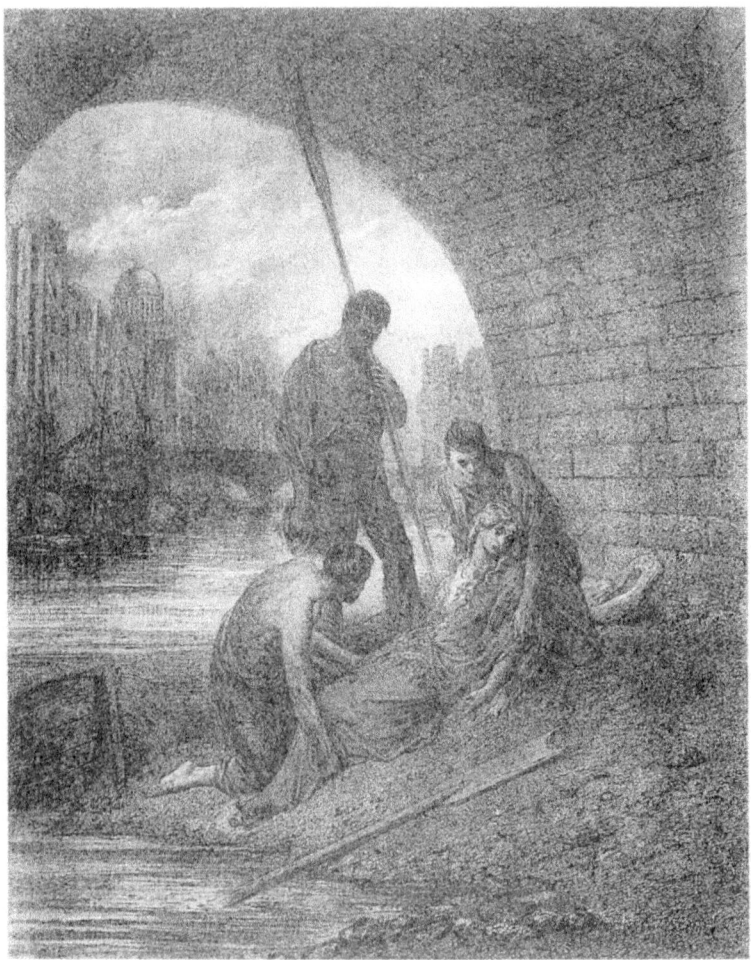

31 Gustave Doré. Wood engraving by L. Stocks. 'The Bridge of Sighs – Take Her Up Tenderly' from Thomas Hood's *Poems*.

seen from the Thames to the mercantile greatness of Venice seen from its canals. In particular his 1746 painting of 'London: Seen through an arch of Westminster Bridge' provides a 'remarkable, original, and highly influential' image.[28] That the bridge was shown in the course of construction not only alludes to the heroic civil works celebrated, for example, by Pope in his 'Epistle to Burlington' but also to the playful use of picturesque, whimsical, and capricious elements within Canaletto's townscapes. Canaletto's painting was also issued in an engraved form in 1747. In the fifty years following Canaletto the framing arches of the Thames bridges were used in an essentially picturesque way. Samuel Scott's series of paintings of the completion of Westminster Bridge are good examples which date from the mid 1850s.[29] These show as well as scenes of the busy river and the architectural sweep of the river bank the excitement generated by the completion of the architectural project. 'An Arch of Westminster Bridge' now in the National Gallery of Ireland in Dublin shows two workmen completing the installation of the lamps set above the neoclassical balustrade on elegant stanchions. One workman gestures expansively and wonderingly at the new adornment. Further images celebrating the engineering feats of bridge construction were commonplace in the illustrated popular journalism of the 1840s.[30] These illustrations again combine images of overall grandeur and grace with detailed expositions of the achievements of the engineer.

This celebratory and picturesque tradition of depicting bridge arches reaches its Romantic conclusion in the 'moonscapes' of Henry Pether which, painted almost at the same time as Cruikshank's 'The Drunkard's Children', permit a reading of the river view, city skyline, and the inhabitants of the scene which is rich, mysterious, and which denies obvious human presence in order to construct a version of the Romantic sublime. All the connotations of the bridge arch which might interpret it as an emblem of destitution and suicide are repressed in the Romantic intensity of Pether's vision which has reminded modern critics of Caspar David Friedrich. It was even possible for Victorian artists to construct an industrial picturesque, in which the busy commercial activity of the river could be assimilated into the spectacular panoramic sweep of river and skyline.[31]

Against this picturesque tradition of representing the bridge arch, the Victorians also constructed another meaning which it is tempting to call a 'realist' one because it belonged essentially to the developing visual genres of social investigation – the wood engraved illustrations for mass journalism; the developing tradition of social realist oil painting; and, to some extent, the new industrial picturesque typified by aquatints of railway scenes or urban topography.[32] In this tradition the bridge arch took on the force which it still bears – not the gentle contemplative melancholy of Flanagan and Allen's song, 'Underneath the Arches' but rather the social anxiety and helplessness of 'cardboard city' or 'the homeless'. In these formulations the arch becomes menacing and oppressive. The shelter it offers is cruelly ironic, as only those beyond the agencies of social concern, beyond charity, indeed only those almost beyond redemption, find their way to the riverside. This acutely pessimistic narrative of the bridge arch as the last refuge for the destitute, the alienated, the moral weakling, and the criminal (the repressed other of industrial culture) utterly denies the picturesque potential of a received eighteenth-century tradition. In order to establish a unified meaning for the bridge arch in Victorian representational codes, it was necessary to exclude a long standing picturesque tradition in favour of a new, urgent, and avowedly realist one. The urgency of the newly perceived social problems of suicides seem to have banished the aesthetic, commercial, and imperial pleasures found in contemplating the London waterfront from Victorian consciousness at a single blow. This is of course an overstatement – put more moderately, what happens is a displacement of the picturesque into oil painting and watercolours, while the popular prints take over the naturalistic, socially concerned modes of representation available to them.

Similarly, the skyline motif in Victorian representations of suicide became available as a unified and pessimistic construction of meaning through an intersection with another narrative which was central to the Victorian construction of its own social conscience, that of the seamstress.[33] While the use of the river/skyline silhouette as the masthead of *The Illustrated London News* and *The British Workman* gave it an almost iconic and potentially heroic meaning, the skyline became more and more powerfully associated in iconographical terms with the seamstress's garret and therefore with another, slightly different narrative of social despair – that of the hard-working but unrewarded labourer, the willing worker who is doomed to poverty not by moral depravity but by the callous, uncaring organisation of labour and the gender distinctions which structure Victorian industrial culture.

Reading the suicide narrative

This chapter is structured rather differently from the previous three which have been built round a combination of contextual explanations and detailed, print by print expositions of that context. In this chapter, many of the images discussed have already been exposed to close analysis, and I have shown in the notes and text where this has occurred. It is also my hope that by this stage of the book, readers will be well able to pursue their own interpretations of popular mass circulation images. I invite you to construct your own interpretation of Victorian narratives of suicides from the available representations. But I also believe that any detailed expositions of these prints will merely serve to suggest the unanimity and coherence of the image set and representational codes through which suicide is depicted. I have sought to show in this chapter how that unanimity can only be constructed and sustained through the repression of potentially competing further narratives, which were available within the culture and which might have been used to assemble different meanings. I have shown, for example, that the Victorians might have pursued a comic, if cruel, prior literary and visual tradition of regarding vulnerable isolates in the city as gullible dupes. They might have persisted in seeing the Thames as a heroic metaphor for commercial and imperial success – to some extent, in oil painting at least, they did continue to discover this meaning. They might have continued to figure London through the kind of urban picturesque which appears in the prints of urban conflagrations (see chapter 2) or in the world of Pierce Egan and the educated dustman (see chapter 3). But the images assembled here show that, to a remarkable degree, they refused to extend these optimistic accounts of urban life on into the mid-Victorian period, choosing instead to construct a single coherent narrative of anxiety and despair. As chapter 4 illustrates, this process of mediating between competing narratives and constructing unified meanings is a central act of ideological purpose, whether perceived as such or not by those involved in the production of images.

Yet sustaining that unanimity of representation is a very difficult undertaking. In chapter 4, we saw an apparently unified and coherent early Victorian middle class view of the heroic interdependence of work, family, home, and gender roles fractured by the admission into representation of the possibility of the disruptive male drunk, the precisely antipathetic industrial enemy which many of the representations had sought to exclude. In this chapter, we have seen a more sustained apparent unanimity of representation, but under this apparent consistency I have sought to show how the images are in fact determined by a central dichotomy between naturalism and melodrama, between a discourse of active social concern and a discourse of social helplessness which lapses, at its worst, into one of prurient sexuality. In trying to construct suicide in ways which made it accessible to Victorian meliorism, many of these images offer instead only the consolations of horrified spectatorship. Once again, as in the representations of family and work discussed in chapter 4, what becomes apparent in studying these images are the tensions within middle class ideology rather than its unified drive towards hegemonic assertion.

Additionally, in accordance with many previous exhortations to make the study of particular modes of representation central to the

CASSELL'S MAGAZINE.

SATURDAY, JULY 16, 1870.

MAN AND WIFE.
BY WILKIE COLLINS.

SIXTEENTH SCENE.—SALT PATCH.

CHAPTER THE FIFTY-FOURTH.—THE MANUSCRIPT.

1.

"My Confession :—To be put into my coffin ; and to be buried with me when I die.

"This is the history of what I did, in the time remained for some years the only one at home. At the latter part of the time, my mother's health failed ; and I managed the house, in her place. Our spiritual pastor, good Mr. Bapchild, used often to dine with us, on Sundays, between the services. He approved of my management of the house, and, in particular, of my cooking. This was not

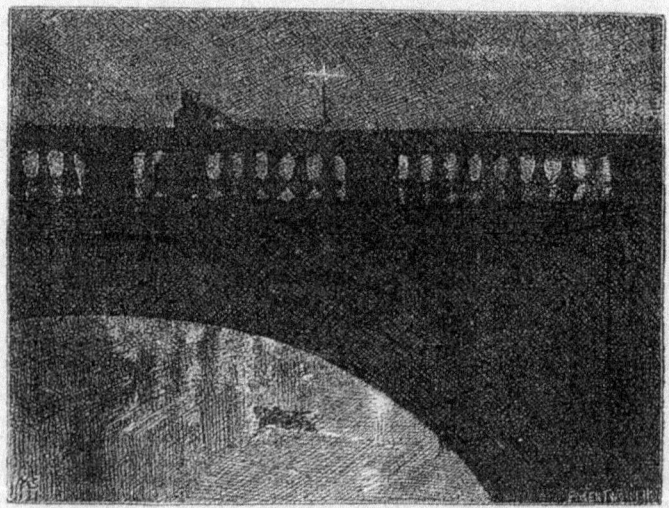

"I WENT DOWN TO THE BRIDGE AFTER DARK, AND LOOKED OVER AT THE RIVER."

of my married life. Here—known to no other mortal creature, confessed to my Creator alone— is the truth.

"At the great day of the Resurrection, we shall all rise again in our bodies as we have lived. When I am called before the Judgment Seat, I shall have this in my hand.

"Oh just and merciful Judge, Thou knowest what I have suffered. My trust is in Thee.

2.

"I am the eldest of a large family, born of pious parents. We belonged to the congregation of the Primitive Methodists.

"My sisters were all married before me. I

pleasant to my mother, who felt a jealousy of my being, as it were, set over her in her place. My unhappiness at home began in this way. My mother's temper got worse as her health got worse. My father was much away from us, travelling for his business. I had to bear it all. About this time, I began to think it would be well for me if I could marry as my sisters had done ; and have good Mr. Bapchild to dinner between the services, in a house of my own.

"In this frame of mind, I made acquaintance with a young man who attended service at our chapel.

"His name was Joel Dethridge. He had a beautiful voice. When we sang hymns, he sang

32 M.S., engraved by P. Wentworth. Wood engraving. 'I went down to the bridge after dark ...'. Illustration to Wilkie Collins's *Man and Wife* in *Cassell's Magazine* 16 July 1870.

explanation of the social meanings, this chapter identifies contradictions within the Victorian use of wood engraving as its dominant representational mode. It is both a naturalistic and representational medium widely used as a means of describing an increasingly complex world to a mass audience, and a medium associated with popular entertainment, with the theatre, the broadside song, and humorous journalism. This double history poses the interesting question of whether the tensions between various meanings identified in the (largely wood engraved) images of suicides discussed in this chapter are more the product of the representational mode than of any social or ideological uncertainty. I do not believe there is any simple answer to this question beyond the reassertion that the interpretation of popular graphic imagery cannot be properly undertaken without widespread recognition of how the chosen mode of representation to some extent determines the nature of image produced.

A coda on Kenny Meadows

I have chosen not to pursue any detailed interpretation of individual images in this chapter for the reasons already stated above. I would, however, like to conclude the text of this book by looking briefly at one image, Kenny Meadows's extraordinary vignette illustration to Angus Bethune Reach's article 'The Last Hour of a Suicide' published in *The Illuminated Magazine* in 1844 (see illustration 30). *The Illuminated Magazine*, edited at this time by Douglas Jerrold, who was a characteristically inventive and entrepreneurial editor and backer of many periodicals in this decade, provides an example of a particularly complex and fascinating mass circulation illustrated journal. Jerrold employed an art editor, Ebenezer Landells, one of Bewick's pupils, who had moved to London to participate in the rapidly growing market for mass produced wood engraved illustration especially for periodicals.[34] Under Landells's guidance, *The Illuminated Magazine* had begun to develop a high reputation for its illustration which, unusually, combined single plate etched plates by big name engravers like Leech with a wide array of vignette wood engraved illustration, and, uniquely, some degree of coloured wood engraved capitals, title pages, and illuminations. The introduction of colour, while not sustained, was a radical step.

Yet, for all its experimental elements, what strikes me most about *The Illuminated Magazine* is the scale and brilliance of its wood engraved vignette illustration, which is used for capitals, end-pieces, indexes, and contents pages as well as for the text. The vignettes are therefore both expository and decorative, and the pleasure in the deco-rative possibilities is immediately apparent, with baskets of flowers and a cherub holding a candle of illumination gracing the contents page alone. The vignette illustrations to the text are often very large in size for wood engravings of this period, and startlingly varied in shape and composition. Interesting in the context of this chapter is a vignette of a river/bridge arch/London skyline/shipping compendium of motifs attached to an article on 'The Monster City' by the Revd Robert Jones,[35] where the right hand half of the image is daringly cut across a fraction of an inch below the top of the balustrade, so that the river-scape is three-quarters obliterated by Jones's text. Nothing could show more clearly the artistic possibilities of the wood-engraving's powers to be aligned with type – here the type overlays the image in a startling and eye-catching way.

Meadows's suicide vignette is a similarly spectacular imposition of a large-scale wood engraved illustration on to the page's composi-tion, thus intruding on any easy complicity between text and illustration. The vignette is divided in technique between an austere, almost Fuseli-like neo-classical linearity in the depiction of the suicide's body lying under a sheet with only her sopping hair and the rise of her breasts to indicate her gender, and the tonally complex, symbolic representation of 'Death' drawn in conjunction with the bridge motif drawn from the conventional repertoire of suicide motifs. Yet what happens in this image is that the conventional motifs of slab, sodden body, and bridge arch are startled out of their naturalistic meaning both by the crude and melodramatic symbolism of the drawing and by the disparities in engraving technique which juxtapose the various elements in the illustration. The image, put simply, decon-structs the conventional naturalistic suicide narrative even as it invokes it. To my mind, the non-naturalistic codes of this image prove infinitely more powerful than the attempts at naturalism largely discussed elsewhere in this chapter. The popular melodramatic tradi-tions of the wood engraving had, and have, much to offer even the most sophisticated reader.

Meadows is an interesting artist to end this book on. Like Seymour, although a decade later, he had to undergo a technical tran-sition from metal engraving to wood in order to survive in a changed mass market. He also had to manage a transition from comic illustra-tion in an eighteenth-century caricature tradition to the more varied topical and serious jobs offered by the new mass market magazines.[36]

Early years of hardship came to an end when he became associated with some of the biggest illustrated book projects of the late 1830s and 1840s which brought him into the mainstream of commercial wood engraving, especially through his close contact with the Dalziel brothers, the best known engravers of artists' drawings of the time. Engen describes him as 'influential but largely unoriginal', and sees his career as the fortunate product of the marketplace.[37] He argues that Meadows's 'own brand of delicate fantasy had been superceded by the more aggressive draughtsmanship of Leech and Doyle' by the 1850s.[38]

Like Seymour, then, Meadows represents the jobbing artists who came to construct so much of their culture's experience into visual images while remaining largely unregarded or unanalysed in their own lifetimes or since. This book has sought to suggest ways in which the pursuit of artists like Meadows, undertaken with some awareness of social history and of the changing modes of representation which transformed popular image making, might enable us to uncover the complex codes through which past societies represent themselves to us. In the process, we shall surely find out more about ourselves.

List of images cited

On the Brink

[1] A. Hervieu
     'He drew near the extremest edge'
     Illustration to Frances Trollope, *Michael Armstrong – Factory Boy* (1840).
     See O. Anderson, *Suicide in Victorian and Edwardian England* (Oxford, Clarendon Press 1987), 204.

[2] Richard Doyle
     'She paused a moment on the brink'
     Illustration for C. Dickens, *The Chimes* (1844).
     See Anderson, *Suicide in Victorian and Edwardian England*, 206.

[3] Hablôt K. Browne ('Phiz')
     'The River'
     Illustration for C. Dickens, *David Copperfield* (1849).

[4] W.S. (engraved by P. Wentworth)
     'I went down to the river after dark ...' (illustration 32)
     Wood engraved illustration to Wilkie Collins's *Man and Wife* published in *Cassell's Magazine* 16 July 1870.

[5] Gustave Doré
     'The Bridge of Sighs' (illustration 29)
     Wood engraved illustration to Thomas Hood's *Poems* (Ward Lock 1878).

[6] Thomas Graham
     'Alone in London'

Oil on canvas. No date.
Perth Museum and Art Gallery.

The Leap

[7]   George Cruikshank
'The Drunkard's Children' (illustration **27**)
Plate 8. 'The maniac father and the convict brother are gone. – The poor girl, homeless, friendless, deserted, destitute and gin mad, commits self murder'.
Glyphograph (David Bogue 1848).

[8]   George Standfast
Wood engraved illustration to G.W.M. Reynolds's *The Parricide* (John Dicks 1847), 113.

[9]   Henry Anelay (illustration **28**)
Wood engraved illustration to G.W.M. Reynolds's *Mysteries of the Court of London* (London, John Dicks 8 vols, 1853 on), vol. 2, 25.
See B. Gates, *Victorian Suicide* (Princeton, University Press 1988), 144.

[10] Frederick Gilbert
Wood engraved illustration to G.W.M. Reynolds's *Rosa Lambert* (London, John Dicks 1853–54), 65.

[11] Anon.
Wood engraved illustration to Dion Boucicault's *After Dark: A Tale of London Life* (1868).
See Gates, *Victorian Suicide*, 147.

[12] Anon.
Wood engraved cover illustration for Charles Selby, *London By Night* (Dicks' Standard Plays 721, 1886).
See Gates, *Victorian Suicide*, 145.

Under the Arch

[13] Kenny Meadows (illustration **30**)
Wood engraved illustration for A.B. Reach, 'The Last Hour of a Suicide' in *The Illuminated Magazine*, vol. 3, (July 1844), 161.

[14] G.F. Watts
'Found Drowned'
Oil on canvas. 1848–50. A version of Hood's 'The Bridge of Sighs'.

[15] Lord Gerald Fitzgerald
Illustration to 'The Bridge of Sighs' in the Junior Etching Club edition of *Passages from the Poems of Thomas Hood* (1858).
See Anderson, *Suicide in Victorian and Edwardian England*, 203.

[16] Augustus Egg
'Past and Present 3 – Despair'
Oil on canvas. 1858.
See Gates, *Victorian Suicide*, 140.

[17] Abraham Solomon
'Drown'd! drown'd!'
Lithograph of an oil painting shown at the Royal Academy in 1860.
See Gates, *Victorian Suicide*, 136.

[18] Gustave Doré (illustration **31**)
Engraved illustration for 'The Bridge of Sighs' in Thomas Hood, *Poems* (London, Ward Lock 1878).

Alone in London

[19] G.J. Pinwell
'Near her betrayer's door she lays her head'
Wood engraved illustration for *Dalziel's Illustrated Goldsmith* (London, Ward Lock, 1865).

[20] Robert Seymour
Etched illustration to first issue of Dickens's *Pickwick Papers* (1837).

Notes

1 Olive Anderson, *Suicide in Victorian and Edwardian England* (Oxford, Clarendon Press 1987).

2 Barbara Gates, *Victorian Suicide* (Princeton, University Press 1988), especially 125–50.

3 See, for example, the extended studies of female prostitution, suicide, and representation in Lynda Nead, *Myths of Sexuality* (Oxford, Basil Blackwell 1988); Helen Michie, *The Flesh Made Word* (New York, Oxford University Press 1987), especially chapter III which is called 'Calling and falling: vocation and prostitution'; Linda Nochlin, 'Lost and "Found": once more the fallen woman' in *Women, Art, Power and Other Essays* (London, Thames and Hudson 1989), 57–85; Lynda Nead 'Seduction, Prostitution, Suicide – "On the Brink" by Alfred Elmore' in *Art History* vol. 5, 310–22; and Lynda Nead, 'The Magdalen in Modern Times' in R. Betterton *Looking On* (London, Routledge 1987), 73–92. While this chapter does not enter extensively into discussions of the Victorian representational codes for prostitution, the literary and visual motifs associated with female prostitution do form an essential element in the wider narrative of suicide, and thus comprise an important context for my discussion here.

4 R.A. Vogler, *The Graphic Works of George Cruikshank* (New York, Dover Publications 1979), 111 and 161–2; H. and M. Evans, *The Man Who Drew The Drunkard's Daughter* (London, Frederick Muller 1978), 134–5. While both authors agree that this plate from 'The Drunkard's Children' is unusually fine for this phase of Cruikshank's career, Vogler insists on its 'eerie' qualities which render it almost 'surreal'. The argument of this chapter is that the print hovers between the naturalistic and the emblematic, but never aspires to the surreal.

5 See note 3 above.

6 See for a representative example of 'picture editor' versions of significant Victorian images N. Bentley's *The Victorian Scene* (London, Weidenfeld and Nicolson 1978).

7 Edward Jenkins, *Ginx's Baby* (London, Alexander Strahan 1870) and *The Devil's Chain* (London, Strahan & Co. 1876). For further commentary on Jenkins's work see: B.E. Maidment 'Victorian Publishing and Social Criticism: The Case of Edward Jenkins' in *Publishing History* XI 1982, 41–71; and B.E. Maidment 'What shall we do with the starving baby – Edward Jenkins and *Ginx's Baby*' in P. Humm, P. Stigant and P. Widdowson (eds), *Popular Fictions: Essays in Literature and History* (London, Methuen 1986).

8   Articles on suicide from the 1840s and 1850s which are not cited by Anderson
     or Gates but which I have found of interest include: A.B. Reach, 'The Last
     Hour of a Suicide' in *The Illuminated Magazine* vol. 3, July 1844, 161–4; [G.H.
     Lewes] 'Suicide in Life and Literature' in *The Westminster Review* 1857, 52–78;
     Harriet Martineau, 'Self Murder' in *Once A Week* 1859, 510–14; and [J.N.
     Radcliffe], 'The Aesthetics of Suicide' in the *Journal of Psychological Medicine*
     1859, 582–602.

9   Thomas Graham 'Alone in London'. Oil on canvas; in Perth Museum and Art
     Gallery. The painting is approximately 3ft by 2ft in size, and was exhibited in
     the 'Robert Scott Lauder's Master Class' exhibition in the National Gallery of
     Scotland in Edinburgh in 1983.

10   The Kenny Meadows vignette is on p. 161 of the article, and is discussed in
     detail in the concluding section of this chapter. See illustration 30.

11   For the development of magazines like *The Penny Magazine* and *Chambers'
     Journal* see chapters 3 and 4. The key secondary studies listed there are R.D.
     Altick's *The English Common Reader* (Chicago, University of Chicago Press
     1957), Celina Fox's *Graphic Journalism in England During the 1830s and 1840s*
     (New York, Greenwood Press 1988), Patricia Anderson's *The Printed Image
     and the Transformation of Popular Culture* (Oxford, Clarendon Press 1991), and
     Louis James's *Print and the People 1819–1851* (London, Allen Lane 1976).

12   *The Illustrated Exhibitor* was a weekly magazine published by John Cassell which
     began in early 1852. While little different in format from many cheap illus-
     trated weekly miscellanies of the period apart from a marked emphasis on the
     useful, decorative, and fine arts, *The Illustrated Exhibitor* was one of several peri-
     odicals to begin to use the 'A Visit To' format to explore industrial processes.
     The 'visit' genre had, characteristically, been brilliantly and definitively formu-
     lated by one of Charles Knight's publications, Dodd's *Days in the Factory* (1843).
     The articles in *The Illustrated Exhibitor* (the first described a gutta percha works)
     were illustrated by a double page spread of wood engravings, which combined
     vignettes and larger framed illustrations. The quality is poor, but the extent of
     the transition from the copper plate to wood engraving by this date could not be
     more clearly marked as the variety of wood engraved formats obviously super-
     sedes previous use of metal engraving for similar purposes.

13   Apart from the comments made in the previous note, the 'Visit to …' format
     persisted right on to the end of the nineteenth century. *The Pall Mall
     Magazine*, for example, still used it in the 1880s and 1890s.

14   My undated McGowan edition of *Barclay's Universal English Dictionary*
     claimed to be 'superbly embellished' by copper plates. The plates, however, are
     crude, sensational, and narrative rather than expository, and suggest that
     McGowan decided to render his potentially stuffy publication more palatable
     for popular taste by spicing it up with engravings which seem closer in feel to
     woodcuts than to the expository precision one might have expected from
     copper plates. Alfred Boime in *Art in an Age of Revolution* (New Haven, Yale
     University Press 1989) offers a useful account of the way in which Diderot's
     Encyclopedie offered a source for the democratising impulse of the
     Revolutionary period.

15   For accounts of the founding and development of *The Illustrated London News*
     and its use of controversial illustration see: S. Houfe, *The Dictionary of British
     Book Illustrators and Caricaturists 1800–1914* (Woodbridge, Antique
     Collectors' Club, revised edn 1981); Anderson, *The Printed Image*; Fox,

Graphic Journalism; and Altick, *English Common Reader*. Careful study of R.K. Engen's *Dictionary of Victorian Wood Engravers* (Cambridge, Chadwyck-Healey 1985) would enable the careful student to construct a large 'cast' of engravers for *The Illustrated London News*. It would be an excellent project to relate this group to their other projects, and attempt to build a network of interconnections, projects, and ventures for professional wood engravers and artists in the 1830s and 1840s.

16 The two standard early appreciations of Victorian wood engraving are Gleeson White's *English Illustration – The Sixties 1855–1870* (Bath, Kingsmead 1970, reprint of original 1897 edition) and Forrest Reid's *Illustrators of the Eighteen Sixties* (London, Faber and Gwyer 1928). More recent books like Percy Muir's *Victorian Illustrated Books* (London, Batsford revised edn 1985) and Eric de Maré's *The Victorian Woodblock Illustrators* (London, Gordon Fraser 1980) have pursued a similar agenda based on aesthetic criteria. I have found that these attempts to describe Victorian woodblock illustration as a 'canon' of fine art a hindrance in trying to write this book. While I accept that, for example, Millais's illustrations for *Orley Farm* do show a brilliant ability to use the wood engraving medium in an original and entirely satisfying way, I have found many individual engravings by little regarded artists which seem to me equally brilliant. While conventional wisdom, for example, sees Kenny Meadows as a rather unoriginal engraver, the illustration by him discussed in this chapter seems of exceptionally high quality. The medium, largely used by jobbing professionals, seems to me to throw up images of utterly variable quality regardless of the reputation of artist and engraver. See Introduction for discussion of the aesthetic issues raised by popular prints.

17 Roger Orme, *Roger Miller* (London, S.W. Partridge, no date).

18 *Ibid.*, 36–7.

19 Edward Jenkins, *The Devil's Chain* (London, Strahan & Co. 1876), xvi.

20 *Ibid.*, 1–2.

21 *Ibid.*, 4.

22 Edward Jenkins, *Ginx's Baby – His Birth and Other Misfortunes* (London, Strahan & Co 5th edn 1870), 224.

23 Jenkins, *Ginx's Baby*, 223.

24 Hesba Stretton's real name was Sarah Smith and she was the author of a number of short improving narratives. These are listed amongst R.D. Altick's Victorian bestsellers. Her most widely distributed work (though, as Altick notes elsewhere, not necessarily the widest read), *Jessica's First Prayer* reached a total print run of 1,500,000 in its long career. These figures make the total for *Alone in London*, distributed together with another text, of 750,000 look rather insignificant.

25 *Dalziel's Illustrated Goldsmith* was published by Ward Lock in 1865 with a hundred plates by G.J. Pinwell. Eric de Maré, who gives the book considerable attention in *The Victorian Woodblock Illustrators*, speaks highly of Pinwell's work, but sees a general difficulty for Victorian engravers and artists in dealing with eighteenth-century subjects (de Maré, p. 161). My argument here is that Pinwell is seeking to appropriate an alien narrative to highly Victorian social purposes, and renders the scene entirely through Victorian iconography regardless of its historical context. To this extent I share de Maré's perception.

26 Linda Nochlin's essay 'Lost and "Found"' is a good account of this image. Her essay also offers some additional images of female suicides.

27 Louis Hawes, *Presences of Nature* (New Haven, Yale Centre for British Art 1982). Hawes's two sections on Townscape (84–112 and 188–202) provide a useful introduction to these issues.

28 See W.G. Constable and J.G. Links, *Canaletto* (Oxford University Press, 2nd edn, 2 vols, 1976), 406–7 and 570–1; J.G. Links, *Canaletto and his Patrons* (London, Paul Elek 1977), 66–7.

29 Even though this chapter traces a 'realist' and pessimistic usage of the bridge arch and city skyline motifs, traditions for representing these motifs as optimistic and picturesque were obviously equally available if in another discourse altogether. For example, Thomas Malton's series of aquatints, 'A Picturesque Tour through the Cities of London and Westminster', was published between 1792 and 1801 and was, according to Christopher White 'responsible for developing the taste for books with views of cities'. (C. White *English Landscape 1630–1850* (New Haven, Yale Centre for British Art 1977), 38). Certainly, in prints and watercolours alone it is easily possible to demonstrate an uninterrupted picturesque tradition of representation of the bridge arch and riverscape complex of motifs. The St Paul's Cathedral/Blackfriars Bridge image for example was used by Samuel Scott (c. 1770), William James Bennett, after G.F. Robson (1810), various Havells in their books of London views, John Preston Neale (1835), and Herbert Menzies Marshall (1880). Illustrations of these paintings an prints can be found in Ian Mackenzie's *British Prints* and H.L. Mallalieu's *The Dictionary of British Watercolour Artists*. While the mood of these images may range from calm, reflective serenity to breezy bustle, the picturesque response remains unbroken by the dark associations of the same scenes exploited by the artists and wood engravers working within the differing discourses of popular image making.

30 *The Pictorial Times* for 30 December 1843 has, for example, an illustrated feature on the rebuilding of Westminster Bridge which uses images of both heroic activity and engineering complexity (as in the images of the Albion Mill discussed in chapter 2) and of the overall beauty and grace of the structure.

31 Edward Angelo Goodall's 'St Paul's Cathedral and Blackfriars Bridge from the River Thames' is one obvious example of the commercial and the picturesque becoming elided together into a single triumphal image. (See Sotheby's sale catalogue for 16 November 1989).

32 See, for further discussion, F.D. Klingender, *Art and the Industrial Revolution* (London, Evelyn, Adams, and Mackay, revised edn 1968).

33 T.J. Edelstein's '"They Sang the Song of the Shirt" – the Visual Iconology of the Seamstress' in *Victorian Studies*, Spring 1980, is the starting place for much subsequent discussion. The constituent elements of the seamstress narrative are perhaps somewhat different to those of the suicide. While the seamstress narrative is crucially one of despair and alienation, the visual representation of the seamstress has a totally different closure to that of the suicide. Usually depicted in a bare garret, side-lit either by a feeble dusk or an equally feeble dawn, weary with the prospect of a night's labour or another day's toil against unyielding deadlines, alone or responsible for sick relatives, the seamstress looks out across, or is set against, the roofline of an uncaring city. Yet the narrative of the seamstress is left crucially unclosed. Feeble as the slanting light often is, it represents hope. The seamstress is generally represented within Victorian iconology as an exploited victim within an uncaring indus-

trial culture, but the possibily of continuance, or even redemption, is seldom denied. Seen against the unified despair and closure of the images of suicide seen in this chapter, the depiction of the seamstress seems to provide something approaching hope, a social problem faced and possibly even resolved in graphic terms at least. The two narratives of 'the seamstress' and the 'suicide' are brought together in a literary text by Hood's 'The Song of the Shirt'. Doré's graphic version of the poem, however, decisively opts for a pessimistic closure without admitting the possibility of redemption.

34 For Ebenezer Landells see Engen, *Dictionary of Victorian Wood Engravers*, 149–50. In acting as the sole supplier of engravings to *The Illuminated Magazine* for a short spell, Landells became a kind of proto-art editor, a key role developed to great effect in the commercial world of London engraving by the Dalziel brothers. Landells was also a key figure in the development of *The Illustrated London News*.

35 *The Illuminated Magazine* vol. III, 286.

36 Engen, *Dictionary of Victorian Wood Engravers* (178–9) contains a long entry on Meadows which provides a detailed account of his varied output. See also Houfe, *Dictionary of British Book Illustrators and Caricaturists*.

37 Engen, *Dictionary of Victorian Wood Engravers*, 179.

38 *Ibid.*

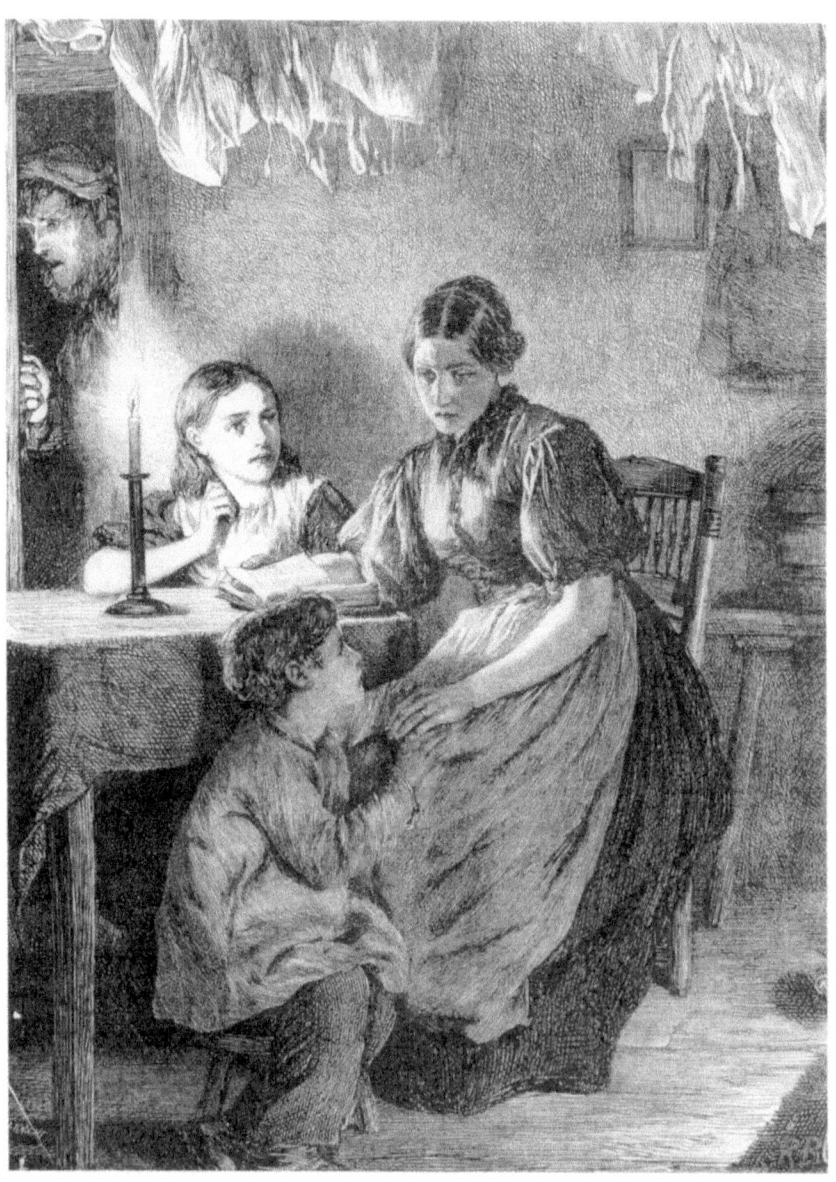

33 'Father Stirling' from *The British Workman* No. 152 (1 August 1867).
Wood engraving signed 'RB' and 'J. Knight'.

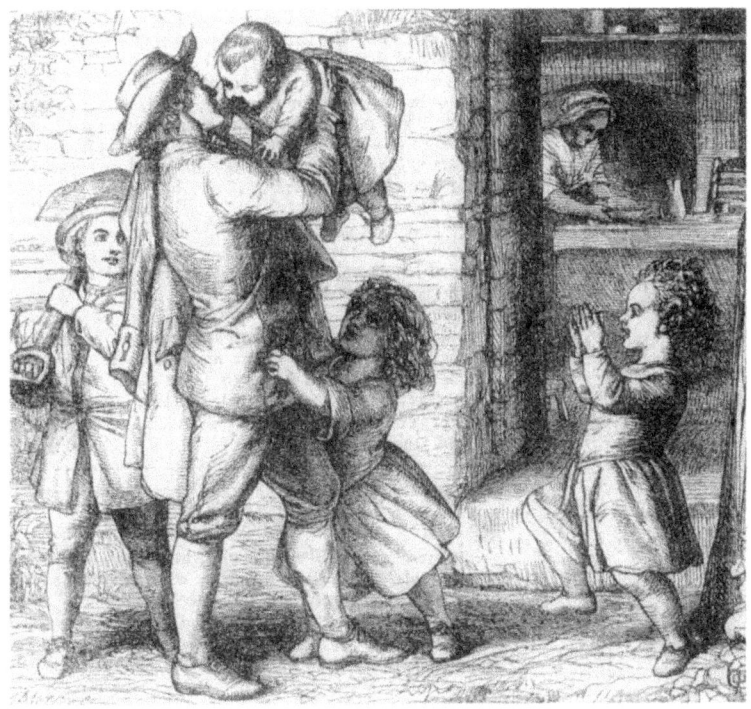

34 'Father's Come' from *The British Workman* No. 137 (1 May 1866).
Unsigned wood engraving.

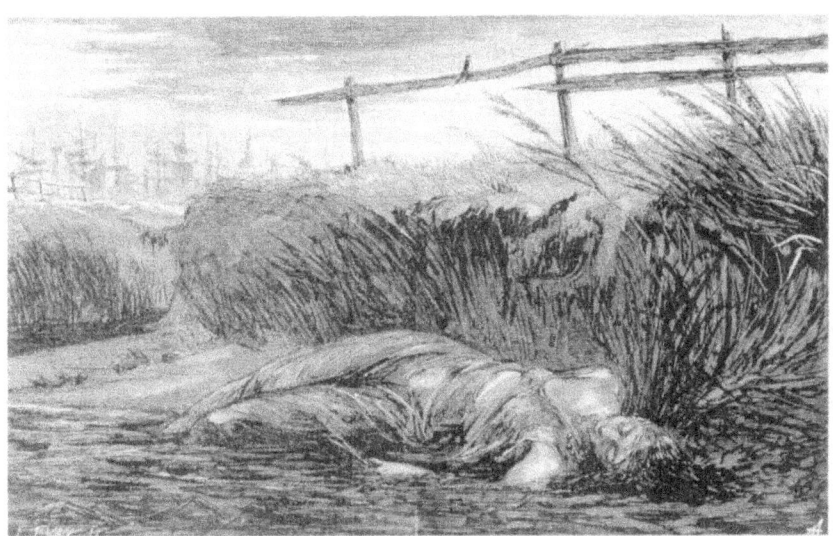

35 'Found Drowned' from *Tinsley's Magazine* vol. 3 (September 1868) 207–9.
Wood engraving by Edmund Evans.

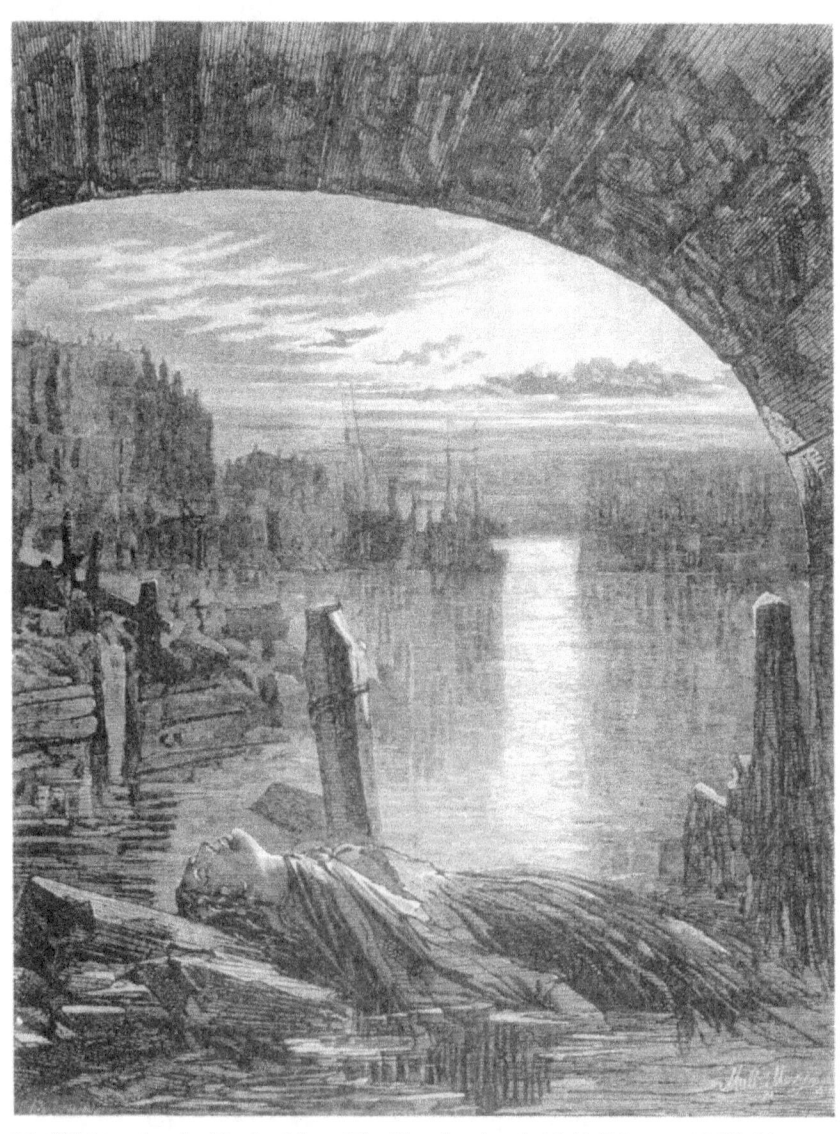

36 'Waiting for the Verdict' from *The Tomahawk* vol. 11 (8 February 1868) 58.
Coloured wood engraving drawn by Matt Morgan engraved by T. Bolton.

❧ BIBLIOGRAPHY

The following listings are divided into sections to try to give readers access to the various strands of interest – technical, historical, and theoretical – which are combined in the study of popular image making. Some degree of annotation has been introduced to point students to texts which are important for the level of detailed information which they contain or for their originality or typicality in using particular theoretical approaches. No aspiration to completeness is intended, and often the annotations point to more extended specialist bibliographies and listings published elsewhere. The organisation of the bibliography, however, does represent the approach to the study of prints exemplified in this book, and seeks to show the various types of knowledge students would need to acknowledge in furthering their studies of graphic images.

Primary sources are not included here, because each chapter offers some degree of self-contained evaluation of available primary sources. The notes and image lists supply full details of the particular images studied. It would prove quite impossible to exemplify all the places a student might look for interesting images made or published between 1790 and 1860 – in effect it would be necessary to list every illustrated periodical, tract, separately published print, illustrated book, and poster from the period. In asking readers not to be overwhelmed by the enormous bulk and diversity of available source material for the study of popular graphic images, it seems most useful here to try to lay out and evaluate those critical discussions and histories of various print genres which help us to describe and order this mass of primary sources.

General history of prints, including dictionaries and lists of printmakers

BMC, see Stephens and George.

F.W. Burgess, *Old Prints and Engravings* (London, Routledge 1924).

S. Calloway, *English Prints for the Collector* (London, Lutterworth Press 1980). Contains a useful artist based bibliography.

F. Eichenberg, *The Art of the Print – Masterpieces, History, Techniques* (London, Thames and Hudson 1976).

C. Fox, 'The Engravers' Battle for Professional Recognition in Early Nineteenth Century London' in *London Journal* vol. 2, no. 1 1976, 3–31.

C. Fox, *Graphic Journalism in England During the 1830s and 1840s* (New York, Greenwood Press 1988). Developed from an Oxford doctoral thesis, this book is an important attempt to link image making to the development of mass periodical literature. Little work has been done specifically on magazine illustration except where it intersects with the careers of well known artists or the history of famous magazines like *Punch*.

J.M. Friedman, *Color Printing in England 1486–1870* (New Haven, Yale Centre for British Art 1978).

R. Garton, *British Printmakers 1855–1955* (Devizes, Garton and Co. 1992).

B. Gascoigne, *How to Identify Prints* (London, Thames and Hudson 1986).

R.T. Godfrey, *Printmaking in Britain – A General History from its Beginnings to the Present Day* (Oxford, Phaidon 1978).

D.G. Gohm, *Maps and Prints for Pleasure and Investment* (London, John Gifford, second edn 1978). Contains an extensive 'Dictionary' of engravers.

T. Gretton, *Murders and Moralities – English Catchpenny Prints 1800 – 1860* (London, British Museum 1980). Best introduction to the cheapest and most crudely drawn strata of the print market.

A. Hayden, *Chats on Old Prints* (London, T. Fisher Unwin 1907).

S. Houfe, *The Dictionary of British Book Illustrators and Caricaturists 1800–1914* (Woodbridge, Antique Collectors' Club revised edn. 1981). A quite wonderful book which combines vast amounts of specific information on individual artists and engravers with an extended introduction which provides a clear and useful account of the social history of image making which is especially helpful on the close relationship between periodicals and illustration. The illustrations are diverse and often unexpected.

M.V. Jackson, *Engines of Instruction, Mischief, and Magic: Children's Literature in England from Its Beginnings to 1839* (Lincoln, University of Nebraska Press 1989). I have deliberately included a representative history of children's literature here because it is an area of interest not discussed in this study. Jackson's book shows some of the contradictions shown in histories of children's literature over the status of illustrations. As Jackson's own illustrations show, children's books were almost invariably illustrated, and these illustrations used the full range of available image making techniques, and were especially interested in colour printing for mass audiences. Her book shows a splendidly wide range of illustrated texts, many of them visually compelling and carefully formulated, and, unusually for academic studies of texts, she also generally includes both text and illustration often by printing a double page spread. So her book offers readers a real chance to see the image/text complex in a wide range of different versions and techniques. But Jackson's text fails almost entirely to capitalise on her illustrations by concentrating exclusively on the *texts* as literature and as evidence of the ideological struggle over educational principles. The result is, literally, only half the picture. Jackson is not alone in taking children's literature as a category made up entirely of texts. Even though the historians of childrens' literature are only too eager to use the decorative potential of their sources to support their own texts, they seldom analyse or even notice the nature of the images which accompany the books, pamphlets, alphabet books, tracts, and ephemera which form the subject of their study.

D. Karshan, *Prints* (Washington, Cooper-Hewitt Museum 1980).

D. Kunzle, *The History of the Comic Strip: The Nineteenth Century* (Berkeley, University of California Press 1990).

S. Lambert, *The Image Multiplied: Five Centuries of Printed Reproductions of Paintings and Drawings* (London, Trefoil 1987). The standard introduction to the history of attempts to reproduce paintings and drawings for a wider mass market.

I. Mackenzie, *British Prints: Dictionary and Price Guide* (Woodbridge, Antique

Collectors' Club 1987). While aimed primarily at collectors, Mackenzie's book illustrates clearly the range and diversity of print-making traditions.

B. Maidment, *Into the 1830s – Some Origins of Victorian Illustrated Journalism* (Manchester, Manchester Polytechnic 1992). Shows how illustration was a key factor in developing a mass readership for periodical literature.

A.H. Mayor, *Popular Prints of the Americas* (New York, Crown Publishers 1973).

C. Roger-Marx, *Graphic Art of the Nineteenth Century* (London, Thames and Hudson 1962).

R. Russell, *Guide to British Topographical Prints* (Newton Abbot, David and Charles 1979).

F.C. Stephens and M.D. George, *Catalogue of Political and Personal Satires Preserved in the Department of Prints and Drawings in the British Museum* (London, British Museum 1870–1954). A monumental piece of scholarship which forms one of the basic resources for the history of popular prints, especially caricature and political and social satire. The catalogue can now be used in many libraries alongside the microfilm version of the prints themselves.

P. Stewart, *Engraven Desire: Eros, Image, and Text in the French Eighteenth Century* (London, Duke University Press 1992).

Printmaking processes

C. Ashwin, 'Graphic imagery 1837–1901: A Victorian revolution' in *Art History*, vol. 1, no. 3, September 1978, 360–70.

F. Brunner, *A Handbook of Graphic Reproduction Processes* (1962).

T. Fawcett 'Graphic versus Photographic in Nineteenth Century Reproduction' in *Art History*, vol. 9, no. 2, June 1986, 185–212.

P. Gilmour, *Artists in Print* (London, BBC Publications 1981). Although concerned with contemporary artist-printmakers, this book does give well illustrated introductions to the main printmaking techniques.

A Guide to the Processes and Schools of Engraving (London, British Museum 1914 and many subsequent editions). A very useful brief summary.

A. Scharf, *Art and Industry* (Bletchley, Open University Press 1971). Section 3 called 'The Mechanization of Art' (72–92) deals with reprographic processes and their social impact.

G. Wakeman, *Victorian Book Illustration – The Technical Revolution* (Newton Abbot, David and Charles 1973). While mainly concerned with later Victorian photo-reprographic methods, this book contains invaluable technical information relevant to this book.

Wood engraving

R.J. Beedham, *Wood Engraving* (London, Faber and Faber, 5th edn 1938).

Douglas Percy Bliss, *A History of Wood Engraving* (London, J.M. Dent 1928).

Dalziel brothers, *A Record of the Work of the Dalziel Brothers 1840–1890* (London 1901 and subsequent reprints). A very important first hand account of the development, role, and status of the professional wood engraver throughout the period when wood engraving was becoming the central mode of popular image making.

E. de Maré, *The Victorian Woodblock Illustrators* (London, Gordon Fraser 1980). Important both as an accessible survey of a key topic and as a useful introduction to the technical history of wood engraving processes.

R.K. Engen, *Dictionary of Victorian Wood Engravers* (Cambridge, Chadwyck-Healey 1985). A mine of important information, especially on the remote corners of magazine illustration. Includes several excellent bibliographies, especially a detailed listing on nineteenth-century wood engraving (xvii–xxi).

A. Garrett, *A History of Wood Engraving* (London, Midas Books 1978).

K. Lindley, *The Woodblock Engravers* (1970).

Metal engraving

B. Hunnissett, *An Illustrated Dictionary of British Steel Engravers* (London, Scolar Press 1989).

C. Wax, *The Mezzotint; History and Technique* (London, Thames and Hudson 1990).

Etching

E.S. Lumsden, *The Art of Etching* (London, Seeley, Service, & Co. 1924).

W. Shaw-Sparrow, *British Etching from Barlow to Seymour Haden* (London 1926)

F. Wedmore, *Etching in England* (London 1895).

Lithography

P. Gilmour (ed.), *Lasting Impressions – Lithography as Art* (London, Alexandria Press 1988). See especially chap. 1 by Clinton Adams on 'The Nature of Lithography'.

F.H. Man, *Homage to Senefelder* (London, Victoria and Albert Museum 1971).

P.C. Marzio, *The Democratic Art – Pictures for a Nineteenth Century America* (London, Scolar Press 1980).

D. Porzio (ed.), *Lithography: 200 Years of Art, History, and Technique* (London, Bracken Books 1982).

M. Twyman, *Lithography 1800–1850* (Oxford, Oxford University Press 1970). A detailed study of the early history of lithography with an extensive bibliography.

Book illustration

R.M. Burch, *Colour Printing and Colour Printers* (London 1910).

T.R. Chester and J.I. Whalley, *A History of Children's Book Illustration* (London, John Murray 1988).

M. Hardie, *English Coloured Books* (London, Fitzhouse Books 1990). First published 1906.

J.R. Harvey, *Victorian Novelists and their Illustrators* (London, Sidgwick and Jackson 1970).

E. Hodnett, *Image and Text: Studies in the Illustration of English Literature* (London, Scolar 2nd edn 1986). Includes chapters on Blake, 'Phiz', and Tenniel.

P. James, *English Book Illustration 1800–1900* (Harmondsworth, Penguin 1947).

C.T. Lewis, *The Story of Picture Printing in England During the Nineteenth Century* (London 1928).

R. McLean, *Victorian Book Design* (London 1963).

R. McLean, *English Coloured Books 1738 – 1898* (London, British Printing Machinery Association Ltd. 1980).

M. Melot, *The Art of Illustration* (New York, Rizzoli 1984).

P. Muir, *Victorian Illustrated Books* (London, B.T. Batsford, revised edn 1985). Contains useful thematic study guides at the end of each chapter.

G.N. Ray, *The Art of the French Illustrated Book 1700 to 1914* (New York, Dover Publications 1986).

Forrest Reid, *Illustrators of the Eighteen Sixties* (London, Faber and Gwyer 1928).

R.M. Slythe, *The Art of Illustration 1750 – 1900* (London, The Library Association 1970). A useful general introduction to both techniques and history.

Gleeson White, *English Illustration – The Sixties 1855–1870* (Bath, Kingsmead 1970, reprint of original 1897 edition).

Caricature

D. Donald, '"Calumny and caricatura" – eighteenth century political prints and the case of George Townshend' in *Art History*, vol. 6, no. 1, March 1983, 44–66.

D. Donald, 'Characters and Caricatures: The Satirical View' in N. Penny (ed.), *Reynolds* (London, Weidenfeld and Nicolson 1986), 355–93.

English Caricature 1620 to the Present (London, Victoria and Albert Museum 1984).

W. Feaver, *Masters of Caricature* (London, Weidenfeld and Nicolson 1981).

E.H. Gombrich and E. Kris, *Caricature* (Harmondsworth, Penguin 1940).

F.D. Klingender, (ed.), *Hogarth and English Caricature* (London, Transatlantic Arts Ltd. 1944).

Edgell Rickwood, *Radical Squibs and Loyal Ripostes* (London, Adams and Dart 1971).

J. Wechsler, *A Human Comedy: Physiognomy and Caricature in 19th Century Paris* (London, Thames and Hudson 1982). An important study which shows how the imagery and iconography of French lithography draws on contemporary social codes and beliefs.

M. Wood, *Folly and Vice: The Art of Satire and Social Criticism* (London, South Bank Centre 1989).

M. Wood, *Radical Satire and Print Culture 1790–1822* (Oxford, Clarendon Press 1994).

Prints as social history

P. Anderson, *The Printed Image and the Transformation of Popular Culture 1790–1860* (Oxford, Clarendon Press 1991). Given its title this book might be expected to offer a theorised account of the ideological drive which underpinned the development of a mass market for graphic images in popular texts. Anderson's book is in fact largely descriptive, but it does offer the only plausible attempt apart from Houfe to offer an extended narrative history of the huge changes which occurred in popular image making during this period.

D. Alexander, 'Kauffmann and the print market in eighteenth-century England' in W.W. Roworth (ed.), *Angelica Kauffmann* (London, Reaktion Books 1992), 141–78.

H.M. Atherton, 'The mob in eighteenth century caricature' in *Eighteenth Century Studies*, vol. 12, no. 1, 1978.

D. Bindman (ed.), *The Shadow of the Guillotine: Britain and the French Revolution* (London, British Museum 1989). The wonderful catalogue of a staggering bi-centenary exhibition which shows – if nothing else – the extent and complexity of the ways in which historical events are represented graphically, not just in prints but also through pottery, funerary statuary, handkerchiefs, coins, medals, broadsides, and even stained glass. Bindman's 'Preface' offers interesting brief comment on the use of visual material as a form of historical explanation.

J. Brewer, *The Common People and Politics 1750–1790s* (Cambridge, Chadwyck-Healey 1986). This volume in Chadwyck-Healey's seven volume 'The English Satirical Print 1600–1832' series, draws on the British Museum collection and offers, with its companion volumes, the most sustained attempt to use satirical prints as an ambitious and self-conscious form of social history. Each volume comprises an extensive introduction as well as an annotated selection of prints.

J. Cuno (ed.), *French Caricature and the French Revolution 1789–1799* (Chicago, University of Chicago Press 1988). An American equivalent to Bindman's catalogue, Cuno's volume moves further away from the notion of caricature as 'illustrative history'. The essays in this volume are as much on genres, visual codes, and iconography as on narrative or historical interpretation.

R. Darnton and D. Roche (eds), *Revolution in Print – The Press in France 1775–1800* (Berkeley, University of California Press 1989). See especially R. Reichhardt, 'Prints – Images of the Bastille' (223–51) and J. Leith, 'Ephemera – Civic Education Through Images' (270–90).

H.T. Dickinson, *Caricatures and the Constitution 1760–1832* (Cambridge, Chadwyck-Healey 1986, 'The English Satirical Print' series).

D. Donald, 'The power of print: graphic images of Peterloo' in *Manchester Region History Review*, vol. III, no. 1, Spring/Summer 1989, 21–30.

M. Duffy, *The Englishman and the Foreigner* (Cambridge, Chadwyck-Healey 1986, 'The English Satirical Print' series).

C. Fox, 'The development of social reportage in English periodical illustration during the 1840s and early 1850s' in *Past and Present* 1977, 90–111.

M.D. George, *English Political Caricature: A Study of Opinion and Propaganda* (Oxford, Oxford University Press 1959).

M.D. George, *From Hogarth to Cruikshank – Social Change in Graphic Satire* (London, Viking 1967, reprinted 1987). Illustrative social history through the documentary use of graphic images at its most scholarly and effective.

L. James, *Print and the People 1819–1851* (London, Allen Lane 1976). A brilliantly conceived anthology which, drawing on the John Johnson collection of printed ephemera held in the Bodleian Library in Oxford, represents the range of popular print through mode and genre. James's anthology insists on the interaction between verbal and visual in popular culture, and underlines the power and experience of relatively unsophisticated audiences in deciphering the emblematic or the symbolic visual message.

M.W. Jones, *The Cartoon History of the American Revolution* (London, London Editions 1977).

M.W. Jones, *A Cartoon History of the Monarchy* (London, Macmillan 1978).

P. Langford, *Walpole and the Robinocracy* (Cambridge, Chadwyck-Healey 1986, 'The English Satirical Print' series).

A.H. Mayor, *Prints and People: A Social History of Printed Pictures* (New York, The Metropolitan Museum of Art 1972). The most ambitious social history of prints not just in historical and geographical scope, but also in Mayor's determination to give due weight to the market, the technical development of printmaking, and the social purposes of prints as well as to great practitioners. An essential introduction.

J. Miller, *Religion in the Popular Prints 1600–1832* (Cambridge, Chadwyck-Healey 1986, 'The English Satirical Print' series).

R. Paulson, *Representations of Revolution 1789–1820* (New Haven, Yale University Press 1983).

R. Porter, 'Prinney, Boney, Boot' in *London Review of Books*, 20 March 1986, 19–20.

R. Porter, 'Seeing the Past' in *Past and Present*, February 1988, 186–205.

I. Roots, 'Prints, politics, and people' in *History Today*, vol. 37, March 1987, 47–53.

J.A. Sharpe, *Crime and Law in English Satirical Prints 1600–1832* (Cambridge, Chadwyck-Healey 1986, 'The English Satirical Print' series).

R. Southey, *Mr. Rowlandson's England* (Woodbridge, Antique Collectors' Club 1985). Uses Rowlandson's prints and drawings to illustrate a contemporary text.

P.D.G. Thomas, *The American Revolution* (Cambridge, Chadwyck-Healey 1986, 'The English Satirical Print' series).

G.M. Trevelyan, *The Seven Years of William IV* (London 1952). An anthology of John Doyle's ('HB') lithographed political caricatures organised as a historical commentary on the reign.

T. Wright, *Caricature History of the Georges* (1867 and many subsequent editions).

Individual artists and printmakers discussed in the text
Thomas Bewick

I. Bain, *Thomas Bewick: An Illustrated Record of his Life and Work* (Newcastle, The Laing Gallery 1979).

I. Bain, *The Watercolours and Drawings of Thomas Bewick and his Workshop Apprentices* (Stocksfield, Thomas Bewick Birthplace Trust, 2 vols, 1989).

I. Bain (ed.), *A Memoir of Thomas Bewick written by himself* (Oxford, Oxford University Press 1979).

A. Dobson, *Thomas Bewick and his Pupils* (London 1884).

F. Hicklin, *Bewick – Wood Engravings* (London, HMSO 1978).

R. Marsack (ed.), *Thomas Bewick – Selected Work* (Manchester, Carcanet Press 1989).

G. Reynolds, *Thomas Bewick: A Resumé of his Life and Works* (London, Art and Technics 1949).

H. Ritvo, *The Animal Estate: The English and other Creatures in Victorian England* (Harvard University Press 1987).

C. Rosen and H. Zerner, 'The Romantic Vignette and Thomas Bewick' in *Romanticism and Realism* (London, Faber and Faber 1984).

M.F. Schulz, *Paradise Preserved: Recreations of Eden in Eighteenth and Nineteenth Century England* (Cambridge, Cambridge University Press 1985).

R. Stone, *Wood Engravings of Thomas Bewick* (London, Rupert Hart-Davis 1953).

D.C. Thomson, 'Thomas Bewick' in H.C. Ewart (ed.), *Toilers in Art* (London, Isbister & Co. n.d.), 323–54.

M. Weekley, *Thomas Bewick* (Oxford, Oxford University Press 1953).

M. Weekley (ed.), *A Memoir of Thomas Bewick written by himself* (London, The Cresset Press 1961).

George Cruikshank

A. Burton, 'Cruikshank as an illustrator of fiction', *Princeton University Library Chronicle*, vol. 35, 1973.

A.M. Cohn, *George Cruikshank: A Catalogue Raisonné* (London, Bookman's Journal 1924, 3 vols).

P. Conrad, 'Wrestling with demons' in *The Times Literary Supplement*, 26 July 1974, 798–9.

H. and M. Evans, *The Man Who Drew The Drunkard's Daughter* (London, Frederick Muller 1978).

L. James, 'Cruikshank and early Victorian Caricature' in *History Workshop Journal*, vol. 6, Autumn 1978, 107–20.

M.W. Jones, *George Cruikshank: His Life and London* (London, Macmillan 1978).

R.L. Patten, *George Cruikshank's Life, Times, and Art*, vol. 1 1792–1835 (London, Lutterworth Press 1992). Likely to be the most extensive and authoritative biographical and contextual study of Cruikshank.

R.L. Patten (ed.), *George Cruikshank – A Revaluation* (Princeton, Princeton University Press 2nd edn – 1992).

R.A. Vogler (ed.), *Graphic Works of George Cruikshank* (New York, Dover Publications 1979).

J. Wardroper, *The Caricatures of George Cruikshank* (London, Gordon Fraser 1977).

Gustave Doré

C.B. Grafton (ed.), *Doré Spot Illustrations* (New York, Dover Publications 1987).

G. Pollock, 'Vicarious Excitements: *London: A Pilgrimage* by Gustave Doré and Blanchard Jerrold' in *New Formations*, no. 4, Spring 1988, 25–50.

A. Woods, 'Doré's London; Art and Evidence' in *Art History*, vol. 1, no. 3, September 1978, 341–59.

Other printmakers

F. Antal, *Hogarth and his Place in European Art* (London 1962).

D. Bindman, *Blake as an Artist* (Oxford, Phaidon 1977).

D. Bindman (ed.), *The Complete Graphic Works of William Blake* (London, Thames and Hudson 1978).

J. Burke and C. Caldwell (eds), *Hogarth: The Complete Engravings* (London, Alpine Fine Arts n.d.).

M. Butlin, *William Blake* (London, Tate Gallery 1978).

R.L.S. Cowley, *Marriage à la Mode: A Review of Hogarth's Narrative Art* (Manchester, Manchester University Press 1983).

R. Engen, *Richard Doyle* (Stroud, Catalpa Press 1983).

R. Engen, M. Heseltine and L. Lamborne, *Richard Doyle and his Family* (London, Victoria and Albert Museum 1983).

R.N. Essick, *William Blake, Printmaker* (Princeton, Princeton University Press 1980).

H. and M. Evans, *John Kay of Edinburgh* (Edinburgh, Paul Harris, revised edn 1980).

D. Hambourg, *Richard Doyle* (London, Art and Technics 1948).

Draper Hill, *Mr. Gillray The Caricaturist* (London, Phaidon Press 1965).

Draper Hill (ed.), *The Satirical Etchings of James Gillray* (New York, Dover Publications 1976).

P. Hogarth, *Arthur Boyd Houghton* (London, Gordon Fraser 1981).

D. Morris, *Thomas Hearne and his Landscapes* (London, Reaktion Books 1989).

M. Paley *William Blake* (Oxford, Phaidon 1978).

R. Paulson, *Popular and Polite Art in the Age of Hogarth* (South Bend 1979).

R. Paulson, *Hogarth* (Cambridge, Lutterworth Press, 2 vols, 1992).

J. Piggott, *Turner's Vignettes* (London, Tate Gallery 1992).

D. Rose, *Life, Times, and Recorded Works of Robert Dighton* (Tisbury, Element Books 1981).

M. Webster, *Francis Wheatley* (London, Routledge and Kegan Paul 1970). Pages 53 to 86 describe Wheatley's prints.

Approaches and readings

Not all the texts listed below deal specifically with prints, although most discuss a range of representational possibilities which often include prints. This section of the bibliography does however focus on what might be loosely called 'theory', and especially on theories of representation which have stressed the formal, generic, and social mediations through which images reflect, refract, or construct the society which they seek to describe or illustrate. Recent studies have focused on the representation of gender, the depiction of landscape, and the complexities of photography as a 'naturalistic' medium as sites for detailed discussion, and the following listings reflect these emphases. While, for purposes of clarity, it seems a useful idea to separate out discussions of theories of representation from more historically oriented study of prints, recent historians, as the Introduction shows, have made much more sophisticated use of discussions of representational codes in attempting to understand what prints might say about the society in which they are produced.

C. Arscott and G. Pollock, 'The Partial View – the visual representation of the early nineteenth century city' in J. Seed and J. Wolff (eds), *The Culture of Capital* (Manchester, Manchester University Press 1988).

J. Barrell, *The Dark Side of the Landscape* (Cambridge, Cambridge University Press 1980). An influential study of the representation of labour and poverty in eighteenth-century landscape painting.

J. Barrell, 'The private comedy of Thomas Rowlandson' in *Art History* vol. 6, no. 4, December 1983, 423–41.

Walter Benjamin, *Illuminations* (London, Cape 1970). Benjamin's famous essay on 'The Work of Art in the Age of Mechanical Reproduction' is a necessary starting place for any study of mass produced 'art'.

N. Bryson, *Vision and Painting – The Logic of the Gaze* (London, Macmillan 1983).

D. Cherry, *Painting Women – Victorian Women Artists* (London, Routledge 1993).

E.G. D'Oench 'Prodigal sons and fair penitents: transformations in eighteenth century popular prints' in *Art History*, vol. 13, no. 3, September 1990, 318–43.

W.M. Ivins, *Prints and Visual Communication* (Cambridge, Harvard University Press 1953). This much reprinted text, despite its age, is often a set book for Art History and Communications Studies undergraduates. Ivins does provide a useful history of the impact of technical developments in printmaking on the images produced, but underestimates the effects of ideological purpose in exploiting new techniques.

J. H. Miller, *Illustration* (London, Reaktion Books 1992). A rare and interesting attempt to relate a graphic genre to recent theoretical work in cultural studies before applying theories drawn from Walter Benjamin and others to Turner's illustrative work and the Victorian illustrated novel.

L. Nead, *Myths of Sexuality – Representations of Women in Victorian Britain* (Oxford, Basil Blackwell 1988).

L. Nochlin, *Women, Art, and Power and Other Essays* (London, Thames and Hudson 1989).

L. Nochlin, *Realism* (Harmondsworth, Penguin 1971).

R. Paulson, *Emblem and Expression – Meaning in English Art of the Eighteenth Century* (London, Thames and Hudson 1975).

R. Paulson, *Representations of Revolution 1789–1820* (New Haven, Yale University Press 1983). A key book through Paulson's ability to bring formal, generic, and literary considerations to bear on the history represented in graphic images.

A. Potts, 'Picturing the modern metropolis – images of London in the 19th century' in *History Workshop Journal* 26, Autumn 1988, 28–56.

G. Pollock, *Vision and Difference – Femininity, Feminism and the Histories of Art* (London, Routledge 1988).

C. Rosen and H. Zerner, *Romanticism and Realism* (London, Faber and Faber 1984). Contains some very interesting work on the emergence of the vignette as a characteristic Romantic genre.

J. Tagg, *The Burden of Representation* (London, Macmillan 1988). Tagg links the invention and early development of photography to its functions as various forms of social control, thus dispelling the notion of the 'neutrality' or 'objectivity' of the camera.

L. Smith 'Polly Put the Kettle On' in *Art History*, vol. 17, no. 3, September 1994, 464–9.

J. Wolff, *The Social Production of Art* (London, Macmillan 1981).

Other secondary sources

R.D. Altick, *The English Common Reader* (Chicago, University of Chicago Press 1957).

O. Anderson, *Suicide in Victorian and Edwardian England* (Oxford, Clarendon Press 1987).

Art and the Industrial Revolution (Manchester City Art Gallery 1968).

J. Barrell, *The Birth of Pandora and the Division of Knowledge* (London, Macmillan 1992).

N. Bentley, *The Victorian Scene 1837–1901* (London, Weidenfeld and Nicolson 1968). A good example of 'picture editor' social history of the kind described in the Introduction, where a wide range range of not always relevant images are used to construct 'the Victorian'.

A. Bermingham, *Landscape and Ideology – The English Rustic Tradition 1740–1860* (London, Thames and Hudson 1986).

D. Blayney-Brown, *Catalogue of the Collection of Drawings in the Ashmolean Museum, Oxford* (Oxford, Ashmolean Museum 1982), vol. 4.

M. Butlin and E. Joll, *The Paintings of J.M.W. Turner* (New Haven and London, Yale University Press, revised edn, 2 vols, 1984).

J. Calder, *The Victorian Home* (London, Batsford 1977).

R. Cooper, 'Millais's "The rescue": A Painting of a "Dreadful Interruption of Domestic Peace"' in *Art History*, vol. 9, no. 4, December 1986, 471–86.

C. Davidson, *A Woman's Work Is Never Done* (London, Chatto and Windus 1982).

H.W. Dickinson and R. Jenkins, *James Watt and the Steam Engine* (London 1927).

R. Dorment, *British Painting in the Philadelphia Museum of Art* (Philadelphia Museum of Art 1986).

T.J. Edelstein, '"They Sang the Song of the Shirt" – The Visual Iconology of the Seamstress' in *Victorian Studies*, Spring 1980.

J. Egerton, *Wright of Derby* (London, Tate Gallery 1990).

H. and M. Evans, *Sources of Illustration* (Bath, Adams and Dart 1971).

H. Evans, *The Art of Picture Research* (Newton Abbot, David and Charles 1979).

H.C. Ewart (ed.), *Toilers in Art* (London, Isbister & Co. n.d.). Chapters on several Victorian woodblock illustrators.

E. Fagg, *The Old 'Old Vic' or, from Barrymore to Baylis* (1936).

C. Fox, *Londoners* (London, Thames and Hudson 1987).

C. Fox, *London – World City* (New Haven, Yale University Press 1992).

B.T. Gates, *Victorian Suicide – Mad Crimes and Sad Histories* (Princeton, Princeton University Press 1988).

T. Girtin and D. Loshack, *The Art of Thomas Girtin* (London A. and C. Black 1954).

W. Graham, *English Literary Periodicals* (New York, Octagon Books, reprint of 1930 edition 1966).

L. Hawes, *Presences of Nature: British Landscape 1780–1830* (New Haven, Yale Centre for British Art 1982).

E. Jones, *Industrial Architecture in Britain 1750–1939* (London, Batsford 1985).

F.D. Klingender, *Art and the Industrial Revolution* (London, Evelyn, Adams, and Mackay, revised edn 1968).

B.E. Maidment, 'Victorian publishing and social criticism: the case of Edward Jenkins' in *Publishing History*, vol. XI, 1982, 41–71.

B.E. Maidment, 'What shall we do with the starving baby – Edward Jenkins and *Ginx's Baby*' in P. Humm, P. Stigant and P. Widdowson (eds), *Popular Fictions: Essays in Literature and History* (London, Methuen 1986).

H.L. Mallalieu, *The Dictionary of British Watercolour Artists up to 1920* (Woodbridge, Antique Collectors' Club, 2nd edn–2 vols, 1986).

H. Michie, *The Flesh Made Word – Female Figures and Women's Bodies* (Oxford, Oxford University Press 1989).

D. Mullin (ed.), *Victorian Plays – A Record of Significant Productions on the London Stage 1837–1901* (New York, Greenwood Press 1987).

D. Napier, 'John Lloyd of Shelton' in *The Antique Collector*, vol. 60, no. 10, October 1989.

V. Neuburg and N. Philip (eds), *Charles Dickens – A December Vision: His Social Journalism* (London, Collins 1986).

V. Neuburg, *Popular Literature – A History and Guide* (Harmondsworth, Penguin 1977).

B. Nicolson, *Joseph Wright of Derby: Painter of Light* (London, 2 vols., 1968).

P.G. Nunn, *Victorian Women Artists* (London, The Womens' Press 1987).

R. Palmer, *A Ballad History of England* (London, Batsford 1979).

J.H. Plumb, *The First Four Georges* (London, Book Club Associates 1974). Another good example of a text by a serious historian edited into a 'popular' book by the use of contemporary prints, engravings, and illustrations.

R.G.G. Price, *A History of Punch* (London, Collins 1957).

P. Quennell, *Victorian Panorama* (London, Batsford 1937).

J.C.Reid, *Bucks and Bruisers: Pierce Egan and Regency England* (London, Routledge and Kegan Paul 1971).

A. Ribeiro, *Fashion in the French Revolution* (London, Batsford 1988).

J.M. Robinson, *The Wyatts: An Architectural Dynasty* (Oxford 1979).

F. St. Aubyn (ed.), *Ackermann's Illustrated London* (London, Wordsworth Editions 1985).

A.W. Skempton, 'Samuel Wyatt and the Albion Mill' in *Architectural History*, vol. 14, 1971, 53–73.

Samuel Smiles, *Lives of the Engineers* (London, John Murray, 2 vols., 1861).

K. Solender, *Dreadful Fire! – Burning of the Houses of Parliament* (Cleveland Museum of Art 1984).

M.H. Spielmann, *The History of Punch* (London, Cassell 1895).

D. Vincent, *Bread, Knowledge and Freedom: A Study of Nineteenth-Century Working Class Autobiography* (London, Europa 1971).

D. Vincent, *Literacy and Popular Culture: England 1750–1914* (Cambridge, Cambridge University Press 1989).

C. White, *English Landscape 1630–1850* (New Haven, Yale Centre for British Art 1977).

EU authorised representative for GPSR:
Easy Access System Europe, Mustamäe tee 50,
10621 Tallinn, Estonia
gpsr.requests@easproject.com

www.ingramcontent.com/pod-product-compliance
Lightning Source LLC
Chambersburg PA
CBHW060841170526
45158CB00001B/206